Miguel, Chief of Yuma Indians about 190

THE DESTRUCTION
OF CALIFORNIA INDIANS

A collection of documents from the period 1847 to 1865 in which are described some of the things that happened to some of the Indians of California

Edited by Robert F. Heizer

Introduction to the Bison Book Edition
by Albert L. Hurtado

University of Nebraska Press
Lincoln and London

First Bison Book printing: 1993

Library of Congress Cataloging-in-Publication Data
The Destruction of California Indians: a collection of documents from the
period 1847 to 1865 in which are described some of the things that happened to some of the Indians of California / edited by Robert F. Heizer; introduction to the Bison book edition by Albert L. Hurtado.
p. m.
Originally published: Santa Barbara: Peregrine Smith, 1974.
Includes bibliographical references.
ISBN 0-8032-7262-6 (pa)
1. Indians, Treatment of—California.   2. Indians of North American—California—History.   3. Indians of North America—Government relations—
1789–1869.   I. Heizer, Robert Fleming, 1915–
E78.C15D48   1993
979.4′00497—dc20
92-37603   CIP

Reprinted by arrangement with Michael Heizer

∞

INTRODUCTION TO THE BISON BOOK EDITION

By Albert L. Hurtado

Robert F. Heizer, the anthropologist who compiled this volume, was angry about the history of California Indians. To understand his wrath, one need look no further than the basic facts of California Indian history. After the arrival of Europeans in 1769, the native Californian population plunged from over three hundred thousand to about thirty thousand by 1860.[1] This appalling rate of decline resulted from disease, cultural dislocation, dispossession, and—to a lesser extent—outright homicide. Newcomers—Spaniards, Mexicans, and Anglo-Americans—were responsible for these shocking developments. Heizer's outraged reaction to this terrible story was not uncommon. Contemporary observers, modern historians, and Indians alike have railed against the human and impersonal forces that devastated the California Indians.[2]

The first European settlements brought disaster. Beginning in 1769, a Spanish military and religious expedition founded a series of Catholic missions, presidios (forts), and pueblos in Alta California. The missions were supposed to Hispanicize and Christianize the Indians of California, and they were partially successful. The Crown authorized the missionaries to create vast farms and livestock ranchos where Indian neophytes provided a convenient labor force. Twenty-one missions became the homes of tens of thousands of Indians until the Mexican government, which ruled California after 1821, disbanded these institutions.[3]

From the Spanish perspective, Franciscan missionaries had humanitarian goals, but they unintentionally introduced diseases new to California Indians, who died at a stunningly rapid pace. During the mission era, the Indian population fell by perhaps one hundred thousand.[4] At the same time, Indians began to form raiding societies in the California interior whence they harried religious and lay stock owners alike. Mission refugees and unconverted Indians discouraged settlement in the California interior until 1839 when John A. Sutter established his famous fortified colony, New Helvetia, near the confluence of the Sacramento and American rivers. Sutter's activities further weakened Indian society in the early 1840s. The Indians were at first cautious, but eventually hundreds of them accepted employment as field hands, cowboys, and soldiers for Sutter. The master of New Helvetia used his native army to compel Indians to work for him as well as to defend his fields and flocks. Sutter's success encouraged Anglo-American immigrants to build farms and use Indian labor in California's Central Valley. Eventually, Sutter became a labor contractor who provided Indian workers to rancheros throughout northern California.[5]

The Mexican War heralded U.S. sovereignty over California. Within a few days of the war's end in 1848, Sutter's workers found gold in the mill race they were building on the American River. News of the bonanza set off a world-wide rush to California. For California Indians, the discovery amounted to a disaster. Hundreds of thousands of white miners invaded the last Indian refuges—the Sierra Nevada foothills and mountains and the northern reaches of the state. Miners had slight sympathy for Indian life and little need for their labor. Some newcomers clamored for wars of extermination and the new state government tried to accommodate them. Meanwhile, federal authorities negotiated treaties that would have set aside reservations, but—acceding to the demands of the state legislature— the U.S. Senate refused to ratify. Then the federal government resorted to a series of temporary reservations that served only a fraction of California natives. Thus, in the 1850s Indians were left substantially at the mercy of private interests and the state government. Between 1848 and 1860, the Indian population plummeted from about one hundred fifty thousand to about thirty thousand. Indian numbers did not begin to increase until the turn of the century.[6]

In the late nineteenth century scholars began to examine California's Indian past. Alfred L. Kroeber of the University of California became the acknowledged leader of these investigators, many of whom he trained at Berkeley. Their research and publications laid the foundation for modern California anthropology. Kroeber was primarily interested in reclaiming cultural knowledge from living Indians. He worked with a sense of urgency because he believed that when elderly Indian informants died, knowledge of California Indian society that predated the upheavals of the gold rush would be lost.[7]

Robert F. Heizer was one of Kroeber's graduate students at Berkeley, but he added a new dimension to California Indian studies: archaeology. Heizer became interested in archaeology growing up in Lovelock, Nevada, where he collected Indian artifacts. He wanted to go to Berkeley, but his high school was unaccredited so he went to Sacramento Junior College. The college president, Jeremiah Beverly Lillard, was an amateur archaeologist who took Heizer under his wing. Heizer and other enthusiasts spent much spare time digging for Indian relics in the Sacramento Valley and this experience confirmed his determination to be an archaeologist.

Before Heizer arrived at Berkeley, Kroeber had dismissed California archaeology because he believed that perhistoric change in California was so negligible that archaeological evidence would reveal little. There was no archaeologist on the Berkeley faculty.[8] Kroeber insisted that he write a dissertation about aboriginal whaling, but Heizer continued to hone his archaeological skills until even Kroeber was convinced that excavation could reveal important information about Indian culture. Heizer also attracted the interest of Berkeley historian Herbert Bolton, who in 1940 arranged California Historical Society funds to excavate a site at Drake's Bay, an alleged anchorage of Sir Francis Drake in 1579. Heizer turned up no Drake artifacts, but found evidence of a later Spanish voyage.[9] Other benefactors helped to finance Heizer's field work. After a brief stint at the University of Oregon and working as a marine pipe fitter in the Richmond, California, shipyards during World War Two, Heizer was called first to the University of California at Los Angeles, and then to Berkeley. In 1947 Heizer was the first archaeologist on the Berkeley anthropology faculty. He extended Kroeber's tradition of California anthropology until his death in 1979.[10]

At Berkeley Heizer established an archeological survey that revealed ever more about the California Indian past. He regarded archaeology as "a kind of condensed social history." Although Heizer is best known for his archaeology of California Indians, he undertook several important non-Indian historical projects, including excavations of Sutter's sawmill and California missions. His publications also include collections of documents, books and articles about the history of California race relations.[11] Heizer also did a great deal of interdisciplinary work with several collaborators. Sherburne F. Cook, the brilliant Berkeley physiologist, who pioneered native

American historical demography, was one of his most frequent coauthors. Cook wrote extensively on California Indian population decline, and his writings influenced a generation of historians and anthropologists.[12] Heizer did not confine his interest in Indians to academic work. He worked on behalf of California Indians' claims against the federal government and consulted with the Legal Assistance Program for California Indians.[13]

Heizer's scholarship and advocacy for California Indians made him determined to publicize how the federal government and white people had victimized them. In 1971 he coauthored *The Other Californians*, a sweeping indictment of racism in the golden state.[14] Three years later he published two documentary volumes bearing on California Indian history in the mid-nineteenth century, the present volume and *They Were Only Diggers*.[15]

Heizer wrote these volumes during a time of great ferment among American Indians and university students. In the 1960s the civil rights, free speech, and anti-Vietnam war movements shook American complacency. The Berkeley campus and San Francisco Bay area became the scene of various political demonstrations and protests.[16] In 1968 Indians founded the American Indian Movement (AIM), which confronted the Bureau of Indian Affairs with militant demands for the return of Indian lands and self-determination. A year later Indians and other minority students founded the Third World Liberation Front and made demands for student control of minority programs at Berkeley. The university administration turned them down. In November 1969 Indians occupied and claimed Alcatraz Island, a former federal prison in San Francisco Bay. The occupiers made various unsuccessful demands of the government until federal marshals removed the last protesters in June 1971.[17]

These upheavals made Berkeley a center of controversy and greatly affected Heizer because of his deep knowledge of Indian history. He identified with protestors and believed that the students who participated in the "exciting days of the Free Speech Movement" were his "best students, not in being political activists, but in being more intellectually alive."[18] In his preface to *They Were Only Diggers*, Heizer was explicit about connecting his interest in Indian history to contemporary American concerns like the Vietnam war. He believed that racism in the past was the parent of bigotry in his own time. He argued that "the breakdown of the family structure and the 'youth revolt' of today are correlated with the deep objections against the longest war which America has ever engaged in—a war which is against 'non-persons' analogous to the California Indians in 1850–

1870. If the 'generation gap' is really that, and by this I mean that if the new generation is not simply accepting the values of the one which produced it, then there is some hope for the future."[19]

Conceived as a documentary volume, this work is also a document of its own time. The texts presented here, Heizer frankly admitted in his introduction to the first edition, appear to be one-sided. He argued, however, that they presented a fair picture of the general conditions that existed in California during the gold rush and Civil War eras. The passage of time and new scholarship seem to have vindicated Heizer's judgment, with but a few exceptions. Because Heizer was determined to illustrate the horrors of Indian life in the mid-nineteenth century, he compiled a volume that portrayed Indians as mere victims rather than as thinking actors upon the historical stage. He might have included documents that showed how Indians fought for their rights and attempted to manipulate the federal reservation system. While it is true, as Heizer argues, that the flood of whites overwhelmed native Californians in the 1850s, Indians actively attempted to shape their destinies, as recent scholarship has shown.[20] The volume also lacks chronological balance. The documents give only slight attention to the years 1847–1852. Heizer presented nothing for the years 1848 and 1849, and just a few selections for 1850, the period when the gold rush exploded and changed California forever. Nevertheless, these pages reveal the hellish world of California Indians during the crucial middle decades of the nineteenth century. When Heizer selected these documents, he intended to shock his readers. I suspect that they will continue to have that effect.

NOTES

1. Sherburne F. Cook, *The Population of the California Indians, 1769–1970* (Berkeley, Calif.: 1976), 1–43 and *passim*. Heizer cites different figures in the introduction (p. vi), but he is considering only a part of California. In any case, estimating California Indian population and its rate of decline is a difficult business that has confounded many scholars. See Albert L. Hurtado, "California Indian Demography, Sherburne F. Cook, and the Revision of American History," *Pacific Historical Review* 58 (August 1989): 323–43.

2. For examples of nineteenth-century opinions, see Hubert Howe Bancroft, *History of California*, 7 vols. (San Francisco: The History Company, 1886–90), 7:476–77; and Stephen Powers, *Tribes of California* (1877; reprint., Berkeley: University of California Press, 1975), 400–401. A recent critical work is Douglas Monroy, *Thrown among Strangers: The Making of Mexican Culture in California* (Berkeley: University of California Press, 1990), 3–96,

passim. A modern Indian critique of the missions is found in Rupert Costo and Jeannette Henry Costo, eds., *The Missions of California: A Legacy of Genocide* (San Francisco: The Indian Historian Press, 1987).

3. Monroy, *Thrown among Strangers,* 1–126, *passim.*

4. Sherburne F. Cook's pioneering essays on California historical demography are collected in Cook, *The Conflict between California Indians and White Civilization* (Berkeley: University of California Press, 1976). See also Sherburne F. Cook and Woodrow Borah, "Mission Registers as Sources of Vital Statistics: Eight Missions of Northern California," in Cook and Borah, *Essays in Population History* (Berkeley: University of California Press, 1971–79), 3:177–311.

5. Albert L. Hurtado, *Indian Survival on the California Frontier* (New Haven: Yale University Press, 1988), 32–71.

6. Hurtado, *Indian Survival,* 125–48, 193–210.

7. Robert F. Heizer, "History of Research," in Heizer, ed., *Handbook of North American Indians,* Vol. 8, *California* (Washington, D.C.: Smithsonian Institution, 1978), 8–10.

8. M. A. Baumhoff, "Robert Fleming Heizer, 1915–1979," *American Anthropologist* 82 (1980): 843.

9. Heizer, "Archaeological Evidence of Sebastian Rodriguez Cermeño's California Visit in 1595," *California Historical Society Quarterly* 20 (1941): 315–28; Heizer, *Elizabethan California: A Brief and Sometime Critical Review of . . . the Drake Expedition, June 17–July 23, 1579* (Ramona, Calif.: Ballena Press, 1974).

10. Heizer, "Robert F. Heizer," in Irving Stone, ed., *There Was Light: Autobiography of a University, 1868–1968* (Garden City, N.Y.: Doubleday and Co., 1970), 210–11; Baumhoff, "Robert Fleming Heizer," 844.

11. Quote is from J. Desmond Clark, "Memorial to Robert Fleming Heizer (1915–1979)," *Journal of California and Great Basin Anthropology* 1 (Winter 1979): 241. For a comprehensive list of Heizer's works see "Published Works of Robert Fleming Heizer," *Journal of California and Great Basin Anthropology* 1 (Winter 1979): 246–67.

12. Albert L. Hurtado, "California Indian Demography, Sherburne F. Cook, and the Revision of American History," *Pacific Historical Review* 58 (1989): 323–43; Wilbur R. Jacobs, "Sherburne Friend Cook: Rebel-Revisionist," *Pacific Historical Review* 56 (1985):191–99; Baumhoff, "Robert Fleming Heizer," 844.

13. Hester, "Robert Fleming Heizer," 103.

14. Heizer and Alan F. Almquist, *The Other Californians: Prejudice and Discrimination under Spain, Mexico and the United States to 1920* (Berkeley: University of California Press, 1971).

15. Heizer, ed., *They Were Only Diggers: A Collection of Articles from California Newspapers, 1851–1866, on Indian and White Relations* (Ramona, Calif.: Ballena Press, 1974).

16. W. J. Rorabaugh, *Berkeley at War: The 1960s* (New York: Oxford University Press, 1989), 1–88, and *passim.*

17. Francis Paul Prucha, *The Great Father: The United States Government and the American Indians,* 2 vols. (Lincoln: University of Nebraska Press, 1984), 1116–17; Rorabaugh, *Berkeley at War,* 85.

18. Heizer, "Heizer," 212.

19. Heizer, *They Were Only Diggers,* pp. x–xi.

20. Hurtado, *Indian Survival;* George Harwood Phillips, *Chiefs and Challengers: Indian Cooperation and Resistance in Southern California* (Berkeley: University of California Press, 1975).

INTRODUCTION

Until 1492 the Europeans did not even know of the existence of primitive peoples. The Middle East and the Far East were known, but Persia, India and China held civilized societies with markets, money, interesting food habits, curious modes of dress and other quaint practices which, however different, were still understandable because these people were all related as members of the Old World "Oikoumene," the network of civilizations which had originated in Mesopotamia and had been communicated eastward to China and Japan and westward to the Atlantic Coast since about 5000 B.C.[1]

After Columbus encountered the New World there followed, literally, the discovery of the rest of the earth by Europeans. And as the earth became known for the first time through voyages of discovery and round-the-world explorations, Europeans became aware that it was populated by men whose existence had never been imagined. Religious, philosophical and "practical" explanations were advanced to account for this unexpectedly large and widespread manifestation of humanity, but in the end these really boiled down to the conclusion that all of the non-European peoples of the earth were of a different "order" of man, and this explanation furnished the rationale for their exploitation in the era of colonization which was to follow the discovery period.

In North America the Spaniards devoted their first

efforts to the subjugation and exploitation of the civilized peoples of Middle American and western South America. North of Mexico there was little to encourage Spanish settlement because there was no stock of gold or silver treasure to be gathered—De Soto and Coronado had proved what poor pickings were to be had in Florida and New Mexico and Texas. In time, however, England and France secured title by discovery and possession to major territorial blocks of North America north of Mexico, and from portions of these, through revolution, war, preemption and purchase, the domain of the United States was expanded. The last great block of territory to come under American control was the Far West which was the chief spoil of the U.S.-Mexican War of 1846-48. The northwesternmost sector of this territory was California which in 1846 contained about 100,000 Indians and a few hundred Mexicans and Europeans. Early in 1848 came the discovery of gold in California, an event which signalled the massive entry of gold seekers. Although the gold played out before long, the new population remained as urban and rural settlers. All parts of California were explored and the more favored parts settled, and in this process the native population of Indians suffered a severe decline in numbers. It is believed that between 1848 and 1870 about 50,000 California Indians died. Many of these deaths were the result of simple and direct homicide; some were due to starvation, and others to disease. The federal government in Washington tried to do something to protect the Indians, but these efforts were largely ineffective. A series of treaties (18 in all) was entered into between the United States and representatives of many of the surviving Indian tribes in 1851-1852, but Congress refused to ratify them. Shortly after this, in 1853, there were established a series of Indian reservations,[2] but these also were largely failures since the natives were not adequately fed, clothed, housed or physically protected.[3] Even though U.S. military forces were stationed on some reserves, the conflict between state and federal laws hampered the actions of the soldiers, and the corruption and venality of Indian Agents in charge of reservations was so great that the money appropriated by Congress to operate the reservations was rarely spent for the Indians' welfare. The federal government situated at the other end of the country at a time when the quickest communication took a month to be transmitted, never seemed to understand the problems which California faced. Federal intervention was ever too little, usually too late, too restricted by the requirement that officials follow regulation procedures which were based on inadequate understanding of the local situation, and supported by too limited funds. Efforts to stop the corruption of Indian Agents by making investigations such as those of J. Ross Browne who held an appointed as Special Agent of the Treasury Department do not seem to have had any notable corrective effect.

Some humanitarian sympathy for the plight of the innocent California Indians was occasionally voiced by an army officer or a newspaper writer, or a citizen, but these expressions led to no improvement in the reservation system, or to any significant change in the general stereotype of Indians as ignorant, treacherous, bestial savages who deserved no rights, sympathy or consideration. Indians were in the way of progress, were collectively responsible, and should either be eliminated or put away out of sight on land which was so useless that no white man would find it of the least value. Californian whites acted as though their survival depended upon the total removal of the "Indian menace." While Indians surely did kill some whites, it is clear that they did so in retaliation or when pushed to desperation. Probably the underlying conviction that the Indian menace must be eliminated derived from the feeling that California was part of the wilderness—a frontier full of menace and danger, and a place where positive action was required to survive. The development of this concept of wilderness in America has been well described by Roderick Nash.[4] In a nation which condoned black slavery and which occupied a continent-wide stretch which had been seized from Indian occupants,[5] we can understand how these attitudes prevailed in the 1850s. Only in this way, also, can we understand the public tolerance of the 1850 California legislative act authorizing indenture of Indians—a thinly disguised substitute for slavery[6]—or the common practice of kidnapping Indian children and women, and openly selling them as servants.

There is presented here a series of documents which deal with the relations of California Indians and Americans from 1847 to 1865. One group comprises letters written by U.S. Army officers to their superiors reporting on Indian matters, and letters written to or by the Superintendent of Indian Affairs in California or by Indian Agents under his jurisdiction. In nearly all cases the originals of these letters are deposited in the U.S. National Archives and have been transcribed from photographic copies in the author's possession. These represent only a sampling of a more extensive series, but they are believed to be adequate as examples of this kind of record. The second category of documents is early California newspaper accounts. Here, of course, the amount of potential material is very extensive, and the selections presented here are intended only as a sampling of contemporary public reporting on conditions of Indian life and actions taken against Indians in the first two decades of American California.

It may seem to the reader that the relations between the Americans and the Indians are shown here as one-sided. Were there no champions of the Indians who insisted that they be treated humanely? Were there no state laws which provided benefits for them in their time of need when their lands were occupied by gold miners and ranchers? Did the federal government, with its experience of nearly a century in dealing with Indians on the advancing frontier, ignore their plight and provide them nothing? The answer to these questions is that the native Californians had no spokesmen in the white settlers; the state provided them with nothing whatsoever to ameliorate their difficulties; and the federal government in Washington merely went through motions in its effort to establish and operate reservations where Indians could find sanctuary, be supported, and encouraged by instruction and training to become citizens. It is a simple fact that in 1850 when California became the thirty-first state of the Union, the one hundred thousand Indians that still survived were not of the slightest interest or concern to most white Californians in terms of their human needs. If they ventured, as they occasionally did, to attack whites, this was not because they were an aggressive and unscrupulous lot of savages, but rather for the reason that they were human beings who had been pressed too hard—had seen their tribesmen and families shot down without mercy and without cause, and they finally understood that they were a people without hope and without a chance. If this evaluation seems too emotional or perhaps too academic, and as one written from the comfortable detachment of looking at events which happened over a century ago, then you have a surprise waiting for you in the pages which follow.

I have sorted out the documents into categories which appear as chapters in the Table of Contents. This attempt at organizing such a diverse lot of material should not be taken as anything but a first and rough topical sorting.

These documents have been gathered in various ways. Many were collected by myself and Dr. Alan Almquist in preparation for writing our recent book, *The Other Californians*. Professor Sherburne F. Cook, a man who knows more about California Indians than any other person, placed his accumulation of data at my disposal, and Mr. Robert Barker of the Washington law firm of Wilkinson, Cragun and Barker kindly made available the exhibits which were submitted to the Indian Claims Commission in the case of *Indians of California vs The United States* (Dockets 31, 37, 176, 215 and 333 Consolidated) allowed under Act of Congress approved August 13, 1946.[7]

Robert F. Heizer
Fellow, Center for Advanced Studies
   in the Behavioral Sciences
Stanford, California

1 — A. L. Kroeber. "The Ancient *Oikoumene* as an Historic Culture Aggregate." Huxley Memorial Lecture for 1945. Royal Anthrop. Inst. of Great Britain and Ireland. 1945. A.L. Kroeber. *A Roster of Civilizations and Culture*. Aldine, Chicago, 1962.

2 — For the rather complicated history of Indian reservations in California see W. H. Ellison. *The Indians of the Southwest: A Century of Development Under the United States*. Univ. Oklahoma Press, 1949, pp. 35-45, 80-94.

3 — J. Ross Browne. "The Indians of California." In *Crusoe's Island*. Harper, New York, 1867, pp. 284-308.

4 — Roderick Nash. *Wilderness in the American Mind*. Yale Univ. Press, 1967.

5 — On this subject the reader can start by consulting W. E. Washburn. *The Indian and the White Man*. Anchor Books, 1964. J. D. Forbes. *The Indian in America's Past*. Prentice-Hall, 1964. W. C. MacLeod. *The American Indian Frontier*. Kegan, Paul, Trench, Trubner, 1928.

6 — On the history and reasons for violence in America see N. Sanford and C. Comstock (eds). *Sanctions For Evil*. Jossey-Bass, San Francisco, 1971. R. Hofstadter and M. Wallace. *American Violence: a Documentary History*. A. Knopf, 1970. H. D. Graham and T. R. Gurr. *The History of Violence in America: a Report to the National Commission on the Causes and Prevention of Violence*. Bantam Books, 1969. O. Kerner (Chairman). *Report of the National Advisory Commission on Civil Disorders*. Bantam Books, 1968. For a more general survey of violence see A. de Rueck and J. Knight (eds). *Conflict in Society*. J. and A. Churchill, London, 1966.

7 — N. O. Lurie. "The Indian Claims and Commission Act." *Annals of the American Academy of Political and Social Science*, Vol. 311, pp. 56-70, 1957.

CONTENTS

ILLUSTRATIONS

Photograph Sources:

from the Lowie Museum of Anthropology, Berkeley, California (LMA), photographs appearing on pages 2, 40, 242, 266, 270, 286, 308;

from the American Museum of Natural History, New York, New York (MNH), photographs appearing on pages 10, 100, 218, 292;

from the Southwest Museum, Highland Park, California (SM), photographs appearing as the frontispiece and on page 174.

THE DESTRUCTION
OF CALIFORNIA INDIANS

Monache woman, Annie Antone, born 1862. Photo 192?

1

SOME EARLY RECORDS

The four documents in this chapter all date from the interim period between 1846 when California was seized by U. S. military forces from Mexico and January 1848, when gold was discovered at Sutter's sawmill at Coloma, Eldorado County. This last event was the trigger which launched the Gold Rush and set in motion the confrontation of the Argonauts and the Indians. These four documents show clearly that the hostility which was to characterize the attitude of whites toward Indians into the 1870s already existed in this interim period when California was under military government.

Fort Sacramento, March 13, 1847

Sir:

On the 3rd ult. and in compliance with Mr [?] request I sent two couriers via Sonoma with a report to you of the progress of the Mountain expedition which I presume you have received e're this. The day after dispatching the couriers two men arrived from the upper part of the Sacramento Valley with a petition of which I herewith enclose your copy. I immediately sent off two couriers with a copy to Capt. Kern then in camp on the California Mountains on the 7th of march, he ordering me to send him a company of the soldiers attached to this Garrison and in compliance with his orders I immediately sent him the best men in the garrison armed with carbines and lances.

Capt. E. M. Kern, the commander of this post has taken charge of the force and proceeded to the disturbed district and will no doubt act prudently. Subsequent to the departure of Capt. Kern for the mountains your order dated Feby. 11th, 1847, was received but in the absence of Capt. Kern, Capt. J. A. Sutter or myself cannot act. We have been left in charge of the business of the Garrison but of course cannot officially from head quarters. You will probably notice the great necessity of keeping up a strong force in this part of the country to protect the inhabitants of the upper part of the Sacramento Valley as well as the settlers of the San Joaquin Valley. The latter valley is inhabited by a brave band of Indians known by the title of "Horse Thieves" and unless properly managed may be troublesome to the inhabitants in that part of the country.

The larger part of the soldiers of this Garrison (in health) are now in active service. You will please inform us as soon as convenient whether you wish the soldiers of this Garrison discharged or not. I would respectfully suggest that a part at least should be kept in service. The soldiers of this Garrison are Indians instructed in the science of war by Capt.

4

J. A. Sutter for the past seven years and can be employed at one half the expense that white men can and are far preferable for this service. Capt. J. A. Sutter has heretofore kept up a strong Garrison at this post at his individual expense which has had the effect of keeping the Indians of both valleys quiet and the settlers have been protected at his expense. But now an enlightened nation has raised her Flag Capt. Sutter will throw down the walls of his Fort that have protected him against the half-civilized Californians and the savage Indians at a great expense and as an American citizen look to that Flag for protection.

I would also suggest the propriety of putting in force the laws of the United States in regard to selling ardent spirits to the Indians. I am induced to do so from the fact of having been witness that a person bought a Bbl Gin and Capt. Sutter was obliged to pay the enormous price of six dollars a gallon for the same to prevent it being sold to the Indians in his employ on the Feather River Farm, some eighty miles above this point. And in my presence the owner of the Launch on which said Gin was brought up told Capt. Sutter that he would bring up a lot of Liquor to sell to the Indian soldiers as soon as they were paid off by the U.S. Government as Capt. Sutter refused to sell or give them liquor. I immediately informed Capt. Kern of the affair and he at once said he would take the responsibility of destroying any article of the kind offered for sale in this part of the country to the Indians. I think that an order from the commander of the Northern District of California prohibiting the sale of ardent spirits to Indians would have a good effect.

Some of the suffering immigrants of the [Donner] Party brought over the California Mountains by the party sent out from this post on the 31st day of January last have arrived at this Fort and are provided for by Capt. J. A. Sutter. Nothing has been heard from Mr. Woodworth since my last communication to you but we shall look for him in some eight or ten days. The weather since my last report has been very unfavorable in the Mountains and we are fearful that they will not be so successful as the party that we sent from this post.

Very Respectfully
Your obdt. servt.
Geo. Mc Kinstry
Sheriff, Sac. Dist.

To Capt. I. G. Hall
Comdg. Northern District California

1:2   Letter, Harrison to DuPont

Sonoma March 17th 1847

Sir

Since sealing the letter which accompanies this, I have seen Dr. Bayle who says that in the late Indian difficulty the whites (Californians) were to blame. They stormed their village and attempted to take some of them into servitude, were resisted and lost one of their number, not however, without killing four of their opponents.

With regard to the keeping of a force here, he says as do all (Gov. Boggs among the number) that it is highly necessary to keep not only the Indians but some of our own bad countrymen.

Very respectfully
Your obt. Servt.
Geo W. Harrison

Capt. DuPont.

Pueblo de los Angeles
April 11th 1847

Sir,

I have been sent to this Section of California, clothed with full powers, both Civil and Military, by Genl. Kearny, the Governor of the Territory. There being no Alcalde in your vicinity I am induced to address you upon the subject of the depredations now being committed by the Indians upon the persons and property of the people of California. You are represented to me as a man of great good character standing among the people whose property it is my wish to protect. I therefore call upon you to visit the different Ranches in your part of the Country and require the inhabitants to turn out one or two good men from each Ranch with a number of spare horses and to assemble here on the 19th day of this month to join the United States troops at this place as well as the people who will be raised here to go upon an expedition against the horse stealing Indians, repel their invasion in the Country and pursue and destroy them.

I shall rely upon you to use your best influence in aiding and carrying these instructions in to effect.

Don Jose Salazar, the Alcalde of this place, will inform you of the number of men and horses required from your vicinity.

I am Respectfully
Your Obt. Servt.
R. B. Mason
Col. 1st Dragoons
U. S. A.

Al Sr.
Don Manuel Arquisola
San Buenaventura
California

[July, 1847]

. . I would respectfully call your attention to the necessity of publishing some decree forbidding all persons from trespassing upon the Indians, there are some who go among them for no good purposes, get into difficulties with them, and are driven off. They hasten to the settlements to ask the assistance of their friends, who in some late instances have armed themselves and returned, to chastise the indians. You will not fail to perceive, that all of our best efforts to conciliate the indians will be of no avail, and we may be forced into an interminable indian warfare, which may cause infinite trouble.

With a hope that the above will meet your approbation, I am

Your very obt. servt.
Henry A. Naglee
Capt. 7th N.Y. Vols.
Comdg Detachment

Col. R. B. Mason
Comdg 10th Mily Dept.
and Governor of California

Courtesy MNH

Shasta man, Kimolly. Photo 190[

2

CONDITIONS OF INDIANS

This selection of documents illustrates the conditions under which the Indians were living after the Gold Rush began. The flood of gold seekers into the state, and in their wake farmers who preempted land, had the immediate effect of reducing, and at times wholly eliminating, the food supply of the Indians (cf. 2:2, 2:6, 2:12). Indians were prohibited from possessing guns—a restraint aimed at reducing their retaliatory effectiveness, but also making it difficult to kill game which was becoming more scarce and shy because it was a source of food for the gold miners. Starving natives might steal food or kill a cow, and such acts led to punitive reaction by the whites. The prevalence of venereal disease (cf. 2:2, 2:14) was one of the results of the contact of the natives and whites. Hostile acts against Indians could not be redressed by legal means since Indians were prohibited from testifying against whites. Nor were Indians allowed to vote. The first legislature of 1850 thus effectively blocked Indians from participating in any way in the government despite the fact that in the Treaty of Guadalupe Hidalgo which marked the end of the Mexican War, the Indians, as former citizens of Mexico, were guaranteed American citizenship.

Camp Wessells California
December 31st 1853

Sir:

I have the honor to submit the following report as my observations of the Indians of this section of California.

When I left Fort Miller, with my Command, destined for the Four Creeks, it was with the belief that the Indians residing on these Creeks, and their tributaries, numbered at the least calculation six thousand. This information I had collected from the reports of gentlemen who had previously visited the Creeks. One of the County officers (of the County of Tulare) in making his report of the number of Indians living on the Four Creeks sets them down at something over nine thousand. I have made inquiries of "hunters" and other men residing on the Creeks who have time and again visited every Indian rancheria on them, from the Sierra Nevada down to Tule Lake. From the information thus gathered with what I have myself seen, I feel confident their numbers will not exceed one thousand all told.

I find that great numbers of them fall victim yearly to the Fever, ague and other fevers so prevalent during the summer and fall months, their mode of living being no guarantee against disease. One of the principal ingredients, with which they sustain life, is fish, and these have truly been supplied by nature in as great abundance as could be wished for by any people, the streams being literally filled with the finest quality of fish.

They take deer in great abundance, the meat of which they use for food. The skins, their chief article of traffic, are dressed. For these they obtain of the traders blankets and clothes. Acorns also are very plentifully supplied. Probably no portion of the State has more oak timber than the Four Creek country or the same area.

The Indians are now and have been ever since our little difficulty about the "ox" on the most friendly terms with the "Whites." When the affair referred to was settled, the Chief's made the most solemn promises to prevent their people in the future from stealing or molesting in any way the "White Settlers." This promise I have as yet no reason to believe has ever been violated on the part of the Indians. Moreover I am inclined to think the chastisement they have received will effectually serve as a check on their conduct for a long time to come.

I am sir very respectfully
Your obt Svt
John Nugens
Bvt. 2nd Lt, 2nd Inf.
Comdg: Detachment
To   Company: "G" 2nd Infantry
Lieut T. Wright
2nd U. S. Infantry
Comdg Fort Miller
Cal

2:2 Letter, Stevenson to Henley

Diamond Springs
El Dorado County
December 31st 1853

Sir:

In accordance with your instructions and the regulations of the Indian Department I respectfully submit for your consideration the following report.

Since my appointment by you as Special Indian Agent for the Counties of El Dorado, Placer, Amador and Calaveras, I have endeavored according to your instructions to ascertain the number and condition of the Indians within my agency, and also to instruct them as to the policy of the Government in their removal to and subsistence upon Military reservations.

The dictates of humanity and the good of our own people alike require the early and effective interposition of the Government in respect to the Indians of this locality. These Indians, some eight thousand in number, are divided into about one hundred and twenty-five separate bands or communities and some of them very difficult of access, and are to be found straggling about every mining camp in the mining regions. Many of them being without any settled place of habitation; and many of them have already imbibed the very worst vices of civilization, and are becoming vitiated and degraded, a pest and nuisance to the localities where they resort. It is a frequent occurrence to find white men living with Indian women and because the Indians dare to remonstrate against this course of conduct they are frequently subject to the worst and most brutal treatment. An occurrence of this kind took place last month near Buckeye Flat, in the County. Two miners had seduced a couple of squaws and were living with them or keeping them as prostitutes. The Indians went to the cabin and demanded their women, when they were fired upon by the miners which resulted in the immediate death of one and dangerously wounding another, and yet there was nothing but Indian evidence that could be obtained to punish these villains, and as the Indian's evidence is not allowed as against a White man in this State, they could not be convicted. The poverty and misery that now exists among these Indians is beyond description and is driving the squaws to the most open and disgusting acts of prostitution, thereby engendering diseases of the most frightful and fatal character. I had occasion a few days since to visit an Indian Camp, and on my arrival found one of their head men or chiefs. I conversed with him on the subject of removing the Indians to a Reservation. He answered me in quite good English saying that he was in favor of that course because he was satisfied that if they remained where they were they must all starve or fall a victim to that fatal disease that the white men had brought among them, but says he "I shall die before their removal can be accomplished, therefore, it matters but little to me." I asked him his reasons for thinking so, when to my surprise he showed me his legs which were

14

covered with ulcers peculiar to the disease I have referred to. He asked me if the Big Chief of the White men would cure them of this dreadful disease if they went to a reservation. I told him yes and, although I had no power or instruction from you to expend any money for medicine or medical treatment, I took him to a Doctor and paid him his prescriptions out of my own pocket, which I have done in many other cases of a like character. In one camp in the Eastern portion of this County I found nine squaws so far advanced with this disease that most of them were unable to walk. I turned in disgust and sorrow from a sight more revolting than I had ever before witnessed. In this diseased, unsettled, dispersed and otherwise unfavorable condition, nothing can be done to reclaim or improve them until they shall be removed to to a place where those evil influences are less likely to surround them.

In all my travels through the country I have invariably found that the better class of Indians are in favor of removing and willing to go to any place where they can have a permanent home, while the more worthless and drunken are opposed to any policy that would in the least interfere with their debased passions and appetites. I believe it is an admitted fact by every person at all conversant with Indian character that the use of ardent spirits stands more in the way of their civilization than anything that can be mentioned. When they are sober they are as easily managed and influenced to do what is right as most other people; but they all seem to have a strong appetite for whiskey, and will use every means in their power to obtain it and once under its influence their reason is gone. They are then ready for any acts of violence, brutality and crime that a savage nature can invent, and although the law in this State is very severe against those who sell them liquor, it is almost impossible to prevent them from obtaining it. I have endeavored to find out by Indians where they get liquor, but they will not inform. I have, however, succeeded in convicting and fining those persons in this county for selling or giving away liquor to Indians, which will have a tendency to lessen the traffic in that article among them. The Indians in this portion of the State are wretchedly

15

poor, having no horses, cattle or other property. They formerly subsisted on game, fish, acorns, etc., but it is now impossible for them to make a living by hunting or fishing, for nearly all the game has been driven from the mining region or has been killed by the thousands of our people who now occupy the once quiet home of these children of the forest. The rivers or tributaries of the Sacramento formerly were clear as crystal and abounded with the finest salmon and other fish. I saw them at Salmon Falls on the American river in the year 1851, and also the Indians taking barrels of these beautiful fish and drying them for winter. But the miners have turned the streams from their beds and conveyed the water to the dry diggings and after being used until it is so thick with mud that it will scarcely run it returns to its natural channel and with it the soil from a thousand hills, which has driven almost every kind of fish to seek new places of resort where they can enjoy a purer and more natural element. And to prove the old adage that misfortunes never come singly the oaks have for the last three years refused to furnish the acorn, which formed one of the chief articles of Indian food. They have often told me that the white man had killed all their game, had driven the fish from the rivers, had cut down and destroyed the trees and that what were now standing were worthless for they bore no acorns. In their superstitious imaginations they believe that the White man's presence among them has caused the trees (that formerly bore plentifully) to now be worthless and barren. In concluding this brief report I deem it my duty to recommend to your favorable consideration the early establishment of a suitable reservation and the removal of these Indians thereto, where they can receive medical aid and assistance which at the present time they so much require.

All of which is very respectfully submitted.

E. A. Stevenson
Hon. Thos. J. Henley   Spec. Indian Agent
Supt. of Indian Affairs
San Francisco Cal.

                                        Head Quarters
                                        Fort Miller Cal
Major E. D. Townsend   Feb 24th 1854
Asst. Adjt. Genl.
Dept of the Pacific
Sir
    I have to report that an inoffensive Indian was barba-
rously murdered about 12 o'clock last night by a white man
at the rancheria within a few hundred yards of this post. The
act was perpetrated in the most brutal manner by one of that
class of lawless ruffians, whose wanton aggressions upon the
Indians in different parts of this State, have so often provoked retaliation.
    The murderer has escaped, but a warrant for his arrest
has been issued.
                                        Respectfully
                                     Yr. Obedt. Servt.
                                        H. W. Wessells
                            Capt. 2nd Infy, Bvt. Major Comdg.

                                        Head Quarters
                                        Fort Miller Cal
Major E. D. Townsend   Mar. 7th 1852
Asst Adjt Genl
Dept of the Pacific
Sir
    Agreeably to the requirements of Circular from Head
Quarters of this Department, dated 18th ult., I have the
honor to submit the following statement, in regard to Indians
in the vicinity of Fort Miller.
    The tribes properly coming under the direct influence of
this post are scattered along the banks of the Fresno, San
Joaquin, King's and the Cah-we-yah rivers, the former being a
branch of the San Joaquin, and the two latter, tributaries of

the Tulare lake. These streams all take their rise in the great Sierra, and flow in a westerly direction, crossed nearly at right angles by the main road from Stockton to the Tejon pass, and Los Angeles. The rancherias on the Fresno are reached in about 20 miles from this point in a Northwesterly direction, those on the Cah-we-yah in about 65 miles Southerly, whilst Rio Reis (King river) is found at 25 miles in the same direction.

The tribes living on the Fresno have suffered much from sickness during the last three years, and from that cause have sensibly diminished in numbers, they may now be estimated at 400 souls including 100 able bodied men, those on the San Joaquin itself, and within ten miles of this post, have a total of 350, of which 80 or 90 are men.

On the Rio Reis [King River], the rancherias extend in detached positions, from the foot hills of the Sierra to the Tulare lake, and are estimated at 250 fighting men, or 1100 souls in all. Whilst those on the Cah-we-yah and its vicinity, will number 800, including 200 able bodied men, these later being within striking distance of the small outpost on Rowena Creek, a branch of the Cah-we-yah.

White settlers have established themselves without apprehension at eligible points on each of the streams already named, for agricultural and mining purposes. The Indians are docile and tractable in disposition, seem willing to live on amicable terms with the whites, and under the influence of a military force, a good understanding generally prevails, interrupted, however, by occasional acts of violence on the part of a certain class of desparadoes, who infest the mining regions of California, who regard oppression towards the weak as a merit, and with whom the life of an Indian, is valued only as that of a wild beast.

The Indians referred to in this statement are armed exclusively with bows and arrows, both in peace and war.

In connection with this subject, it may not be amiss, to refer to a singular and unaccountable aversion mutually existing between these Indians and the Chinese Emigrants, who in point of numbers, are becoming an important element in the population of this sparsely settled frontier. These latter regard the Indians with feeling of terror and abhorrence, with a vague notion that they are a species of cannibals, whilst the former view the strangers with the contempt due to an inferior being, ridicule their language, manners, and personal appearance, and impose upon them with impunity, when they can do so with safety to themselves.

Respectfully
Your Obed Servt
H. W. Wessells
Capt. 2 Infy, Bvt. Major Comdg.

2:4 Report, McDaniel and McQueen to Henley; letter, Henley to Manypenny

Office of the Superintendent
of Indian Affairs
Hon G. W. Manypenny   San Francisco Cal Oct. 14, 1854
Commissioner of Indian Affairs
Washington D. C.

Sir

For the information of the Department, I herewith enclose a copy of the report of Special Agents McDaniel and McQueen upon duties assigned them as shown by the report.

It is sometimes necessary to employ Agents temporarily for a special duty, who are discharged when that duty is performed.

Thos. J. Henley
Sup. Ind. Affairs

Benicia 4th Oct. 1854
Sir

In conformity to your instructions we proceeded to inspect the localities and condition of the Indians at the following places. First at the Bariessa Valley on the Peuta

[Putah] Creek we found something like one hundred and fifty Indians whose condition is that of slavery. We made inquiry in regard to the kidnapping referred to in your letter of instructions and found the Bariessa family in possession of a numerous gang of Indians at work on their Ranch of different tribes, all of whom had been driven in from the valley and mountains of Stone [Stony] Creek by violence, and they and certain Sonora Mexicans living with them are constantly in the practice of selling the young Indians, both male and female to whomsoever will purchase them. And we have ascertained to whom they have sold several of them, which testimony can be had to prosecute to conviction of this crime, but which we declined doing at present until we have further instructions from you. We then proceeded accross the mountains to Popes Valley where we found fifty or sixty Indians in the employ of Mr. Pope and living on his lands, but heard no complaint there of kidnapping, neither do we believe it to exist. From thence we proceeded to Kiota [Coyote] Valley and found on Mr. Stirling's land seventy five (75) Indians or there abouts who appeared to be doing well. From thence we proceeded to Clear Lake, the home of the Indians in this part of the country, whom we found cultivating the soil and living in abundance, contented and happy. They numbered seven or eight hundred. The country is eminently adapted to their wants, abounding in fish, grass and game. We found these Indians residing on land said to have been granted to Mexicans, and now belonging to Broom Smith and others, which grants have been rejected by the Board of Land Commission. There are two lakes, said to be thirty five miles long, connected by a narrow strait and from four to ten miles wide, of pure fresh water. This lake [Clear Lake] is about one hundred or one hundred and twenty miles from this place, surrounded by mountains and canions on all sides, entirely isolated from all arrible lands for a distance of twenty miles. From these facts we are decidedly of the opinion that this Lake is admirably adapted and is pointed out by nature for an Indian Reservation if private rights can be disposed of so as to disencumber it of conflicting title. There are also some few squatters on this valley and others as we hear are preparing to remove there. From this place or from Nappa there is a road which has been used by several waggons and had been found a tolerable mountain road capable of all necessary purposes of transporting the necessary supplies for the reservation.

We have also made diligent inquiry in relation to a Valley situated fifty miles north of Bariessa Valley on Peuta Creek, which has been mentioned as a suitable place for an Indian Reservation, and from whence the Bariessa's and their confederates drive in the Indians when they want them to harvest their grain, build their fences, and their homes, or for other purposes. This Valley, from the best information we can procure, is not of sufficient body of good land to warrant a reservation. The water which flows into the Sacramento near Calousa is said to be brackish, although there is said to be springs of pure water in the neighborhood, possibly on the land. We are also informed that the Valley is inaccessible for a waggon road, being surrounded by high and rugged mountains. We also found it our duty to make diligent inquiry of the country lying up Russian River above the settlements, and are of opinion that there is no Valley of sufficient extent and quality of soil to justify an Indian Reservation, although there is said to be numerous tribes of Indians there, all of whom are wild and hostile, but which we did not visit, as it would require a force of twenty or thirty men to penetrate their country and explore their land. We having but one man with us thought it improvident to attempt it, but the information we procured may be relied on.

All of which is respectfully submitted,
We have the honor to be signed
With respect
Your obt. Servts.
Wm. McDaniel on Special Duty
Wm. McQueen

To Thos. J. Henley Esq.
Superintendent of Indian
Affairs for California

2:5　Letters, Enyart to Henley; Henley to Manypenny

Fresno Reservation

To Thos. J. Henley　　　　　　　　Nov. 3rd 1854
Sup. Indian Affairs
San Francisco

Sir

According to your request I herewith submit you a report of the number of Indians at present living upon the Reservation under my charge here and also my opinion as to the number of Indians in the San Joaquin Valley.

No. of Indians residing on the Fresno Farm

TRIBES	CHIEFS	NO.
Chow-chilli	Niaque & Pojolil	30
Chook Chanches	Co-oquis	220
Pohonicha	Notoopa	90
Potohanchi	Bautista	100
	Whole No.	440

The above tribes are all living upon the Reservation doing all the work that is required to be done under the supervision of two or three White men. We keep constantly employed about 25 to 30 selecting five or six alternately every week from each Tribe, then dividing the labor between them.

They have gathered very few acorns this year owing to the great scarcity and are almost entirely destitute of anything to eat and consequently are dependant upon the Reservation for subsistence. I have started some on the River to catch fish and others are hunting wild game, but they never think of preparing anything of the kind for any length of time ahead.

They are all very much pleased with the Reservation and appear very willing to work. There is also the Pit Kachi Tribe,

Capt. Tom Kit, living on the San Joaquin River near Fort Miller, numbering 250, and who I am informed intend also to come over here in a few days, which will then make our whole number here this Winter 600., unless some other tribes should come over from the Merced River. They have heard of the intention of establishing a Reservation here all over the country and seem anxious to come without any solicitation.

In addition to the Indians enumerated above there are from the best information I can gather

upon the Merced River about	300
on Tuolumne River about	350
on Stanislaus River about	100
Dents Ferry on the Stanislaus River about	250
Scattering through the country	100
in all	1,100

This will I think comprise the whole number of Indians in Mariposa, Stanislaus, and Tuolumne Counties. I think that heretofore the number of Indians has been over estimated in this Valley and that at the most they will not exceed 2,000 in all.

There is no doubt but that the whole of them can be collected upon this farm without any difficulty. I think this place well adapted for the purpose and that within the year it will be the most prosperous Reservation in the State.

We will have under cultivation this coming year about five hundred acres of wheat, seven hundred acres of barley and two hundred acres of corn and vegetables.

The fence around the new field of 800 acres is nearly completed. We are now only waiting for the rain so as to be able to commence plowing.

I intend to start up the River a few miles next week with a small party of Indians and put them to mining, and if they are successful, I shall keep the most of them at work this winter. They are all much in need of clothing and blankets. If I succeed in mining, I shall be able to make them clothe themselves. All of the Indians at present here are very

23

temperate, not being accustomed to the use of liquor. No spirits is allowed them in any shape on the Reservation.

Hoping that I may be successful in carrying out your ideas and desires here

I remain Respectfully Your obt. servt.
(signed) D. A. Enyart
Office of the Superintendent of Indian Affairs
San Francisco Dec. 11, 1852

Hon. G. W. Manypenny
Commr. Indn Affrs.

Sir

I have the honor to send you the above report of the Special Indian Agent at the Indian Farm on the Fresno.

Very Respectfully
Thos. J. Henley

2:6   Letter, Henley to Manypenny

Office of the Superintendent
of Indian Affairs
Hon G. W. Manypenny   San Francisco Dec. 8, 1854
Comm. Indian Affairs
Washington D. C.

Sir:

The following is an extract from a letter of the Special Agent for the Northern portion of the State.

In speaking of the Trinity Indians he says, "Besides the failure of the Salmon to get above the Flumes at Scotts Bar and the increasing wildness of the game and the effect of the law prohibiting the whites from selling them powder (which difficulties all the Indians labor under), besides these the war-

24

riors of the Shasta tribe are almost exterminated, leaving a large number of women and children, some old men and women, some blind and crippled, and all in almost a helpless condition. These have come over and remained in this neighborhood, and I have furnished them with beef, which together with what beef I have furnished other Indians in necessitous cases ammounts to about 2,000 pounds at 17 cents per pound. Now I am well satisfied if you were here you would with the pitiful condition of these Indians in full view have furnished them more than I have. But I feel uneasy lest you may not approve my conduct or might think I was taking too much responsibility in the matter. This is the reason I write again, and also request you to see Lieut. Bonnycastle. For rest assured, I would not furnish these Indians one pound of beef on government accounts (though I might have the mortification to see them starve) if I did not feel satisfied that you would approve it. If you desire me to furnish no more, say so by letter, and I will furnish them no more. I hope you will not think me sensitive, but I want to know whether my conduct as an officer is approved or I incur responsibility—the necessity of which might be absolute and the propriety of which might seem clear to my mind, still by possibility it might not seem so clear to you."

Very Respectfully
Your obt. Servt.
Thos. J. Henley
Sup. Ind. Affrs.

2:7   Letter, Dougherty to Henley

Col. T. J. Henley   Bodega Dec. 12, 1854

Sir
As special Indian agent for the counties of Sonoma, Napa, Marin and Mendocino, I submit the following report.

In pursuance of instructions I visited the Indians located on Russian River & in the Valleys of Ukiah, Sanel & Massatakiah & brought down between three and four hundred, who according to your suggestions, were distributed to labor among the settlers.

They remained from about the middle of September until the latter portion of November when they returned home perfectly satisfied, all having received clothing such as they required consisting principally of Blankets, Pantaloons, Shirts, etc. and in addition thereto taking home with them hoes, picks, shovels, hatchets, axes and other articles of necessity. Under my management, they earned between three and four thousand dollars, every cent expended upon themselves, and the only expense chargeable upon the government is the sum of ninety dollars, the cost of taking them to their homes. On arriving there, they (the Indians) freely distributed among their friends the proceeds of their labor. There is about 4,000 Indians in the above mentioned localities.

I fully set forth the views of the Government in reference to the providing a reservation on which they could do their own work and support themselves, which seemed to meet their general approbation, and I have no doubt they will easily be persuaded to adopt the views of the Superintendent. In connection with their management as well as their protection I am compelled to state that a band of scoundrels, generally fugitive Americans and Spaniards, are in the habit not only of carrying off Indian children, but also committing outrages upon their women, and I have not as yet the power to suppress it. If the authority of the U.S. Marshall could be exercised, many of them could be caught and on adequate proof convicted in the U. S. Courts. I would also request that sufficient arms be furnished to the Agent, to equip half a dozen men, who among the settlers can always be procured to assist those depredators.

If stringent means be adopted to break up these bands, it would not only be beneficial to the Indians, but a great benefit to the settlers, for the cattle and horse stealing belongs largely to their business, and I would earnestly recommend that prompt measures be taken to drive them from the counties. In conclusion I would recommend that a band of Pamphalo Indians about one hundred and thirty residing near the settlements, should be immediately forced to join the main body about 70 miles above their camp in the resort of the above mentioned Spaniards and Americans, and by so doing you thus relieve the settlers from the thieving of the Indians but will do much to disperse those who make it their rendezvous.

I remain
Your Obt. servt.
M. C. Dougherty

2:8 Letter, Wooman and Johnson to Henley

Cow Creek March 25th 1855

Dear Sir

Your favor of Feb 5th, through some cause unknown, was not received by the undersigned till the 21st inst., hence you will readily perceive the reason of receiving no earlier answer, and also why neither of us or Mr. Dribelbis met you at Nome Lackee. Agreeably to your suggestion, most gladly would we have done so, as many facts touching the Indians in this section could have been laid before you, which none can be conversant with save those who have passed months among them. It is much to be regretted that some provision the past winter had not been made for those northern Indians by way of feeding and collecting them at certain points as preparatory steps for their final move to some selected point either in their immediate homes or farther remote. But from the tenor of your communication such discretionary power is not vested in the Supt.

Notwithstanding the extreme mildness of the past winter many of these Indians have perished—literally starved—and such must have been the fate of many others but for the scanty rations furnished by Miners and Settlers living near and among them. Prominent among the many reasons that might be urged in their behalf is the well known fact that they are a numerous powerful and war-like race, capable of immense mischief to the whites as in winters past too many can bear witness, with salmon their great article of food mostly cut off and opportunities of plunder daily increasing and yet preferring a lingering death of starvation to a life of robbery and theft. True of late a few petty thefts have occurred and ever will occur while hunger impels, and for every such offence one must be hung or even a whole Ranch surprised and shot; the citizens believing the like summary chastisement their imperative duty as self protection, so long as the Government offers no aid or other means of redress. You write of having made application for power to establish two additional Reservations, with a design of locating one in the Pitt River Section. We rejoice at this and cannot urge too much in its favor, and the Indians nothing could please them better: they are willing and anxious that a location should be furnished them in their own mountain homes and would at any time gladly settle upon and improve the same. At the same time the mass of them are averse to leaving the mountains for the valley: even yesterday one of the Chiefs from high up on the McCloud River made mention of the fact that many of his men had perished the past winter while afraid to come into the lower hills for roots and clover, fearing the whites would compel them to remove onto the Reserve below. We have heard it has been represented at Nome Lackee that settlers in the Pitt River Section are opposed to their removal on the ground of their being useful as laborers. Such is not the fact. Not one in fifty ever think of working, those who work being confined to a few boys and adults who are fed and clothed and live the same as hired help.

The citizens are opposed, however, to the removal of those living immediately among and around them, while those higher in the mountains are left to swarm in upon them to murder and plunder. While the friendly Indians remain, the wild mountain ones dare not venture in on such excursions. Is there no law by which persons can be punished for taking Indians and Squaws against their will to Shasta and other places and selling them? We think so.

A certain one (perhaps the plural might be used) carries on quite a flourishing traffic in this business.

Very Respectfully
Your Obt. Servt.
Geo. Wooman
D. C. Johnson

Col. T. J. Henley
Supt. Ind. Affrs.
California

2:9   Letter, Stevenson to Henley

Diamond Springs
El Dorado County
June 18th 1855

Thos. J. Henley Esqr.

In compliance with your letter of instructions of May 8th 1855, I have the honor to submit the following report.

The No. of Indians in El Dorado County as near as can be ascertained at present are as follows: to wit, about "Coloma" 300—"Hangtown" 250—"Indian Diggins" and vicinity 350—"Pilot Hill" 300—"Diamond Springs" 250—on the various branches of the "Consumnes" River including "Grizzly Flat", "Leak Springs" and "Pleasant Valley" 300.

The above statement of the number of Indians in the County of El Dorado is as near correct as I could get it in the time allotted to me to make this report. The Indians are living in small squads or "ranchoreis" all over the County, some of them very difficult of access: others in the immediate vicinity of our mining towns who lead such a wandering unsettled life that it takes a long time to number them correctly.

The Indians in the County are peaceable in their character, but their condition is wretched in the extreme. They live on grass, seeds, acorns, pinenuts, clover & insects. The Squaws in this County lead a life of prostitution, contracting disease and disseminating it among the Indians, the terrible consequences of which no language can portray. I have found some 50 that were dying with this awful disease. They are all fond of the "fire water" and get beastly intoxicated every opportunity they have. Their situation as it is is truly a pitiable one, and calls aloud for action on the part of the Government. They are desirous to know when the policy of the U. S. will be extended to them, and I think there will be no trouble in removing them to reservations.

I have purchased a horse of Mr. Brown for which I gave $200 dollars. The receipt for the money is herewith transmitted. I will be at your Office when I will settle with you as per vouchers for my traveling expenses. (I will be down next month) You will send me as soon as possible $200 which I will require to prosecute my labours in the interior of this County.

All of which is respectfully submitted.

Edwd. A. Stevenson
Special Indian Agent

Thos. J. Henley Esqr
Supt Indn Affairs
San Francisco

2:10   Letter, Ord to Mackall

Benicia Cal—August 9th 1856

Sir:

In obedience to instructions I left here on the 20th ult. and proceeded to San Bernardino, The Sycamore Grove—to San Gorgonio Pass, going and returning via Indian villages and to "Jurupa" and "Chino" Ranches with a view to select a suitable site for a military post and to obtain information as to the temper and condition of the Indians and other inhabitants.

As the country is much changed since last reports, the Indians and people differently occupied, I will state how I found them, and it can be then understood where a military post is wanted.

At Los Angeles, I found the Americans and Mexicans arrayed against each other. Some thousands of Mexicans annually pass through, and a large number live at this place. They are well armed and hostile, and a U. S. force is more imperatively demanded to prevent a revolution of these discontented foreigners than to keep down the Indians, who are simply the servants of the whites. Should the Indians attempt a servile insurrection, it would be due to the insidious influence of the Mexicans.

I visited all the Rancho's within twenty miles of San Bernardino as well as that place, and I found, except a few left in their villages to watch the crops, that the Indians are all quietly labouring on the farms, cattle ranches or in the villages, as servants to the whites, according to the laws of this State (abstract of which is appended).

It will be seen that by this law the overseer of a large rancho has but to be a "justice of the peace," and he is enabled to buy and keep Indian servants "as he may want them, and to punish them at discretion within a limit." The system thus legalised provides labour in a hot climate where otherwise there would be none, and it being a continuation of the system to which the Indians were accustomed under the Mexican rule, it works well. Each of the large cattle rancho's near Los Angeles and San Bernardino has from fifteen to thirty Indians permanently occupied on it. They are numerously employed by the Mormons at San Bernardino, so Genl. Rich, the head Elder informed me; and the Mayor of Los Angeles stated to me that there are about four hundred Indians continuously employed in that town. Their pay averages about six dollars a month. I myself have employed these Indians both as private servants and on public service, and

31

they are the best and cheapest the southern country affords. The State laws, as will be seen by the abstract, makes no provision for any rebellion of the Indians against this system of servitude, and they have generally been submissive and appear contented under it.

In some instances these servile Indians have been deluded and disappointed by promises of aid from Washington, which promises were never realised. These promises are made by men who have been, claim to be or are acting as Indian Agents, as the Indians have been told of moneys meant for them of which they get little or nothing. Of course, they fancy they are deprived of their rights.

In too many cases, especially in San Diego and San Bernardino Counties, where the country is mostly a dry desert or barren mountains and where employment for the Indians driven from the few moist patches by the squatters is scarce, complaints have been frequently made by the Indians (compelled to yield the irrigable patches whereon they have lived) to State and military authorities. Of course, as the Squatter law prevails, the poor Indians have no redress.

I am aware that a portion of what are known as the Tulare Indians were for a time gathered on a reservation near the "Tejon" Pass, but they became dissatisfied and most of them left. This attempt of the General government to provide for unprovided Indians near the mines and beyond the cattle ranchos is praiseworthy, and if the Genl. government could have controlled the white men who occupy the Indians' country and selected honest men, not politicians, to have managed their reserves, the plan might have been of service to the Indians. But the interests of the managers of these reserves and the interests of the Indians are incompatible. Besides the laws of the U. S. governing the first and the laws of the State governing the last are at variance, hence no good can result from the reserve system as at present managed.

At San Bernardino I found that the Mormons were attending to their crops and families, and as they have small crops and large families and have discontent and dissension at home, they have no time for interfering in Indian affairs.

Their common people are ignorant, and I should think from what I saw and heard, timid, so that being under excellent control of shrewd Elders, these Elders will preserve peace without and good order within, as well as possible, because their community is surrounded with unscrupulous squatters and dissenters, anxious for an excuse to drive them from the country at San Bernardino.

The Mormon Valley is an extensive bottom or meadow where the head of the Santa Anna River quits the bold escarpments of San Bernardino Mtn. This meadow is mostly fenced, in small squares. So their village is a village of corn fields, surrounded with barren mountains and desolate plains and affords no grasing except for the private cattle. The Indians have made no forays through the Cajon for three or four years. On the contrary, cattle are now driven by its owners for the benefit of the better grass, through the Cajon Pass, to the banks of the Mojave River, whence the Indians used to come to steal. Hence I think there is neither use nor economy in a Post at San Bernardino or at Sycamore Grove, where there is neither wood, water or grass sufficient.

The necessity for a military Post in San Gorgonio Pass depends on its being the travelled route to the Jila River. Parties are now out on the desert to ascertain if a line of Stage Coaches cannot be put through the pass to the "Jila." As soon as this route is permanently adopted by immigrants, a military post will be necessary in the San Gorgonio pass as near as practicable to the desert (the upper weavers is the site I would select) for the protection of travellers against the Desert and Colorado River Indians (who now murder small parties). The country is generally a desert, the roads over plains with water at long intervals—the climate very hot. Hence, Infantry could be of but little service, and I think it would be a good place to try the camels, at the upper Weavers, should lumber be required. It is within eight miles. Water, too, is there enough for a large command if used economically—and plenty of good grass—but the reservation should be set aside and the squatters now there bought out and others kept off for the entire control of the water would be necessary to the post.

Should troops be immediately stationed at any place between the "Tejon" and San Diego, Los Angeles is the proper point of some place in its vicinity, for it is the head quarters for all information. Supplies of all kinds can be had cheaply and dragoons especially can reach any of the settlements likely to be threatened with trouble in a day or two. The American part of its population is not more than one eighth the whole number, and the foreigners, native Californians and Indians are not so well disposed towards the American Government but they could be tampered with by parties disposed to produce civil commotion or revolution.

Respectfully submitted with a reference to the map of a survey of R Road Routes, by R. S. Williamson and and J. G. Parke U. S. T. Engrs. and J. W. Smith, C.E., for plans and distances.

Respectfully your Obdt Servt
To   E. O. C. Ord, Capt. 3rd Arty.
Major W. W. Mackall
Asst. Adjt. Genl. Hd. Qrs. Pac. Div.
Benicia California

2:11   Letter, Henley to Mix

Office Supt. Ind Affs
Chas E. Mix Esqr.   San Francisco June 19 1858

Sir

In referring to my communication of this date in reference to the killing of Indians by white persons for fancied or real aggressions by Indians.

I have to report the arrival of James Cunningham from the Matole Station near Mendocino with the intelligence that the settlers in that vicinity have attacked, killed or driven away all the Indians who had been collected at the station, and are now raging an indiscriminate war upon all who can be found either in the valley or in the mountains. He saw on the day he left for this place several Indians shot without any known provocation. He reports that a party of thirty men were then in readiness to start for Shelter Cove and other places upon the coast for the avowed purpose of attacking and destroying all the Rancheries in that vicinity.

Those Indians are peaceable and well disposed, and this is a most outrageous and murderous expedition.

I have of course no remedy for such outrages. Mr. Cunningham has been directed to return and endeavor as far as possible by peaceable and conciliatory policy to disuade the whites from this severe and inhumane policy and to pacify the Indians and prevent them if possible from resorting to retaliation and revenge, which would generally fall upon the heads of innocent persons. There is great excitement among all the Indians in the entire coast country, and very bad feeling exists among the whites and there is a prospect of serious difficulty during the Summer. Every precaution, however, in my power will be adopted to prevent it. In this case one or two special agents will be kept travelling during the Summer to meet any emergency that may arise.

Very Respectfully your
Obt Svt
Thos. J. Henley
Supt. Ind Affrs.

2:12   Newspaper editorial, Sacramento, 1855

Indian War

The accounts from the North indicate the commencement of a war of extermination against the Indians. The latter commenced the attack on the Klamath; but who can determine their provocation or the amount of destitution suffered before the hostile blow was struck.

The intrusion of the white man upon the Indians' hunting grounds has driven off the game and destroyed their fisheries. The consequence is, the Indians suffer every winter for sustenance. Hunger and starvation follows them wherever they go. Is it, then, a matter of wonder that they become desperate and resort to stealing and killing? They are driven to steal or starve, and the Indian mode is to kill and then plunder.

The policy of our Government towards the Indians in this State is most miserable. Had reasonable care been exercised to see that they were provided with something to eat and wear in this State, no necessity would have presented itself for an indiscriminate slaughter of the race.

The fate of the Indian is fixed. He must be annihilated by the advance of the white man; by the diseases, and, to them, the evils of civilization. But the work should not have been commenced at so early a day by the deadly rifle.

To show how the matter is viewed on the Klamath, we copy the following from the Crescent City *Herald*. The people look upon it there as a war of extermination, and are killing all grown up males. A writer from Trinidad, under date of January 22d, says:

I shall start the two Indians that came down with me to-night, and hope they may reach Crescent City in safety, although I think it exceedingly doubtful, as the whites are shooting them whenever an opportunity offers; for this reason I start them in the night, hoping they may be out of danger ere morning. On the Klamath the Indians have killed six white men, and I understand some stock. From the Salmon down the whites are in arms, with determination, I believe, if possible, to destroy all the grown up males, notwithstanding this meets with the opposition of some few who have favorite Indians amongst them. I doubt whether this discrimination should be made, as some who have been considered good have proved the most treacherous. I understand that the ferry of Mr. Boyce, as also that of Mr. Simms, has been cut away. Messrs. Norton and Beard have moved their families from Elk Camp to Trinidad; they were the only white females in that section that were exposed to the savages. I have no doubt there will be warm times on the Klamath for some weeks, as the Indians are numerous, well armed and determined to fight.

36

Condition of the Indians
in Tuolumne County

The Tuolumne *Courier* draws the following picture of the miserable condition of the Indians in and about Columbia:

For months past our feelings have been shocked at the condition of the Indians who are located about this neighborhood. There is no sympathizing care extended to these frail relics of humanity, as the storms sweep over their miserable huts and unclad bodies. Their intercourse with civilized communities has been accompanied with the ordinary results which other tribes have experienced under similar circumstances: prostitution, intemperance, and vice, in their most revolting aspects. As soon as the grey light of morning appears, they may be seen prowling round in search of miserable offal, for which they must compete with the dogs. At midnight their savage howls may frequently be heard, as they return to their sleeping places, half crazy from the poisonous drink which they have imbibed from some of the low groggeries about the outskirts of the town. A few weeks ago, one of their number murdered another in the vicinity of the Catholic church, while raving with madness from the above cause. But there is no law enforced for these poor wretches. It is no one's business to look after and to protect them. Why do not our citizens ask the Legislature to have them removed to one of the reservations, where they will be comfortable, and be afforded an opportunity of learning some of the Christian ways of civilized beings?

Condition of the Indians in the Middle Mines

The condition of the Indians in the vicity of Jackson, Amador county, demands the immediate attention of the Indian Agent in this State, for while appropriations have been made for the relief and removal of the Indians in almost every part of the State, those of El Dorado, Amador and Calaveras counties have been entirely neglected. Some time ago an agent was appointed in El Dorado county, but he has not taken any action in the premises. A more miserable or degraded race of beings never existed than the Indians in this vicinity, for in addition to their slothful and filthy habits, they have acquired all of the lower order of vices of the white man, which they indulge in without a particle of that moral restraint which governs more or less the actions of the white man. It is no uncommon sight in Amador county to see half a dozen of these miserable creatures reeling about the streets in a disgusting state of drunkenness, indulging in the most obscene language and actions, which cannot fail to excite in every breast a feeling of compassion for the Indian, and an outburst of honest indignation against the fiend-like white man (God save the mark!) who furnishes them with the poison by which they elevate the character of the brute creation by a favorable comparison with "God's image."

Justice not only to the whites, but the Indians themselves, demands their immediate removal from among us, and unless this is done, in a few more years the race of Digger Indians in the vicinity of Jackson will become extinct. The most loathsome diseases, the natural consequence of their contact with civilization, prevails among them to an alarming extent, and while it is carrying the red man rapidly to the grave, it exercises the most demoralizing influence upon society, by a familiar association with the idea of lechery which the most depraved and abandoned mind can possibly conceive. Amador *Sentinel.*

Clear Lake Indians

The Napa *Reporter* does not give a very favorable idea of the condition of the Clear Lake Indians. It says:

The Indians at Clear Lake are about 150 in all, and have under fence and in cultivation, after their fashion, about 100 acres. They have been hemmed in more and more each year by settlers who have taken up pre-emption claims, and even now remain only by sufferance. Most of the settlers are friendly to the Indians, and disposed to do all in their power for their comfort, but there are, we are very sorry to say, some exceptions. The Clear Lake tribe has dwindled from 10,000 in 1849 to a mere remnant of about 500 in all. The aged warriors state that they have a sorry time of it—being often pinched for food and clothing, while the younger men, by laboring on the ranches can supply themselves and wives with all that is necessary. Our informant states that while even the old chiefs have scarcely so much as a dirty shirt to hide their nakedness, many of the young men are well dressed after the American fashion, and their women furnished with gay dresses and even hoops!

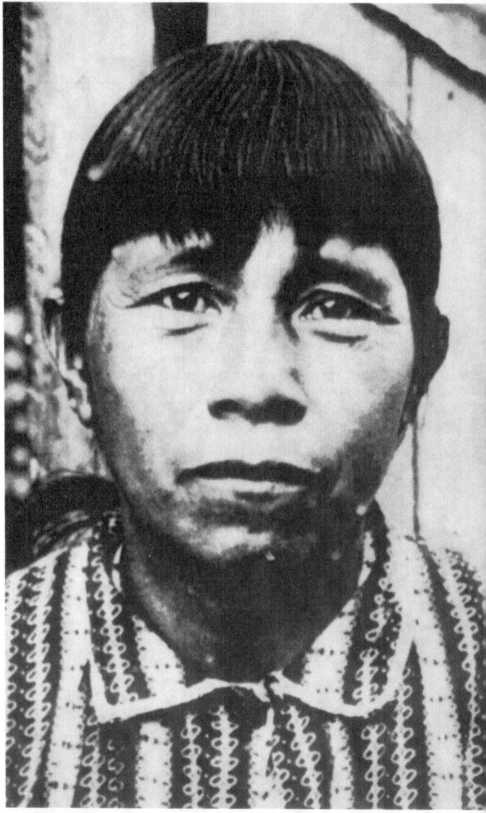

Courtesy LMA   Monache woman. Mrs. Ben Hancock. *Photo 190*

REGULAR AND VOLUNTEER TROOP ACTIONS AGAINST INDIANS

This section is concerned with actions of volunteer and regular troops against Indians. Such actions were usually justified as necessary to punish Indians who had attacked or killed whites or had stolen livestock. Indians, of course, did attack whites and steal cattle for food, not because they were unregenerate savages, but in retaliation for white atrocities and for their loss of livelihood resulting from seizure of their lands and the scarcity of food. A cycle of White-Indian retaliation was thus established. Federal troops seem, on the whole, to have acted with discipline and restraint, but they were often under extreme pressure by the local settlers to kill as many Indians as possible, and conflicts between federal and state laws were common. It is clear that the white settlers in California wanted the Indians to be wholly eliminated because they were considered a danger to peace and security.

Cantonment Far West Cal.
16th May 1850

Sir

I have the honor to report the following circumstances and my proceedings relative to a recent murder committed in this vicinity by Indians. Viz:

A message was received by me on the the the 8th Inst. from James Walsh residing on Wolf Creek some twenty two miles up the Imigrant Road, between Bear Creek and Yuba River, that on the day previous (the 7th) some twenty Indians had made an attack on Samuel H. Holt and his brother George Holt, who were quietly working in or about their saw mill, located on said creek and about half a mile from Walsh's cabin. Samuel H. Holt was killed and George severely wounded by arrows. Their cabin was robbed at once of all valuables and subsequently both cabin and saw mill have been burned to the ground, supposed to be the work of the same party of natives. On the moment of learning the facts, having but 8 privates for duty, I detached Lieut. Hendershott, one corporal and five privates to the scene of the murder, with orders to arrest, if possible, any of the guilty party. Doct. Murray accompanied the command to render professional aid to the wounded man Holt, and I am glad to report his opinion that said wounds are not mortal. Lieut. H. returned on the 11th without having found any save one Indian, who was seen loitering near the scene of the depredation and whom he secured under the possibility of his being a look-out of the war-like party, but no body of Indians was found and the previous camps were entirely abandoned, which in connection with other facts, convinces me that the culprits have escaped to the south over Bear Creek.

From the same reliable source, I am informed of the probable cause of this otherwise inaccountable affair, as Messrs. Holt have been all winter on the most friendly terms with the Indians, and even more, have treated them kindly and hospitably. It seems that on or about the 6th Inst. some ten white men made an attack on this Indian camp and killed two (if not three) Indians, under the impression that said Indians or some others had stolen and killed some of their cattle which were then missing. But behold the very next day, after having boasted of their feat the lost cattle were found. It may readily be supposed that, in revenge, the natives fell upon the Holts as the most available victims and considering that after such outrages, all white men were equally at fault. And thus has one been murdered, another severely wounded and their property been destroyed the work and earnings of many months (for with the mill were consumed some thousands of feet of lumber) purely in consequence of a lawless aggression of white men in the first instance!!

Such affairs are becoming quite frequent and unless some steps can be taken to stop them, it may be found that a more innocent class—the emigrants of this season from the East—may become victims to the Indian love of vengeance,— Crossing the Sierra too, as they will, with bitter apprehension, so near the operations of their countrymen in the mines, and broken down partially, as many will be, after a long overland trip and perhaps not so well supplied with ammunition.

With the present reduced state of my command, a military station here or at any other point in this valley, serves as the merest pretense of protection or aid of any kind to the inhabitants, as I have not the force or ability to send ten bayonets a mile from the camp on any duty whatever. So far as the mining population is concerned, they are competent to their own defense beyond all doubt, and since the State Legislature is complete, any difficulty among themselves, I should presume, could be managed by the civil authorities.

On the occasion before referred to in this letter I took the precaution to instruct Lieut. Hendershott to render any assistance which might be wanted by a sheriff or his deputy (as I understood he was near the scene of outrage at that time) in arresting the white men who appeared to have been the first aggressors, but he had no call of that nature.

If there be any Agent of the Indian Department for this valley, I would respectfully suggest that he be advised to make an excursion among the natives with an Interpreter to notify them, at least, of what will be their probable fate unless they discontinue their thieving and submit with a better grace to being shot down, although it may seem strange to them, thus to be intruded upon by the whites, for so far as my information goes the whole mining district of this valley is still Indian Territory and as yet never treated for or even notice given that they must vacate their hunting grounds in favor of our gold diggers.

Respectfully Submitted by Sir.
Your Obt. Servt.
H. Day
Capt. Comdg.

To
Asst Adjt. Genl.
Hd. Qrs. 10 Mil Dept.
Monterey

3:2   Letter, Judah to Wright

Fort Jones Cala.
January 31st 1854

Sir,

I have the honor to report that I left Fort Jones with twenty six men of my Company on the 16th Inst, and reached Cottonwood, thirty miles distant, on the 18th where

I was joined by twenty four Volunteers from that place, with whom I marched on the 19th nine miles to a good camping ground, within four miles of the cave occupied by the Indians, and then made a reconnaissance to within two miles of that point, finding two of the dead bodies, referred to in the copy of that letter I had the honor to forward you, from the citizens of Cottonwood. On the next morning I started for the Cave, over a rough and broken trail, the ground for the last two miles being admirably suited for an ambuscade, for which, from the character of the previous attack by the Indians, I was prepared. I met with no opposition and posted myself about three hundred and fifty yards in front of the cave, protected by a slight ledge of rocks, and from which the Indians at its mouth were distinctly visible. The cave was situated upon an opposite slope, and an attacking party would be subjected to a continual fire up to its very mouth, unprotected by tree or rock. The cave can only be entered by a small aperture, behind which is thrown up a breast work of heavy timber. A desultory fire was for a short time made by my party, without my orders, which was occasionally returned by the Indians. I had brought with me my animals and packs in the hope of finding a safe and suitable encampment from which I might operate, but after a diligent search, no one could be found supplying wood and water, and at which it would not have required the detail of at least half my force as a guard against surprise. I then deemed it my duty to propose to Capt. Grieger (Comdg the Volunteers) to storm the cave, a proposal to which I think for good reasons, he did not consider it safe to accede. There is a point upon the top of the cave which could have been more easily and safely reached than the one I assumed, but from which the entrance could not be reached. From my own observations, added to the absence of a safe and suitable encampment, I decided it was proper and safe to postpone an attack, and return to Camp, which I did starting immediately for Cottonwood accompanied by Asst. Surgn. Sorrel and Lieut Crook, whom I despatched the following morning to Fort Jones for a mountain Howitzer, with which I hoped to reach the mouth of the cave from the position I had vacated. At the same time I dispatched an Express to Fort Jones for provisions of which I had brought a supply but for ten days for my own Command, but which were quite exhausted by the necessity for supplying the Volunteers. I returned to camp the next day with fresh Beef for the Command. During this time the cold was intense, probably reaching at times as low a temperature as 20° below 0 Fah. as I find that at Yreka, which is of a much lower altitude, that during my absence the mercury had fallen to 15° below 0. We were also subjected to several severe snow storms, against which, having no tents, we were unprotected. On the 21st I was prostrated by unusual exertion and exposure, which induced a paroxism of a chronic complaint under which I am laboring, and incapacitated me for further exertion. Capt. Smith with Lt. Ogle, arrived on the 23rd with the howitzer, and left with the command on the ensuing morning for the cave, to which I did not feel myself able to accompany him.

The details of his attack he will probably communicate. Its result was a determination to desist from any further hostile movement. Capt. Ben Wright, a celebrated Indian partizan fighter, and others of experience in Indian warfare, in common with the whole party, agree that a point and direct attack (the only possible one) would be attended with a loss of life incommensurate with the object to be attained (if possible to succeed at all). As the top of the cave can be safely reached and occupied, it is generally believed that the Indians can be only forced to evacuate, by drilling down and blasting its roof. On the morning succeeding the return of Captain Smith, with the command, our encampment was broken up and I reached this Post this evening. I am pleased to acknowledge my extreme indebtedness to the officers of my company, Lieuts. Bonnycastle and Crook, and Asst. Surgeon Sorrell, without the aid of whose intelligence and activity I could not have conducted an expedition so hastily executed and at a season of the year so unpropitious. The men of the command evinced extraordinary endurance and uniform good conduct.

Very Respectfully
Your Obt. Servt.
Henry M. Judah
Capt. 4th Infantry
Commdg

Col G. Wright
Comdg N. Div. of Cal
Fort Reading
Cala.

3:3 Letters, Buchanan to Townsend (2); Lothian to Buchanan

Head Quarters, Detachment 4th Infantry
Fort Humboldt, Cal., Oct. 11th, 1854

Sir,

I have the honor to report the return of the party under Capt. Judah, on the 9th inst. and to enclose his report of the expedition. From this it will be seen that the murderers of Mr. Wigman were captured after a very fatiguing pursuit, which was judiciously conducted by Capt. Judah. These prisoners are now in confinement in the guard house, where I shall keep them until called for by the civil authority or until I receive instructions concerning them from the General as I have no specific instructions as to the disposal of prisoners under such circumstances as the present. I should be pleased to learn whether my present course is in accordance with the General's views. I have some doubts in my own mind as to which is the proper Court to try them, the State or United States District Court. I have, however, addressed a letter on the subject to the County Attorney for this County, of which the enclosed is a copy. I also enclose a copy of my instructions to Capt. Judah.

I am Sir,
Respectfully
Your Obt. Servt.
Robt. C. Buchanan
Bvt. Lt. Col. Capt. 4th Inf.
Commdg

To
Bvt. Maj. S. D. Townsend
Asst. Adjt. Genl.
Dept of the Pac.
Benicia Cal.

Head Quarters Detachment 4th Infantry
Fort Humboldt, Cal, Oct. 19th 1854

Sir,

I have the honor to enclose for the information of the General, Commanding, the reply of the County Attorney to my communication of the 10th inst. heretofore enclosed.

From this letter of Mr. Van Dyke, the newly elected Attorney, it will be seen that there is no disposition on the part of the State authorities for this County to take charge of these Indians, and I therefore request, if not already done, that full instructions be given me in relation to disposing of them. The act referred to by Mr. Van Dyke is not applicable to the case, and he ought to be aware of it, as I presume he must be, as it is merely quoted in order to shift the responsibility from the civil authorities of the State to myself, for it is perfectly evident that I cannot "issue process or order under the authority of the United States." The offence is one against the peace and dignity of the State of California, I imagine, as it was committed on one of her citizens, and in a portion of territory claimed to be under her jurisdiction, and hence the offenders are clearly to be tried by her Courts and punished according to her laws. It would seem strange that I should arrest these men under any other authority than that of the United States, for it is well known to the Attorney that I have neither the authority nor inclination to meddle with the laws of the State, except so far as my plain duty, *as in this case*, enables me to assist in bringing offenders against them to justice. He knows that I was sent here "to protect this section of country against the Indians," and in the execution of the duty assigned me, arrested these two Indians who had committed a murder on the person of one of the citizens of the State, within the limits of this County. The simple explanation of the difficulty is this: The people of the County do not want to go to the expence of keeping these prisoners until the next regular term of the District Court, and the County Attorney in his letter only reflects that feeling. This feeling is so strong that the "Humboldt Times" openly advocates the organization of a "Committee of Vigilance" instead of a trial by law, as is shown by the enclosed extract from last Saturday's issue. If this course is to be adopted, it strikes me that it will hardly be necessary for me to apprehend any more Indians, as I certainly shall not turn them over to any but the properly constituted authorities, and then only upon a requisition made in due form of law, or in obedience to the orders of the Commander of the Department. In conclusion, I would respectfully request that I may be furnished with an immediate answer to this communication.

I am, Sir,
Respectfully
Your Obt. Servt.
Robt. C. Buchanan
Bvt. Lt. Col. Capt. 4th Inf.
Commdg.

To
Bvt. Maj. E. D. Townsend
Asst. Adjt. Gen.
Dept. of the Pac.
Benicia
Cal.

[Copy of newspaper clipping referred to in preceding letter, name of paper and date not ascertainable from clipping]

A Vigilance Committee

We are opposed to "mob law" as is practiced in some of the States, but have ever, since our residence in this State, approved of the formation of Vigilance Committees, consisting only of respectable citizens, men not liable to be led away by excitement, but who could cooly and dispassionately adjudge the merits of a question or the guilt or innocence of a prisoner, outside of a court room. If there ever existed a necessity for such an association, it is in our county, as has been fully shown within the past two months. A citizen of the county has his dearest rights trampled on, his sanctuary polluted, he himself slain, basely assassinated, the wife of his bosom not satisfied with dishonoring his bed, is proven to have instigated, encouraged and excited her paramour to take his life. The murderer is arrested, sufficient testimony is elicited to have hung both, but by an unfortunate omission, the woman is not indicted. Her testimony though of minor import to prove her complicity in the murder is used for the State and she unfortunately for justice occupies a place in the witness, instead of the criminal box. The facts of the case are clear, the prisoner is convicted and after sentence makes a confession which if published in his own language would not only harrow up the feelings of our readers but disgust them. The answers of the woman to questions put by the District Attorney were too obscene and filthy to find a place in any paper.—The prisoner has been allowed to escape and the woman is at large. So much for justice.

A few weeks ago, an honest and industrious citizen of Weott river was killed by the Indians; one of the murderers was killed by friendly Indians in their endeavors to capture him; this week two others were captured and are now in confinement at Fort Humboldt awaiting the requisition of the civil authorities. We would regret to see them taken by the civil authorities and confined until the April term of the District Court which could only be done at an expense of several thousand dollars, which to our already over taxed people would be far too onerous, and at the same time if the pleasure of the criminal were consulted they would prefer to be hung up at once. The most important feature of the last murder is that suspicion is fastened upon a white man who if Indian testimony was allowable, would be hung. Collateral circumstances alone are almost sufficient to convict him.

While we can but commend our citizens for their law abiding conduct, we at the same time, wish it understood that we are opposed to a resort to such extreme measures as the usurpation of the laws and administering of justice except in extreme cases—such as we have had lately. In the absence of a Court house and a secure jail as is the case in this county, there exists a necessity for the organization of a committee of citizens to aid our officers in the arrest and safe keeping of criminals.

Head Quarters, Detachment 4th Inf.
Fort Humboldt, Cal, Nov. 18th 1854

Sir,
I have the honor to report that I have released the two Indian prisoners from confinement at this Post. I received your communication of the 1st inst. on the 7th and the next day addressed a note to the Sheriff, informing him that they were here ready to be turned over to him, as I was not authorized to detain them, and that if he should decline taking them they would be released. A copy of his note is herewith enclosed in order that the General may be aware of the singular ground taken by the State of California in relation to Indians apprehended for crimes against its own laws. As it was out of the question for the United States to make

arrangements for the support whilst in jail of these two Indians, I released them.

As I see by the papers that several officers have arrived in California, I venture to hope that a Subaltern will soon be sent to this Post, when his services are very much needed.

I am, Sir, Respectfully
Your Obt Servt
Robert C. Buchanan
Bvt. Lt. Col. Capt. 4th Inf.
To   Commdg
Bvt. Maj. E. D. Townsend
Asst. Adjt. Genl.
Dept of the Pac.
Benicia, Cal.

Bucksport, Nov. 9, 1854

Sir,
I received your note of the 8th requesting me to take charge of two Indians who are in confinement at your quarters, accused of being accessary to the murder of one Mr. Wigman. I will take charge of said Indians, provided that provision be made by the United States for the support of such prisoners, as per stated under the Head of Miscellaneous Provisions respecting Sheriffs and their officers, Page 718, Sect. 41, Compiled laws of California; unless such provisions be made, I cannot take charge of the said Indians as Sheriff.

I am, Sir,
Very respectfully,
Your Obt. Servt.
Peter Lothian
To   Sheriff of Humboldt County
Robt. C. Buchanan
Brt. Lieut. Col. U. S. Army
Commanding

52

Fort Jones, Cal. March 26 1854

Sir

Having received information from the Indians of Scott's Valley that the band of Indians, under a Chief known by the whites as "Bill" and inhabiting a cave near the Klamath River were desirous of placing themselves under the protection of the Troops at this Post, and receiving at the same time frequent reports from the citizens of Cottonwood of the hostile intentions and threats of this same band, I deemed it my duty to ascertain if possible, the truth in the matter. Having employed an Interpreter and taking two Indians from this Valley with me. I started on Tuesday last with the intention of going to the cave, and on Wednesday afternoon reached a creek within a mile of that point, and from its swollen state finding myself unable to cross, I was forced to remain here, causing one of the Indians with me to swim the creek. I sent word to Bill of my being near and ready to talk with him. Bill was out hunting at some distance from the cave, but one of his people started immediately to inform him of my wish, and early on the following morning, Bill, with some ten of his men arrived opposite my camp, bringing with them an axe, with which two trees were felled across the stream, when they came into camp. After some customary forms had been gone through, the Indians visited me with Mr. Rosborough, the Indian Agent, who had joined me, and Mr. Steele the Interpreter, to sit with them around the Camp fire, when all of them shook hands with us and expressed great pleasure at being able to talk with me. I then told Bill that my object in coming out to see him was to ascertain if he wished to come in to Fort Jones and that if he was willing to go with me. I had there a party of Soldiers, at the Klamath Ferry, the nearest point to the white settlements, for the purpose of protecting him and his people from any attack by the whites.

Bill replied that he was willing to go to Fort Jones with

me, but that many of his people were sick with fever, unable to travel and that he had no means of transporting them. He said that he preferred remaining at the cave as there was more game there than in Scott's Valley, if he could be assured of remaining unmolested by the whites, but that he was very anxious to be at peace with us, and that he would come in to Scott's Valley if I wished, so soon as his people were sufficiently recovered to travel.

He then gave me a history of his difficulties with the citizens of Cottonwood, his statement being the same as that made by him to Capt. Smith 1st Dragoons in January last, and confirming the accounts of the origin of the difficulty, I had before received from reliable sources. The whites began the fight and Bill defended himself and drove them off.

Before leaving I made Bill promise me that his people should molest the whites in no way by stealing stock or otherwise, telling him that any acts of the kind would be punished. After I had mounted my horse to leave, Bill repeated to Mr. Steele, that if John, a Scott's Valley Indian was sent over to him, he would return with him to this Valley.

On reaching the Klamath Ferry on my return, I found several of the lower class of the Cottonwood population there, for the purpose, as I heard afterwards, though nothing was said at the time, of getting into a disturbance with the Indians in the event of their being with us. This however I presume to have been mere talk, as these men were of the party attacking the Indians in January, and as at that time they did some pretty good running and very little fighting there was not much danger of their attacking the same Indians when under the protection of a few well armed Soldiers.

I am Sir
Your Obt. Servt.
J.C. Bonnycastle
1st Lieut. 4th Infy.
Commdg.

Co. G. Wright
Comdg. North Mil. Dist Cal.
Fort Reading

54

War Department
Washington, July 25, 1854

Sir,

I have the honor to transmit, herewith, for your information a copy of a report made by Lieut. J. C. Bonnycastle, 4th Infantry, commanding Fort Jones, California, concerning Indian affairs in the neighborhood of his Post, and announcing the death of Tipsha-Tyee, the Rogue River Chief, and the murder of the Shasta Chief, "Bill", by the whites.

Very respectfully
Your obt Servt
Jefferson Davis
Secretary of War

Hon. R. McClellande,
Secretary of the Interior

Fort Jones, Cala May 28, 1854

Sir,

I have the honor to report that about 12th, inst. I was informed by one of the Indians encamped at this place, that an outrage had been attempted on a white woman living between Yreka and the Klamath River during the absence of her husband, by an Indian called "Joe" of the Shasta tribe; and that the Indian had been prevented from accomplishing his purpose by the resistance of the woman and by the arrival of some white men on whose near approach he fled. I immediately sent Lieut. Flood to inform the chief of the Shastas, "Bill", that I required the unconditional surrender of the Indian "Joe" that he might be punished.

Lieut. Flood with the Indian Agent Mr. Rosborough saw the chief and made my demand known to him. Bill made an effort to extract a promise that Joe should not be hung and at the same time expressed himself as being angry that the offence had been committed. I had, however, directed Lieut. Flood to require an unconditional surrender of the Indian, for two reasons—because I wished to test the protestations of friendship I had received from these Indians, and because intending, as I did to hand the offender over to be tried by civil authority I could not answer for his being only punished strictly according to law. After some hesitation, Bill promised that the offender should be delivered to me at the Fort, within two days. Three days having elapsed and having heard nothing of Bill, on the 16th inst. I started from this Post with all of the force at my disposal for the purpose of compelling the surrender of Joe. On reaching Yreka my camp was visited by two of the principal Indians of the Scotts valley band, who expressed themselves as very anxious that Joe should be given up, and endeavoured to obtain a promise from me that he should not be hung.

This promise I refused to give for the reasons already stated, but agreed that in case the offender should be surrendered before I reached the Klamath River I would return to Fort Jones, satisfied, but if I was forced to cross the river to get him, I told them that I should hold the tribe responsible for his misconduct and that I should engage the services of a large band of De Chute (Oregon) Indians to aid me in catching and punishing them.

Early the next day I resumed my march without holding any further communication with the Indians, although solicited to do so, but before having marched ten miles, I was overtaken by an old Indian, formerly chief of the Shastas and three other Indians, all mounted. The old chief was very anxious that I should go with him to see that the woman had not been hurt, and it was with some difficulty that I could make him understand that the intention was almost as culpable whether successful or not. Indeed the Indian could not see why I spoke of the offence as being of such magnitude, when their squaws are constantly run down, sometimes by men on horses, and raped.

Having ascertained where I intended camping that night, getting me to promise that I would await there his return the

56

next day, the old man with the other Indians pushed on for the camp of the Shastas, in the mountains, promising before he left that Joe should be given up the next day.

I encamped then at the willow spring, within a few miles of the Klamath, on the night of the 17th inst. and purposed remaining at this point until the evening of the next day, in order to give Bill every chance of remaining at peace with us; but just at dark, a messenger from Cottonwood arrived with the information that at noon that day a pack train had been attacked on the Siskiyou Mountain by Indians, and one of two men with the train killed, the other barely escaping.

The Siskiyou range being the country through which the Rogue River chief known as "Tipsha Tyee" and his band roam, I at once concluded that it was he who had attacked the train, and this being a blow at the interest of almost all of the citizens of this section of the country, I resolved to follow him up as rapidly as possible with the hope of being able to catch and punish the Indians engaged in the murder. My promise to the Shasta Indians to wait their arrival at my camp, with the necessary preparations for quick movement, prevented me from leaving until mid-day, when the Shastas not having arrived we started for the Siskiyou, leaving our pack animals under a guard and every man carrying one blanket with ten days rations of bread and pork. That night we reached nearly the top of the mountain. From Willow Spring I sent Lieut. Flood back to Yreka to inform Lem-testis, the chief of the De Chutes of my being called off in another direction, and early on the morning of the 18th he overtook me at the point where the murder had been committed, accompanied by some thirty eight of the De Chutes well mounted and anxious to aid in the capture of Tipsha. These Indians having made a long march, contrary to my wish, I was forced to remain that day on the mountain with them, that their horses might rest and graze.

At daylight on the 19th taking the trail of Tipsha we started across the mountain and marched more than twenty-five miles, mostly over a very rough country. The De Chutes being well mounted and riding anywhere, with practiced eye detected signs of the retreating Indians, when but few whites could have detected any indication that they had passed. By the sign, the De Chutes asserted that six Indians were engaged in the murder.

Late in the afternoon we reached a point where the signs indicated that the Indians had recently encamped, and halting, spies were sent out, who on their return reported that two Indians had gone off to the northward, up a valley with the mules taken from the train, while the other four with seven horses, stolen from some drovers two nights before, had gone in the direction of the *cave* on the Klamath, and that one Indian, afoot, had been traced, going up the valley, quite recently, after the Indians with the mules. This Indian they believed to be one of some adjacent tribe, who having come to visit the camp at which we were halted and finding it deserted was returning to his home. The direction taken by the Indians with the horses, inducing me to believe that the murder had been participated in by the Shasta Indians, I determined to pursue *them* and to inflict severe punishment. Following their trail then at nightfall we encamped, and at daylight next morning moved on toward the cave. About 10 o'clock the De Chute scouts discovered the Shasta camp and bringing back the information, we hurried forward with the expectation of engaging them before they could gain their stronghold.

On reaching the brink of a tall bluff, opposite to another on the top of which the Shasta camp was, we were hailed by an american, who called out that Capt. Goodall was with the Shastas and wished to see me. Supposing that he was there to inform me that the Indian "Joe" had been given up and that he knew nothing of my having tracked the murderers of the Packer to this camp, I told Capt. Goodall to come over to me, when I expected, that on learning the facts I had to communicate, he with the three men with him would join me in an attack on the Shastas. However, on reaching me, he informed me that Tipsha had come into the Shasta camp about thirty six hours before, and had proposed, after telling them of the murder he had just committed that they should join him in waging war on the whites, and that instead of agreeing to this, the Shastas had killed Tipsha, his son and his son-in-law, the fourth Indian with him escaping, and being doubtless the Indian whose foot tracts the De Chutes had seen the evening before. Capt. Goodall further stated that these Indians were very anxious to remain at peace, that the Indian Joe had been brought in, about two hours after I had left my camp at the Willow Spring, where I had promised to wait, and had then gone on to Yreka, where he remained two days, when he had returned with him to the Shasta camp. That immediately on killing Tipsha, two Shasta Indians had brought his scalp with that of his son to him in Yreka, soliciting his interference to prevent my attacking them when Tipsha's trail should have led me to their camp, when by authority of the Indian agent he had come out. Sending my company and the De Chute Indians to find a camp, accompanied by Lieut. Flood, Capt. Goodall, the chief Lem-tes-tis, and one or two others, I passed over to the Shasta Camp, where I was received by the Indians with every demonstration of confidence and friendship. After expressing my approbation of their course in killing Tipsha, I demanded that the horses be taken from him and the boy Joe, should be given up to me, to which they gave prompt assent, and Capt. Goodall volunteered to bring Joe in with him the next day, to which under the circumstances I agreed. Having talked with them for some time, assuring them of my friendship so long as they behaved and advising them to come in and learn to work & c., I told them to catch up the horses taken from Tipsha as I wished to take them with me, this was done at once, and after at their request giving them a paper, requesting that they might not be molested by the whites, I mounted and rejoined my company in camp, from which we moved on that night to the Klamath, and on the next day, camping beyond Yreka. I rode into town for the purpose of making some arrangement with Mr. Rosborough as to the disposition of the Indian Joe, when he should be brought in by Capt. Goodall. On reaching Mr. Rosborough's room I found Capt. Goodall had just arrived there and to my astonishment and regret, he had neglected to bring Joe. He gave several excuses for his omission but deeming none of them sufficient, I spoke very plainly to him of his violation of a voluntary promise and told him that having started out to get Joe, I was determined to have him, even though I was compelled to retrace my steps. Capt. Goodall, who had omitted to bring the Indian with him, not thinking of the importance attaching to his voluntary surrender, admitted his error and told me that he would start back that night and get him. The Indian Agent having given to Capt. Goodall a note authorising him to bring in Joe, he started the same night with the chief Bill, who was in Yreka, for the Shasta camp, and I returned with my command to Fort Jones.

Capt. Goodall knowing that both the Indian Agent and myself desired the Shasta Indians to come into Scotts Valley, determined without my knowledge to endeavour to induce the whole band to come in at once, and on his way to their camp unguardedly stated such to be his intention, in conversation with several white men. Having reached the Shasta camp, the band readily agreed to accompany him to Fort Jones, and on the morning of the 24th inst. they all started, the Indians numbering, men, women, and children some sixty. Reaching the Klamath Ferry in the afternoon of this day, they camped some two hundred yards above the ferry, when the chief Bill with five of his men wishing to cross the river for the purpose of bathing, left their arms in camp and went with Capt. Goodall to the ferry; on arriving opposite the ferry they saw four white men with the De Chute chief Lem-tes-tis, the latter of whom had that same day promised me solemnly not to molest the Shastas, advancing to the waters edge on the opposite shore, with rifles. Capt. Goodall at once seeing that the Indians were to be attacked, told them to run, and called to the whites not to fire, that he was acting by authority. Five of the Indians with him ran, the chief Bill being lame was unable to do so, they were all fired into, both by the whites on the opposite side of the river and by others on the same side with the Indians. In fact, they were completely surrounded by whites and the De Chutes who had been hired to engage in this villainous affair.

The chief Bill was severely wounded at the first fire, two other Indians were killed and two others escaped very badly wounded. A white man named Mr. Stuart went up to Bill for the purpose of scalping him, while yet alive, but Bill struggling with him, got his knife away, when this man after having beat him about the head with his pistol, shot him several times, after which he was scalped by a man named Brickey I understand, when not yet dead he was thrown into the Klamath River. Most of the Indians having escaped into the adjacent chapperal, where they lay concealed, the whites began a search for them, during which an Indian from behind his bush, unfortunately shot and killed a white man named Mr. Kaney.

The De Chute Indians who had not done much towards killing the Shastas, plundered their camp, stealing four children, six or seven horses and several guns, and one of them, I am informed, at the instigation of the man Brickey indecently mutilated one of the murdered Shastas and afterwards the Band started with their plunder for Rogue River.

Before dark of the same evening, the Shastas who had escaped, came opposite the Ferry house and called the cottonwood men cowards &c, dared them out to fight, an invitation which these men declined, preferring the shelter of a heavy log house on which the Indians fired repeatedly for more than an hour.

Capt. Goodall came on to Fort Jones at once and informed me of this cowardly and brutal murder on the part of the whites. When mounting six men on mules, with Lieut. Flood I started for Cottonwood for the purpose of obtaining such information as might enable me to bring the whites to punishment, and by sending Lieut. Flood on to Fort Lane to recover the children &c stolen by the De Chutes that they might be returned to the Shastas. I ascertained the particulars of this murder to be as already stated, but could obtain no information as to the names of more than three white men engaged in it, these were Brickey, Mr. Stuart, and E. M. Geiger.

Mr. Rosborough accompanied me and made every effort to obtain information for the purpose of bringing the murderers to trial. We should have obtained writs for the three men named and Judge Peters of the District court, who took a warm interest in the matter, would have caused a grand jury to be summoned that they might be indicted, had Mr. Rosborough and myself not been perfectly well aware that in this Section of the country, action of this nature would only result in the escape of the guilty parties, the greater number of the populace vilely regretting, not that they have among them such murderous scoundrels, but that since the assassination of the Shastas was attempted, it had not been completely successful. The Shastas vowed vengeance against *all* the whites, and I feared that innocent persons living on farms within their reach, might be made to suffer for the acts of those who sought immunity from retribution in the town of Cottonwood.

I however sought the Indians whom I have had encamped here during the winter and explaining the whole matter to them and telling them that I had sent to recover the stolen children &c and that I would make every effort to have the guilty whites punished.

I directed them to see the Shastas, and to tell them that the soldiers and many white citizens were friendly to them; that if I had known they were coming in I should have been at the Ferry with a party of soldiers to protect them, and that I wished them to retaliate only on those men who participated in the murder of their chief, that if they killed no other whites I should have nothing to say.

From this act of treachery, I feared that any influence I might have with these Indians, any confidence which my treatment of them might have inspired, was all lost, but much to my surprise and gratification, on night before last, just after my return from Cottonwood, two of the Shastas, one a boy, brother to the murdered chief, came into Yreka, and sent word to Mr. Rosborough and myself that they wished to talk with us.

Yesterday morning early they came to Mr. Rosborough's room and we had a long talk with them. They stated that they knew the men who had attacked them, that they were satisfied that *all* the whites were not treacherous and finally promised to endeavour to induce the remainder of the band to come to Fort Jones. Mr. Rosborough fed them, made them some presents and took them under his protection, as even in Yreka there are white men who would murder these two unarmed Indians, if they could do so with safety. The Shastas are to send me word if they will come here and in case they wish to do so, I shall have a party of soldiers to protect them on their way, as I should have done before had I known that they intended coming in.

Capt. Goodall deserves the highest praise for his constant and humane efforts in behalf of these Indians, by which he has lost much time and money and has moreover rendered himself disagreeably unpopular with the vagabond mass of the community. It was unfortunate that he attempted to bring the Indians in just when he did, or that intending to do so, he should have avowed his purpose to whites on the road, but he had not arrived at the same just opinion of the character of many of the mining populace as that which had already forced itself on me, some months since, when with the same object in view, I took care to have a party of soldiers at the Ferry.

Mr. Geiger proposes leaving for the Atlantic States on one of the Steamers leaving San Francisco on the 15th of June, and I would respectfully suggest that if possible, he be arrested in San Francisco to be tried there before the U. S. court. I shall endeavour to send an affidavit with reference to his participation in the murder by the next express. This is the course proposed to be pursued by Mr. Rosborough with reference to the other men engaged in the matter, so soon as he can get their names.

I would respectfully call the attention of the commanding General to the fact that these Indians when attacked, held a paper from one intended to guarantee their safety, while Mr. Goodall was acting with the written authority of the Indian Agent, and I hope by that the most severe measures may be taken against the murderers.

In conclusion, I feel called on to express my admiration of the firmness and energy of Mr. Rosborough, the Indian Agent, with reference to this murder and to express a hope that he may be promptly supported by the Superintendent of Indian Affairs, in his effort to bring the murderers to justice.

With reference to the first portion of this communication; the pursuit of "Tipsha Tees" over a rough mountainous country making long and fatiguing marches, the energy and zeal of asst. Surgn. Louel, Lieuts. Crook and Flood and the men of company "E" 4th Infantry is gratefully reported for the information of the commanding General.

I am Sir
Your obt. Servt.
J. C. Bonnycastle
1st Lt. 4th Infantry

To
Maj. Genl. John C. Wool,
Comdg. Dept. of the Pacific
San Francisco, Cala

3:6   Report, Judah to Mackall

San Francisco, Cal.
April 27, 1858

Sir:

I have the honor to enclose herewith a Report in compliance with instructions from Dept. HeadQs of 6th Inf.

Would it be determined that I proceed to Fort Jones before taking any further steps in reference to the Indian disturbances. I should be glad to leave San Francisco today in order to take the boat from Sacramento tomorrow morning and will report in person at an early hour this morning.

Very respectfully
Your obt. Svt.
H. W. Judah
Capt. 4th Infy

For
Maj. W. W. Mackall USA
Asst. Adj. Genl.
San Francisco
Cal

Red Bluffs, Cal.
April 19, 1858

Sir:

I have the honor to report that agreeably with your instructions of 6th inst. I have completed the investigation of the circumstances attending certain alleged Indian outrages upon Antelope and Payne's Creeks as set forth in a certain memorial by citizens of Shasta, Colusa, and Tehama counties to the Governor of this State, and have ascertained that the following are the facts in the case, as elicited by extended enquiries among the most reliable citizens belonging to the counties concerned (particularly those residing in the vicinity of the alleged outrages) and by a personal visit to the scene of the disturbances in Antelope and Payne's creeks from which I returned an hour since.

As far as I can ascertain, all of the injuries committed by Indians upon the property and lives of settlers within the counties named during the past few years have been perpetrated by Indians ranging upon the tributaries to the Sacramento on its east side and in the vicinity of Red Bluffs and Tehama. Stock (live) has been stolen by Indians from the settlers since their occupation of the county and the guilty parties punished without retaliation by the Indians upon the lives of the latter until March 1854 when the first white man named Jose was killed by Indians. Jose was employed by a man who had a short time previous been leader of a party of whites organized for the purpose of chastising Indians. The second white man was killed in June last; his name was Makin; all accounts of this man concur in representing him to have been guilty of repeated enormities against Indians, killing them upon slight provocation, and appropriating to his own use their squaws in such numbers and at such times as best suited his convenience. The third killed was a man named Corby, a partner of Makin's. Corby had collected a party of four Indians to assist him and a few whites in a search for his partner Makin (before he knew of his death); while exercising the terrifying process upon one of the Indians he (the Indian) drew a concealed weapon and killed Corby: the remaining Indians were then dispatched forthwith. I am not sure but that October should be substituted for June as the date of the last mentioned occurence. The fourth and fifth whites killed were the old man Allen and his son, under circumstances as [illegible]. This occurred in February last. This last murder might have been in retaliation for one committed but a few days previously by a party of whites upon the person of a squaw. This squaw was one who had been forcibly retained by Makin previous to his decease, and was undoubtedly one of the conspirators to his death which was effected by treachery through her assistance. Since June last two attempts at the chastisement of the Indians by small parties of whites have been made without success, or at least any good result, and at this time there is no doubt from what I have seen and heard that property and (under certain circumstances) life is insecure in the vicinity of Antelope, Payne's and Mill creeks. I will now state "by what Indians these excesses have been committed." There is no evidence of the permanent occupation of the ranges mentioned by a larger party of Indians than from fifteen to twenty, called the

"Noseys" most of whom have lived with the whites in menial capacities and have left them through various discontents, but with increased capacities for evil aggravated by the posession of ten or a dozen good rifles which they are said to be capable of using with dexterity. These Indians have undoubtedly united and enjoy the cooperation of their brethern upon creeks north of them and particularly those ranging high up on Feather River, the latter acting as agents for the former in the barter of stolen stock for ammunition and other supplies. The country which affords these Indians concealment upon Antelope and Mill Creeks is one of the roughest imaginable, being a continuous series of precipitous canyons over and through which it is near to impossible to follow or look for Indians with any chance of success should they know (as they always can through observation and sources I will hereafter mention) that a competent party is in their pursuit. This last fact the result of my own partial observations and concurred on by all who have belonged to parties of whites operating against those Indians, combined with the uncertainty of their migratory visits for predatory purposes: the physical inadaptability of recruits to such laborious service, and the inappropriate character of their arms (bright barreled muskets) influenced me not to undertake the summary chastisement of the Indians with the recruits under my command, as an attempt almost certain to result in failure.

Before suggesting a probable remedy for the annoyances complained of by the settlers near the localities referred to, I beg to state that the Dept of Indian Affairs in this State was requested by those citizens (or a portion of them) about a year ago to aid them in recovering the friendship of those Indians in the hope of averting the very disturbances which have since occurred. The reply of Col. Henley was unsatisfactory, and restricted his Dept to the simple act of receiving the Indians upon some reservation should they wish to locate thereupon. It may not be inappropriate in me to add that this course of the Indian Dept. in this State has been uniformly consistent as far as any opportunities of judging extends, and is calculated to ignore the popularly received opinion that that Department is entrusted with means by the judicious exercise of which the friendship of Indians may be secured and their depredations upon the lives and property of whites thereby prevented. It is in connection with the above facts that I report the existence of numerous ranches of Indians upon the Sacramento River and the creeks tributary thereto the males of which are used by large farmers for purposes of labor. These ranches undoubtedly add many discontents to the ranks of the Indian depredators, while they at the same time afford them a secure asylum from pursuit, with in many instances immunity from suspicion of implication in the excesses of their more positively (known to be) hostile friends. One of these ranches in particular on Battle Creek near the farm of a Dr. Worzen is reported to me as positively obnoxious to the suspicion which can justifiably attach to them all, and in my opinion until they are broken up and the Indians removed by the proper Department, there will be no immunity from loss of life and property by the settlers in their vicinity. As the summer approaches the Indians divide themselves into small parties of four and five in number and go further back into the mountains, visiting the valley for predatory purposes. This can, I think, be positively if not altogether checked in connection with prompt action of the Indian Dept. (as suggested and necessarily preliminary thereto) by the employment of from fifteen to twenty good men inured to mountain service, as a permanent escorting party during a portion of the summer months. Their efforts might also predispose the Indians for the favorable consideration of any measures towards their permanent pacification which the Indian Department might see fit to initiate.

Having decided after a careful consideration of the circumstances so narrated that it was my duty to proceed no farther before laying them before the general commanding and awaiting further instructions on the premises, I placed the Sacramento River between the town of Red Bluffs and my command (which I left in good order under charge of

Lieut. McCall 4th Infy arrived from Fort Jones for that purpose) and determined to report in person instead of awaiting instructions in camp as calculated to facilitate an adjustment of what has been to me a perplexing question of duty and better enable me to reach my post in time for muster, should the general commanding decide upon my return to that post.

Very respectfully,
Your obt. servt.
H. W. Judah

To Maj. W. W. Mackall, USA   Capt. 4th Infy.
Asst. Adjt. Genl. Dept. of Pac.
San Francisco, Cal.

3:7   Letter, Sorrel to Townsend

Fort Jones Cal
Aug. 2, 1855

Sir:

Since the departure of Capt. Judah, events have here transpired of a nature sufficiently important to render necessary a report of the same to Dept. Hd. Quarters; together with the action I have taken in consequence thereof as temporary commander of this Post.

Immediately after the occurrences which led to that officer's departure for the scene of hostilities, the exasperation of the whites became so great that Indians of all ages and sexes, wherever found, would willingly have been sacrificed to its unbecoming rage; the men whenever seen were either shot or hanged, and among the latter were two Johns claimed to belong to one of the Chiefs of this Valley, and who visiting Yreka, was then seized and executed, solely on suspicion. At once the vicinity of this valley, indulging fears lest the

Indians here would retaliate, assembled in armed bodies with the avowed purpose of "exterminating" this miserable and inoffending people, who protesting that tho they saw with pain their innocent relations so mercilessly slaughtered by the Whites, yet were anxious to live as formerly on terms of peace and friendship. Feeling it to be my duty, both to restrain an impending out-break, and to protect these well-disposed Indians from the infliction of cruelties at the hands of the Whites, I returned to the spot whither in fear they had fled, and prevailed upon them to place themselves under my protection. This morning the entire band was brought in, and are now disarmed and located upon the Military Reserve. In view of these facts, and of the imperative necessity which, in order to secure their own safety, and peace and quite here, will closely confine them to the Reserve. I have assumed the responsibility of supplying them food, consisting Flour and Beef in such quantities as a due regard to economy, and the requirements of nature may warrant. This I will continue to do as long as circumstances may render it necessary or until the wishes of the Commg. General of Capt. Judah shall be made known to me.

When it is known that there is a manifest disposition upon the part of the larger number of Indians of this portion of California, to resist the daily encroachment of the whites; and even now organized bands are openly in arms, and already frenzied with success and rage; I trust it will seem to the Commg. General, the part of wisdom, in caution and humanity, to prevent the general tide from being swelled by the occasion of the Scott Valley Indians, who for so long a time have lived in peaceable contiguity to the whites, and who yet wish to continue their friendly relations.

Yesterday there arrived at this Post from Scott Bar, 19 women and children, who by the humane interference of several good citizens of that community, escaped with their lives, and made good their way here, where they now enjoy the protecting hand of the government. Thus, together with the band I brought in today consisting of Tyee Jack, the "old man" and their people will swell the number now living here to about 100.

Last night I received intelligence from some good citizens of Hamburg Bar, Scott River, that my presence was deemed requisite to preserve the lives of some 50 women and children there collected, but as my absence from the Post even under these circumstances is deemed inadmissible, I am obliged to relinquish them to their fate.

In conclusion, I would earnestly entreat the Commg. General to bring to the notice of the Sup. Ind. Affairs for California, the immediate and absolute necessity for the presence of an agent invested with full power and means to make suitable provisions for the well disposed Indians here.

I am Sir, Very Respectfully
Your obt. Svt.
F. Sorrel
Asst. Surgn.
(In the absence of Capt. Judah) Commg. Fort Jones

Bt. Maj. E. D. Townsend
Asst. Adjt. Genl.
Dept. Pacific
Benicia, Cal.

3:8   Letter, Henley to Wool

Office Supt. Indian Affairs
San Francisco California
August 14th 1855

Maj. Genl. J. C. Wool
Comdg. Pacific Division
Benicia, Cal.

Sir: I am in receipt of yours of 10th inst. The suggestion to send a special Agent to the vicinity of Fort Jones cannot be adopted. By my instructions of the 17th of May last I am expressly prohibited from employing Special Agents; nor have I any authority to provide for the Indians in the manner suggested. The law provides only for "colonising and subsisting Indians on three Military Reservations" and the appropriation cannot be diverted to any other end. The accounts of Capts. Judah and Jones for provisions furnished "Indian allies and Indian prisoners" I have no authority to pay, but if those gentlemen will forward the bills to me I will send them to the Commissioner of Indian Affairs for his decision.

I regret that the Commanding General is of the opinion that he cannot allow the assistance of the Military to convey Indians to the Reservations. The Indians respect the Military but know very little of the civil authority. I could mention several instances where a small escort of Soldiers would enable me to take large numbers to the Reserves, and in many instances to prevent those conflicts that are of such frequent occurrence in mining districts. The Indians, especially those who have hostile intentions, will not leave their old haunts without some coercion, but when once removed they immediately become satisfied and contented. I will give one instance: I have twice had the Trinity Indians collected together for removal to Nome Lackee Reserve. They are anxious to come. A portion of the tribe is now there. Those that remain are in a destitute and suffering condition, and there is constant danger of an outbreak such as lately occurred at Humboldt in Yreka County. Some of their squaws are kept by white men. They will not remain if the tribe leaves and the white men will prevent the tribe from going to keep their squaws.

Our force of white men is necessarily small. In the last instance in Trinity County there were but two white men. When the removal party was ready to move, those owning squaws came into Camp with their revolvers and drove the women away. Then a considerable portion of the Indians refused to go and the removal was defeated.

It is my intention to leave here on Friday in the Steamer Columbia for Humboldt, Klamath and Yreka and should be glad to bear any communication the Genl. may see proper to send the officers in Command in that region in regard to their cooperation with me in whatever it may be necessary to do for the restoration of peace in that quarter.

Respectfully
Your Obt. Servt.
T. J. Henley
Supt. Indn. Affairs

3:9   Letter, Judah to Townsend; affidavits

Fort Jones Cal
August 23rd 1855

Sir:

I have the honor to enclose herewith an affidavit and an explanatory letter to Judge Hoffman of the U. S. District Court for Northern California for such action in the case as the Major General Commanding may deem advisable.

Since my last communication I have been exceedingly annoyed by men (white) too lazy or cowardly to scout in the mountains, who seem determined to create trouble among the peaceable (disarmed) Indians collected upon this reserve. I have found it necessary to keep a strong guard over the Indians at night upon several occasions with my entire command held in readiness to carry out my intentions, which are to meet force by force. Justice to the disarmed Indians, my promise of protection and the dignity of the service seem to me to demand the action I have determined against any armed irresponsible band of men who contemplate such an outrage as that of coming upon the reserve to kill and slaughter the inoffensive Indians collected upon it by me for protection against such attacks. I have openly and freely told the citizens that the reserve should be held inviolate and if they attempt to interfere as they have threatened it will be with a full knowledge of the reception prepared for them. At the same time I have made arrangements to be sufficiently apprised of the approach of any armed party at night to enable me in time to formally warn them off by [?] before I will come into collision with them, and it appears to me that the exersise of such forbearance is all if not more than could be demanded of me under the circumstances.

An express reached me on the evening before last at a late hour with the particulars of the outrage which is contained in my affidavit. I proceeded at an early hour yesterday morning to Yreka returning late in the evening. I found considerable alarm in the Indians camp from the report that a large body of men were coming down to take by force two Indians, Hamburgh John and John the Chief of the Scott's Valley Indians. I was forced under the existing state of things to make again my usual preparations to repel any such attempt.

Although I do not believe that the men can be found actually daring enough to attempt what is so frequently threatened, still the same measures are necessary upon my part as though the contrary were the case, rendering my position one of extreme anxiety and annoyance.

It is my earnest hope that you will approve of my course in the case of the recent outrages and that they may be brought under the cognisance of the U. S. authorities.

Very respectfully
Your obt servant
H. M. Judah
Capt. 4th Infy
Comdg Post

To
Maj E. D. Townsend U. S. A.
Asst. Adjt Gen. Dept. of Pacific
Benicia
Cal

Fort Jones Cal
August 23rd 1855

Sir

The accompanying complaint and affidavit has been enclosed to Maj. Gen. Wool, Comdg Dept. of Pacific, for transmission to you should my course in relation to the matter involved be approved by him and in reference to which I have the honor to submit the following explanations.

Incident to the recent murder of white men upon the Klamath River in this vicinity has been the assemblage of a large number of citizens, organized into companies ostensibly for the purpose of chastising the hostile Indians. Among such assemblages are to be found many men who do not fail to develop qualities and propensities which would disgrace the savage himself and evinced of acts of barbarity with the circumstances of which I am familiar (too shocking for repetition). During the popular excitement incident to Indian operations against Indians these acts have overlooked when justice should have demanded the interference of legal authority in the Indians behalf. Many such outrages have been recently committed in this vicinity which have been thus necessarily overlooked, but the excitement I have alluded [?] to has subsided and outrages similar to that detailed in my affidavit are perpetrated by men for whose enormities there is no palliation and who would appropriately ornament the gallows.

There is a positive and actual necessity for at least one conviction similar to that I am anxious to effect and I believe should the present attempt to secure one be effectual, it will more successfully operate to prevent future outrages upon Indians, and the consequent murder of white men than the presence of any military force, howsoever large that could be placed in this section of the State.

In view of these facts and of that "that the Indian title to this portion of California has never been formally extinguished" I thus lay the matter before you in the hope that you may adjudge the case as one within the jurisdiction

75

of your court. Since reading a section of an Act of Congress I found in the Digest of N. S. Laws (relating to Indians) upon page (422) I have perhaps allowed myself to be more sanguine as to your decision on the matter than I should be, although I am gratified to know that should it be adverse to my wishes every effort will be made by the authorities of Yreka to secure the ends of justice towards the parties concerned. The Sheriff of this County left Yreka on yesterday with a warrant for the arrest of the prisoners who will be retained in custody as long as possible without an examination. At any rate an effort will be made to avoid any action by the State District Court until your action in the case can be known.

Very respectfully
Your obt servant
H. M. Judah
Capt., 4th Infy.
Actg. Indian Agent

To
Hon. Odgen Hoffman
Judge U. S. Dist Court for Nor. Cal
San Francisco
Cal

State of California) Before Hon. J. Montgomery Peters,
County of Siskiyou) Judge of the Eighth Judicial Dist.

Personally appeared before me, J. Montgomery Peters, Judge of the 8th Judicial District of California, Henry M. Judah, Captain in the United States Army, and acting Indian Agent for Northern California, who being first by me duly sworn deposes and says that he is informed and believes that an Indian was shot at in Scott's Valley, in said County and State, on or about August 20th, 1855, by a party of men, consisting of William Maul, George Usery, as he is informed one McClane and another as he is informed by the name of Gillespie, that these men were seen by upon the day previous to the attack upon the Indian, armed with rifles, and that they were seen on the day before by Captain McClary and

John Bateman, and one Martin, prowling around or near the Indian Rancheria on the lower end of said Valley, and said deponent further avows that the tribe to which the Indian belonged was peacable towards the whites, and said deponent further says that he is informed, and believes that upon the following day to wit on the 21st day of August A. D. 1855 the above named William Maul being accompanied and encouraged by the others above named unlawfully killed with malice aforethought an Indian boy named Billy by the whites (Indian name Emmashewyka) at Hamburgh Bar on Klamath River in said County and State, by deliberately and without cause or provocation shooting him with a Rifle, from the effects of which shot the boy died in about half an hour, and that the brother, and sister of the boy were at the time with others of the same tribe in Scott's Valley under the protection of said deponent, the boy Billy having been left at Hamburgh Bar when the others were removed, on account of sickness, with his mother to attend him, in the charge of Mr. White at that place, and the said deponent further says that he verily believes under existing circumstances in this County that it would not be possible to have these parties convicted and punished under the laws of the State of California, and therefore wishes this complaint, together with the accompanying affidavit of Charles L. Thurman, to be transmitted to the Judge of the United States District Court of Northern California, to be used under the laws of the United States, and further deponent saith not.

Subscribed and sworn to
me this 22nd day of   H. M. Judah
August A. D. 1855   Capt., 4th Infy.
  J. Montgomery Peters   Actg Indian Agent
  Judge of the 8th Judicial Dist.

State of California)
County of Siskiyou)

Personally appeared before me, Judge of the 8th Judicial District of California, Charles L. Thurman, who being sworn, deposes and says that on the 21st day of August A. D. 1855, he saw William Maul personally known to him, go up to the house at which the Indian boy Billy (Indian name Emmashewyka) was staying, and take the boy by the arm, and pointing as if for the boy to run, which he did, and that when the boy got about ten steps from him, he saw him raise his rifle and fire, aiming in the way the boy went, and upon going up, this deponent found the boy shot in the back, the ball having passed into the left breast, and still breathing, and that he believes the boy died in about half an hour, and this deponent further says that he saw one George Usery also known personally to him, and two other men by the names of McClane and Gillespie, as he is informed, going up with William Maul towards the place where he shot the Indian boy, and afterwards saw them go off with said Maul, and that from their actions, he verily believes that they were accompanying and encouraging the said Maul in perpetrating the murder, and the deponent further says that he has known the Indian boy Billy since last March, and that as far as he knows, he has been harmless, and inoffensive, and that he thinks the boy was about fourteen years of age, and further deponent says not.

Sworn to, and subscribed
before me this 22nd day   Charles L. Thurman
of August 1855   his (x)   mark
  J. Montgomery Peters
  Judge of the 8th Judicial Dist.

Headquarters Dept. of the Pacific
Benicia   15th September 1855

Sir

Some hundred and fifty men, women and children,
mostly women and children, whose husbands have been
killed by the White inhabitants of California, are now on the
Military Reserve at Fort Jones, and fed by Capt. Judah.

I would again call your attention as Superintendent of
Indian Affairs, to this subject in order that some provision
should be made for their subsistence. Can they not be
received at the Reservation of Nome Lackee or some other
Reserve which you may have selected? If you will receive
them at the Nome Lackee Reserve, I will direct Capt. Judah
to send them down accordingly. It appears to me something
ought to be done for these miserable creatures, who it
appears were not in the wrong, and whom the White inhabitants are determined to exterminate.

I am Very Respectfully
Your Obt. Svt.
John E. Wool
Major Genl.

Hon T. J. Henley
Supt Ind Affairs
San Francisco, Cal

Fort Jones Cal
Nov 1st 1855

Sir

Dictates of humanity towards the Indians of this valley,
irrespective of any duties resulting from my relations as acting Indian Agent, urge me to appeal to you officially for
some recognition of their rights to the protection and
assistance of the Indian Department, of which you are in this
State the Chief.

As far as I can learn, you have never officially visited this portion of California, and since the withdrawal of the Agency from Mr. Rosborough, must be necessarily ignorant of the condition of the Indians in this vicinity, their wants and many necessities. The Indians of Scott's Valley have maintained their friendly relations with the Whites, with a singular forebearance, and by their sincerity have won the good will of the community in which they reside.

They have, as far as I can learn, never received any presents of any description nor any assistance from the Indian Department beyond a scanty supply of food to save them from starvation. Even this was in one instance withdrawn by you, while there remained nearly two feet of snow upon the ground in Scott's Valley. The facts are that but for the assistance rendered by the commissary Department of Fort Jones, the Indians would ere this have starved, and but for the charities of the Whites bestowed in blankets and clothing, they would have perished ere this from cold, for this climate in the winter is a severely cold one.

I have at this time one hundred and twenty six Indians living for protection within a few hundred yards of my quarters. I supply them with flour and beef because they absolutely require it, and cannot subsist themselves. At the same time this duty, I believe, to appertain to your Department rather than to mine. Winter is actually upon us, and the Indians must in some manner or other be provided with shelter, blankets and clothing. If the Indian Department in this State cannot do this at an early date, please inform me of the fact, and I will make an effort to receive relief of some kind from Washington, believing as I do that its charities (to say nothing of rights) would be secured in favor of the Indians, as I their Agent represent.

Very respectfully Your Obt Servt.
H. M. Judah, Capt. 4th Infty, Acting Ind Agent

Thos J. Henley Esqr
Supt Ind Affairs
San Francisco Cal

Fort Jones, Cala.
December 13th, 1855

Sir

I had the honor to address you nearly two months since through Maj. Genl. Wool upon the subject of the Scott's Valley Indians, to which I have received no reply.

As I anticipated, winter has set in with unusual severity, and about one hundred and thirty Indians collected around my post for protection against the whites are in a state of destitution it is pitiable to witness. The ground is covered with snow against which they have no protection, either in the way of clothing or shelter. I have no means with which to supply them with materials for the construction of huts, neither is it in my power to cover their nakedness. I have thus far kept them from starvation, and it may be that the citizens of the Valley, as they have heretofore done, will assume another portion of your duties in assisting them with clothing, for they must have it or perish with cold.

Something must surely be amiss either in the organization of the Indian Department or the administration of its affairs in this State; when Indians who have so signally entitled themselves by their good conduct to consideration, should have been and are entirely neglected and unprovided for.

The duties of this Agency withdrawn from Mr. Rosborough (one of the most efficient ever appointed) are in connection with my active duties in the field, under the circumstances which have demanded this and my previous letter of the most disagreable description. If relief is not afforded by you or at least some satisfactory answer elicited to this and my previous communication, I shall lay copies of them both before the proper authorities at Washington, referring to the people of this Valley for confirmation of the facts I have stated, as notoriously true.

Very Respectfully Your Obt Servt
H. M. Judah, Capt. 4th Infty
Acting Indian Agent

Col. Thos. J. Henley
Supt. Ind. Affairs
San Francisco Cal

Capt. H. M. Judah
Comdg. Ft. Jones

Sir: I am this day in receipt of yours of 1st Nov and 13th Dec. This is the first information I have been able to get (though I have made frequent inquiry) in regard to the Indians at Fort Jones to which you allude. It is true I have not paid an official visit to Ft. Jones. I am not, however, ignorant of the condition of those Indians. The enclosed correspondence will acquaint you with the fact that I had already made such provision for them as met the approbation of the Commanding General, an arrangement entirely consistent with the plan of colonizing the Indians on Reservations, and perfectly within the scope of my powers. I was informed by Genl. Wool in Sept. last that he had dispatched an officer to Ft. Jones to remove them to Nome Lackee in conformity with this arrangement, and I was for some time in the daily expectation of their arrival. It was only very recently that I was informed they were not to be sent. Of the cause of this or the influences which prevented the removal I am not advised. It must be obvious to you that I could not have been expected to provide for the subsistence of those Indians at Ft. Jones at the time that I was expecting their arrival at Nome Lackee, where ample provision had been made for them.

Your letter of 1st Nov. was not forwarded to me from Genl. Wool's office until this date, or it would have received an immediate answer. I have been informed verbally by Genl. Wool and Maj. Cross that the reason why those Indians were not removed was because they were unwilling to leave their present location. Now what I understand to be my duty on this subject is to provide as speedily as possible for their reception of all suffering Indians on the Reservations. This I have done, and have no doubt of being able at all times to receive and take care of Indians situated as those are to which you allude, and although it may appear and no doubt does appear to you that "something must surely be amiss either in the organization or administration of the Indian Department in this State" I am at a loss to perceive the particular appropriateness of the rebuke.

In regard to the question of providing for those Indians under existing circumstances, if they have under the advice of the Acting Agent declined the relief and protection offered them at the Reservation, it would seem to be a doubtful question whether they are entitled to any other.

I have no doubt of the meritorious character of those Indians, but I regard the policy of feeding those who refuse to go to the Reserves as injurious to the policy of colonization as contemplated by the System now in operation.

Respectfully Your Obt Servt
Thos. J. Henley
Supt. Ind Affairs

Office Supt. Ind. Affairs
San Francisco Cal
December 29th 1855

Sir

I herewith enclose copies of letters addressed to me by Capt. Judah, Comdg. Fort Jones, in relation to subsisting Indians at that Fort and my reply thereto.

The facts are I believe briefly as follows. The Indians, I have no doubt, are and have been for a long time in a suffering condition, and I have on two occasions afforded them relief. The officer in command at the Fort has done the same thing. They have become accustomed to this relief, and are now burdensome to the authorities at the Fort. To be relieved of them the proposition was made to remove them to the Reservation if I would receive them. This I consented to do, and an officer was dispatched to effect their removal, but the Indians, I am informed, were unwilling to leave the place, as it was their old home. Genl. Wool is of opinion that no coercion should be used in removing Indians to Reservation; they were therefore permitted to remain. It is not my opinion that these or any other Indians will ever consent to remove if they are fed and kept in idleness in the vicinity of their old homes.

I desire further instructions in regard to this and similar cases which are frequently occurring within this Superintendency.

Respectfully Your Obt Servt.

Thos. J. Henley

Hon G. W. Manypenny   Supt. Ind. Affairs, Cal.
Comm. Ind. Affairs
Washington D. C.

3:11   Letter, Smith to Wright

Fort Lane, O. T.
January 31, 1856

Colonel,

I have the honor to report that on Sunday the 22nd Lieut. Crook, accompanied by D. Sorrel arrived at this post, having been sent by Capt. Judah for the mountain howitzer, and informed us of a difficulty between the inhabitants of Cottonwood and the Indians, supposed to be in considerable force in that vicinity. On the morning of the 23rd I left this post, taking with me Lieut. Ogle, a detachment of 15 men and the howitzer, and arrived on the 3d day at Capt Judah's camp on the Klamath some five miles below the cave, where it was reported the Indians were fortified. I found that Captain Judah had been to the cave with his company and a party of volunteers to reconnoitre, and had returned to his camp to await the arrival of the howitzer. Here I found two companies of organized, besides my independent volunteers, numbering in all about fifty men at camp, and also before joining Capt. Judah I received from reliable persons important information in relation to the origin of the difficulty. I was convinced that the whites (miners) were the aggressors, and very much to blame for their unprovoked attack upon the Indians. The first attack was made by a party of men organised in Cottonwood, who styled themselves the Squaw

84

Hunters, whose avowed purpose was to get squaws by force if necessary, headed by a man who was one of Ben Wright's party at the time he attempted to poison the Murdoc Indians, and others of his stamp. During the first attack at the cave, the chief, Bill, was encamped with his immediate family some ten miles above, on the river, and he absent in Yreka; but fearing another attack, collected his little band together at the cave and prepared to defend themselves against a similar outrage. In this first attack, the whites killed seven Indians (3 men, one of them a brother of the chief, who was approaching the cave unconscious of danger, with a deer upon his back, 2 squaws and 3 children) without resistance on the part of the Indians. After the entrance of the cave had been barricaded, the whites immediately spread the report that the Indians had collected a strong force at the cave for the purpose of war and plunder. A party of 28 men then went out under the pretense of getting some stock they said the Indians had stolen, a mere rumor, and in a fair fight the Indians defeated them killing four of their party, one Indian killed.

With this information I left for the cave on the morning of the 26th (preceded by Capt. Geiger and 17 men who volunteered to take post on top of the cave) with 20 men of Capt. Judah's company and 13 dragoons with the howitzer and some 30 volunteers, leaving Captain Judah sick in camp with a guard of 8 regulars and some volunteers. The cave is in the side of a perpendicular rock or palisade of mountain about 300 feet above the valley, the ascent to which is steep, and the approach directly in front, so that 25 men, with the barricade, could defend it against a charge of 100. The barricade is on the inside and an excellent one, and had I attempted to charge it, it would have been done by the regulars altogether at a great sacrifice of life. After making a proper disposition of the Volunteers and Lieut. Bonnycastle with his company in front of the cave, the cannon was placed on the only eligible position and several shells fired; this gun was then advanced, but the elevation being so great that a trench had to be dug to lower the trail. Two shells only entered the mouth of the cave, but done no damage as I afterwards ascertained owing to the peculiar shape of the arch of the entrance. The Indians were anxious for a talk and had it not been for the clamorous portion of the Volunteers, the difficulty would have been settled without firing the second shot. We encamped that night in front of the cave, and Bill sent three squaws to my camp under the protection of the interpreter to ask me to have a talk. Early next morning I went up to the cave, accompanied by a citizen, Mr. Eddy, residing in that vicinity, and heard what the chief had to say: all of which corroborated previous information, and in addition his great desire to be at peace with the whites. He said he had been living on friendly terms with the whites both in Yreka and Cotton Wood but had left the latter place on account of the ill treatment of his women. I found only the small band of Shastas in the cave, numbering in all not over fifty, and one boy on a visit from some other tribe. They had previously occupied caves higher up the river, but this being more commodius furnished them comfortable and secure winter quarters. I directed the chief to remain in the cave for the present, feeling assured that the ill-disposed portion of the community would massacre indiscriminately men, women and children if brought out.

What justice can be expected of a community that will furnish poison and approve of its being administered wholesale to the Indians: just such characters were the instigators of this affair.

The Volunteers collected all the Indian ponies (12) and brought away nine (maliciously shot one) contrary to my wishes. I regret to have to report the death of Captain Geiger: he was shot while in the act of looking over into the cave from his position on top, a rash act that he had but a few minutes previous cautioned his men against. He was an estimable man and universally beloved. After informing the Volunteers of the result of the talk, we marched back to Captain Judah's camp on the afternoon of the 27th. The volunteers continued on to their homes. I directed Captain Judah to return with his company to Fort Jones, and early in the morning of the 28th I set out with my detachment and Howitzer for this post which we reached yesterday afternoon.

The ground was covered with snow, and the weather intensely cold. Thermometer ten (10) degrees below 0 three days before we left during which time Captain Judah was in camp on the Klamath. I cannot speak too highly of the energy and activity of the Soldiers and officers concerned.

Very Respectfully, Your obedient Servant
A. J. Smith
Col. G. Wright   Capt. 1st Dragoons
Comdg. Nor. Dist. of Cala
Fort Reading, California

3:12   Letter, Winder to Burton

Mission of San Diego Cal
April 29, 1856

Sir

In obedience to your instructions of April 21 st. I proceded to the Rancho of San Jacinto in the vicinity of San Gorgonio. On my arrival there I sent for Juan Antonio the principal Capt. of the Cawilla Indians from whom I learned that the Indians were all quiet, having at present no serious difficulty with the Whites, but the Whites were encroaching upon the lands now occupied by the Indians. He complained that the commissioners had promised to send him farming utensils, and told him to live on this land where he would not be disturbed, neither of which promises have been fulfilled.

He says that the Indians living around him have raised small crops this year, but the greater portion of the tribe were almost entirely destitute of the means of subsistence owing to the failure of their crops.

I ascertained from other sources that the whites were in the habit of taking the gardens or other lands from the Indians without paying them either for crops or improvements and on the other hand the Indians being without food steal the cattle of the Whites and threaten to burn the houses and drive the Indians off, unless the Government should take steps, very soon, either to remove the Indians or prevent further depredations. These causes, you will readily perceive, must lead to a troublesome and expensive war.

At the request of Juan Antonio, I promised to notify him, several days previous to the departure of the next expedition in order that he may assemble his Captains to hear what was said. I feel satisfied that this chief will do all in his power to preserve peace and keep the Indians quiet, which however, cannot be a great while under present circumstances, and I am of the opinion that it would be cheaper to issue Beef to these Indians, than to fight them, at all events until some Superintendent of Indian Affairs is appointed who will attend to the duties pertaining to the office.

I was informed that a Mr. Spitler, an American living near Juan Antonio, is the only man who has endeavored to prevent trouble, and that he has not only been very efficient in settling all disputes; but has fed and protected the Indians as far as lay in his power, this I believe to be true as Juan Antonio appeared to have confidence in him. He is an old Soldier and was severely wounded at the battle of San Pasqual. I would therefore respectfully suggest that something be done to remunerate him for his trouble as he is a very poor man and scarcely able to assist the Indians.

I would further suggest that measures be adopted to mark the boundaries of the Indian lands, and that the whites be prevented from encroaching further.

I enclose herewith a letter from Mr. Rains, the Sub Agent at Temecula, from which you will perceive that the San Louis [San Luis Rey] Indians are also in destitute condition and will therefore be compelled to steal cattle in order to prevent starving: also the great danger of an outbreak, should the threats of the whites be carried out.

For many years these Indians have been in the habit of cultivating their fields without fencing, but at present the cattle of the whites overrun and destroy their crops and they have no means of redress.

The foregoing facts will I think show the absolute necessity of adopting at an early day some means for protecting

88

the Indians from the Whites, and to prevent the former from stealing the cattle of the latter.

> I am Sir Very Respectfully
> Yr. Obt. Servt.
> Wm. A. Winder
> 1st Lt. 3d. Arty.

Capt H. S. Burton USA
Comdg. Mission San Diego

3:13   Letter, Livingston to Mackall

> Fort Miller, Cal.
> August 17, 1856

Sir:

The citizens of King's river, about twenty in number, principally those living about the farm of McWilliam Campbell, known as the Indian farm, on the 11th inst. pursued some Indians who had left the river for the mountains, and killed three men and one woman. They claim that the Indians stole a horse on the 10th inst. belonging to Mr Patterson of the same place. They demanded the thief and told the Indians that if he was not given up they would kill them all. From these threats the Indians were frightened into going into the mountains, but were firm in saying that none of them had stolen the animals.

They attacked the Camp as aforesaid on the morning of the 12th and then returned to the settlements. They destroyed all the property found in the camp, and took several indian horses. These they still hold as spoils of war. It is a matter of great doubt if the Indians ever did steal the animal. The chief said he would find out if it was stolen, and would give some of his own horses to make up the loss. The whites then on the 13th at night went to a ranch of Indians on Dry Creek within 12 miles of this Post, and at daylight burned and destroyed everything they could find. The Indians had been notified of the intention of the whites and had left for this Post. Mr. Campbell, in charge of the King's River Indian farm, knew of all this and did not notify me of it. The whites probably used endeavors to prevent his informing me, as he says they did. I knew nothing of it till the Indians came in for protection. It was the intention of the whites to kill all the Indians. These are a well disposed band of Indians, raising some grain and vegetables and not interfering with the whites that I have ever heard of. The whites justify this act on the ground that some of the horses taken in the mountains belong to the Dry Creek Indians, that they were a part of the guilty ones. Before going against these Indians they gave Mr. Campbell notice that he must remove every Indian from the Indian Farm before a specified time or they would kill them. Mr. Campbell did not inform me of this either, but removed the Indians to this river, and visited me only this morning. Many Indians have come into the Fort and many more will come. There is not supplies here to feed them all, and with at least a nominal Indian Agent on either side, they are very poorly provided for. Many of the Indians who ran to the mountains were those that were brought to the River during former troubles in Tulare County, and placed by proper authority on the Farm. The acts of the whites so far seem to me to be utterly lawless. Those owning stock on King's River allow the stock to feed upon the Indian's acorns, and some even say, assist them to them.

The Commanding officers of Posts are not authorized, as I understand it, to make purchases for the support of Indians where there is a well organized Indian Department whose business it is to attend to the welfare of Indians. The Indians must be fed and collected in suitable spots or they must be allowed to go to the mountains where they can collect their own food. In this latter case every theft or evil that is committed will be charged to their account and they will be hunted and shot down. Several men on King's River have worked many Indians reaping a considerable pecuniary benefit thereby and in return treated them worse than slaves. This has caused a great many jealousies among the whites and is continually working evil. I shall collect all the Indians living in the foothills and threatened by the whites, at the Fort for protection till instructions can be received from Department Hd. Quarters. It is impossible, of course, for me to give protection to every little band while scattered through the country.

If the animal has been stolen, I shall be able to ascertain the fact and produce it if possible.

The Indian Agents have never fed or attended to one tenth part of the Indians here. Still the whites appropriate their country and drive them from it.

Respectfully Sir,
Your obt. Sevt.
La Rhett L. Livingston
Lt. 3rd arty.
Comdg Post

Maj. W. W. Mackall
Asst agt. Genl.
Benicia, Cal.

3:14   Letter, Rundell to Bates

Camp Cap Eele
Klamath Cal
March 4th 1857

Sir.

I have the honor to report every thing as usual in this Section. On the night of the 19th Feby. two men (one named Lewis commonly called "Squire" and the other Lawson, generally known as "Texas") came to an Indian ranch (Wasch) about a mile above this camp on the opposite side of the river. They commenced abusing the Indian Squaws, and one squaw, while endeavoring to protect her daughter, was stabbed by Lewis very severely in the back and shoulder, who also stabbed the father of the girl twice in the arm. They then seized two other squaws whom they forced to remain with them all night. I was informed of the circumstances the next morning and immediately called upon the Indian Agent to have the men arrested. He arrived here on the 22nd and immediately proceeded to Orleans Bar for a warrant. In the mean time, on the 22nd, the two men Lewis and Lawson came to this camp, but not meeting with a favorable reception they left and went back up the river. On the way they stopped at the same ranch, but the Indians having seen them in time, the Squaws ran to the hills. The man Lewis enraged at the escape of the Squaws, seized a club and without provocation, attacked and brutally beat an Indian boy named Tom, so that it is doubtful whether he will recover. I immediately stationed a guard at that ranch to protect the Indians from further outrages. The man Lawson was subsequently shot by Capt. Young, and Lewis has been bound over in $5,000 to appear for trial. He is now in jail at Crescent City. If the proper steps are pursued to insure his punishment, it will have more effect here than an army of Soldiers. He is, I believe, the first white man who has ever been arrested for anything of the kind in this neighborhood, though, his offence compared with others that have taken place on this river is a mere trivial matter. The Indians were very much excited at the time, but by means of my Interpreter I succeeded in pacifying them.

I would request if the Command remains here that it be increased, as one of my men is laid up from Rheumatism, and another severely scalded so that but thirteen men are left.

I am Sir
Very Respectfully
Your obdt. Servant
C. H. Rundell
Lieut. 4th Infantry
Comdg.

To
Lieut F. H. Bates
Acting Asst. Adjt. Genl.
Northern Dist. Cal.

Progress of the White Crusade
Against Indians in the North

The Red Bluff *Beacon* gives some particulars of the success of a "subscription party" in clearing Tehama county of
its Indians, who are certainly very troublesome and dangerous to the white settlers. Says the *Beacon*:

The news reached us, from a reliable source, on Monday, August 1st, that sometime during last week the party
sent out with John Breckenridge, under pay raised by subscription, met a party of five Indians and one white man,
between the headwaters of Butte and Deer creeks, with
whom they engaged in a severe running fight, which only
lasted a short time, when Mr. B. and his party succeeded in
forever silencing, so far as the straggling band is concerned,
hostilities. The red men of the party, as well as their pale-
faced leader, of whom the country is well rid, are now sleeping the sleep of death. As a trophy, or sort of remembrance
that there was a man so base as to lead on a band of savages
to deeds of butchery and theft, the scalp of the white man
was taken and brought away by Mr. Breckenridge.

The day after this encounter, a large rancheria was discovered, and preparations made for surrounding it during the
night. This they only partially succeeded in, owing to the
smallness of the company, which only numbers about a
dozen men. They succeeded, however, about daylight next
morning, in killing ten Indians, including one squaw, who
threw herself between a white man and one of the bucks just
at the moment of firing off the rifle of the former.

This gallant little army is still in the mountains, and
were to attack a much larger rancheria, near the head of Deer
Creek, on Saturday night last, the result of which engagement
has not reached us.

On Sunday afternoon, about an hour before sunset,
while the occupants were absent from home, the houses of

Mr. Roundtree and Mr. Anderson, some four and a half miles above Mayhew's Crossing, on Deer Creek, were set on fire by Indians and entirely consumed, as well as their hay stacks, fencing etc. The smoke and flames soon aroused the neighborhood, but no Indians were to be seen. Owing to the close proximity of these ranches to the foothills, they were enabled to easily escape and secrete themselves. Their tracks were plainly visible next morning, and no doubt remains as to its being Indians who committed the deed.

The inhabitants of the valley along the foothills are all moving in towards the river for protection. Mr. King of Vermont Mills, removed his family down to Mr. Mayhew's on Sunday last, and Mr. Sadorus and family have gone down below Mr. Keefer's on Rock creek. Others, we understand, are leaving every day for more secure quarters.

No doubt now remains that the Indians have white accomplices, and that they receive their supplies of arms and ammunition from white agents. The rancheria stormed last week was found to contain flour, sugar, dishes, and nearly all the comforts usually found in the cabins of white people. It is understood that there are some forty or fifty white brutes living on the head-waters of Butte creeks with squaws, in a state of concubinage, and that uphold and protect the Indians in all their depredations. These people doubtless encourage the Indians to steal from the citizens of this valley, and perhaps divide with them in the spoils a large number of American horses and cattle that have been taken from our citizens, and it would be well for General Kibbe's company, before the contemplated campaign upon which he is about to enter is over, to make strict inquiry into this matter and if, as we suspect, there are white receivers of the stolen property taken from this valley, from time to time by Indians, to endeavor to have them brought to justice. The man who was shot last week was, we learned, a stranger to the party that killed him. The conclusion is, by those who live in the vicinity, that he was, in all probability, one of the Butte creek squaw men.

Memoranda on the Pit River "War," and Gen. Kibbe
Pitt River Valley, Jan. 15, 1860

To the Editor of the *Bulletin:* In looking over a communication published in your issue of 29th December, 1859, and signed "General" Kibbe, Q. M., Adjutant General, & c., in command of volunteers, I notice several inaccuracies, which, in justice to some of the parties named therein, I hope, through the medium of your columns, to correct.

In the communication referred to, it is stated that Napoleon McElroy had done nothing to merit his murder. Now, I know he had killed one Indian and squaw and wounded a third, and the reason assigned for this was that some Indians had stolen a deer from him. For this McElroy and his friends thought the Indians would murder him; for this, perhaps, Birney, an inoffensive man, was killed.

Callahan was perhaps murdered from having lived with Lockhart a year previous, against whom the Indians charged numerous murders. Mr. Kibbe seems to place great importance on the fact that numerous "caches" of roots and other Indian stores were found. This can easily be explained, and with great credit to the Indians, in this way: Heretofore, these Indians have been subsisted through the winter by the United States Government. Early this spring, and throughout the summer, they were repeatedly assured that the Government would give them nothing this winter. Thus, by hard work, they had ample supplies, that were destroyed.

With reference to the "guns" lent by the commanding officer of Fort Crook, upon inquiry I have been informed they were lent to Frank McElroy with a perfect understanding, and repeated promises from himself, that he would not harm any of the valley Indians, but, on the other hand, intended co-operating with a detachment of dragoons which were just starting in pursuit of the very Indians who murdered his brother—a detachment of dragoons having just come in after finding his brother's body and assisting him to bury it. This same detachment, by the way, killed two or three Indians and wounded another, which were perhaps all the band which murdered McElroy.

Mr. Kibbe, says that the body of McElroy was found in Hat Creek, his arms and legs cut off and awfully mangled. I saw the body before it was buried, and the arms and legs were all there—Mr. Kibbe's assertion to the contrary notwithstanding. The murderers of Birney had previously, through the assistance of some Valley Indians, been arrested by the dragoons and turned over to the civil authorities at Shasta.

Mr. Kibbe says that the party above referred to, after having pursued the Indians, came on the rancheria, and in the onslaught, through excitement, & c., killed women and children. This is a grave mistatement of facts. The Indians attacked, or butchered, had been living at a place called "Roff's Ranch" for a long time. There the "bold" volunteers crept on them before day, and, without informing Roff or any of the cattle-herders thereabouts, marched on the ranch, killed about nine men, the balance escaping. The women and children remained, trusting to confidence in the honesty of an American, whom they believed would not murder women and children. In this they were mistaken; for not only in the "excitement" of the moment, but throughout the greater part of the day, they searched around among the "haystocks" with the hatchet, and split the children's heads open. In this way there were over forty women and children butchered—the whites exceeding even the Indians in their butchery.

In conclusion, permit me to add that Mr. Kibbe, with his volunteers, and at great expense to the State, took off about three hundred Indians, of whom a large proportion were women and children. Had a proper demand been made through the United States military authorities, one officer with half a dozen men, including the guides and interpreter, would within ten days, have taken not only these identical 300 Indians, but perhaps 200 more, with the simple expense of the cost of transporting them wherever the Superintendent of Indian affairs might have wished.

Nearly if not quite all the Indians removed by the "General" were harmless. If there be any warriors among such a miserable, cowardly race, he has left them amongst us. The best parts for catching fish have been taken up by the Americans at Lockhart's Ferry and McElroy's Bridge, and thousands of cattle swarm through the valleys. The Indians were accustomed to find their roots, and were not permitted to go among the cattle to dig.

I see that Mr. Kibbe—I am tired of calling him "General"—styles his expedition a war!! I would like to know how many guns or rifles he found among the Indians. When McElroy's body was found, he had a bullet hole through his head. If Kibbe was well posted he would know there is a heap of white Indians around.

As a taxpayer—and I have been one for five years—I sincerely hope that such gross injustice will not be committed as to call upon the people of California to meet the expenses of such a "war." When will California get rid of her great "generals"?

3:17 Newspaper article, San Francisco, 1864

Pursuing the Indians on the Northern Coast

A correspondent of the Mendocino County *Herald,* writing from Camp Grant on 24th June, says:

The Klamath Indians and those tribes about Hoopa and the Trinity country, being in the upper or extreme northern portion of the District, are beginning to see the error of their ways, and are coming in and giving themselves up. Whole tribes have already done so, and with proper management it is presumed that almost the entire bands of strolling, thieving, murdering savages will surrender by the next winter, and be taken to some place of security, where in all time to come depredations upon the whites will no more be heard of. The number of prisoners on the peninsula at Fort Humboldt, has swollen from 50 or 60 (at the commencement of the campaign) to several hundred, and more are being added to it every week.

The most exciting Indian hunt that has yet been made by any scouting party of this whole battalion was when Capt. Simpson sent out a detachment under Sergt. Harris to cooperate with citizens led by the old mountaineer and invincible Digger-hunter Steve Fleming. The Indians from the neighborhood of Hay Fork had killed an Indian boy and five horses within gunshot of Steve's and the citizens thereabouts came and applied to Capt. Simpson for assistance in catching them. This he promptly rendered them and sent out the detachment with instructions to follow them till they were taken, if it should take all summer. There were 7 of this company, 4 from the vicinity of Fort Seward and 4 domestic Indians that acted as trackers and also packed the provisions for the party. They were afterwards joined by 4 or 5 citizens of Hay Fork. Probably a more experienced and determined set of men never got together for scouting after Indians. To give your readers some little idea how keenly such a party scents the track, and how unflinching they are in following them up, it is necessary to tell that these men followed this band of about 9 bucks, 6 squaws and 2 children, for forty-two days and nights over one of the most ragged, rough and dangerous countries on earth. Now down some dark and dismal canon hundreds of feet below the usual level, (if such a term may be applied to such a country) then clambering up the steep and rocky hills, then through miles of the densest thorny thickets, after leaving the track for a time by reasons of the game leaving little or no trace in creasting streams, walking on fallen trees, and over dry leaves, and finally traced them to the settlement on Hay Fork right into a house, and ascertained they had the day before robbed the house of gun, pistol, blankets, &c. They retraced their steps, still on the track, into the south of Trinity country, and found they (the Indians) had been joined by others, and the sergeant went to Fort Teque for assistance. Major Wright sent out 30 men with three Lieutenants, all under the command of Sergeant

98

Harris–Steve Fleming as guide. The third day out they came upon the Indians and killed 9, and took 2 squaws and 2 children prisoners.

Another correspondent of the same journal, writing on 28th June, from Camp No. 27, North Fork of Eel river, says:

On the 7th instant a scouting party brought into camp 17 Indian prisoners, who state that they are the last of their tribes in the mountains of Mendocino County. The truth of their assertion I have not the least reason to doubt, as several scouting parties were simultaneously sent in different directions, which scoured the country for 20 miles around, and each on their return reported no Indian signs, except the charred remains of rancherias and the bleached bones of their inmates. Some of the last band of Indians brought in are old acquaintances—they were recognized as having broken away from different escorts while en route to Fort Humboldt; but being continually harassed by the scouts, they at length surrendered, and are now with the remainder of their tribe in the safe keeping of the district commander, to whom they were forwarded on the 14th instant; thus closing the exodus of a large tribe of hostile Indians, whose depredations were to the Northern settler of the country seriously annoying, and which it was said would take years to extirpate, but was, by a small company, led with energy and armed with discretionary power, cleared from their fortresses in the short space of six months.

On the 23rd instant, when in sight of Trinity Mountains, in a heavy thunder storm with rain, 1st Sergeant Magutie came suddenly upon an Indian brave. Unfortunately, before he had time to order the man not to fire upon him, he received two balls through the head. He was a fine looking Indian, indeed everything about him stamped him of a different tribe to those we have been dealing with. His bow and arrows were of superior description, and were brought to camp as a curiosity.

Courtesy MNH   Maidu man, Lawson Anderson, born 1860. *Photo 190*

RESERVATION MATTERS

The federal government entered into a series of treaties, eighteen in all, with the California Indians in 1851 and 1852. One of these treaties is referred to in Document 4:1. Congress refused to ratify the treaties, largely as a result of the political pressure which the California senators were able to exercise. As an alternative, the federal government began in 1853 to establish reservations in various parts of California where the landless Indians could be gathered and protected. The theory was good, but it fell short in practice. By and large, Indian agents who were appointed to operate these reservations were dishonest, unscrupulous, unqualified, and cared little for the welfare of the people they were charged to help. Corruption and conflict of interest were so apparent that J. Ross Browne was appointed in May, 1857 to investigate the operation of the reservations and to report his findings. This he did in a series of letters, a few which are presented here. Notwithstanding Browne's findings, nothing was done to correct the situation.

Hd. Quarters, Fort Miller, Cala.
August 26, 1852

Sir,

I have the honor to state that your communication marked "Confidential" of July 30th, 1852, was only received by me day before yesterday, and of course too late to be of service at the council which took place on Caweah river on the 15th inst.; but the spirit of the communication was carried into effect as far as practicable.

Cattle had been ordered by me for the purpose of feeding the indians; and they were on their way to the Caweah river when the news of the death of Major Savage threw every thing into confusion, and in consequence the cattle were abandoned. In consequence of no cattle arriving I issued to the indians subsistence stores which I had on hand. Quite a number of indians came into the council but upon learning there were no bribes provided for them, they returned to their homes, leaving their chiefs to represent them in the council.

I should have remarked that the beans which were on their way to the post were "indian property" from Major Savage' rancherie, and were under charge of his men, who refused to draw them any further when they heard of his death. I had promised the indians beans at the council, which promise as yet has not been fulfilled.

This, together with the nullity of the papers which they hold from the Commissioner, guarantees to them certain lands, upon certain conditions, I fear will cause great dissatisfaction among them unless something can be done immediately to convince them that the Americans are acting towards them in good faith.

Each chief was provided with a copy of the articles agreed on between them and the Commissioners.

In a letter recently received by me from the Governor,

he states that there is no prospect of the treaty passing the senate, and until it does pass it is good for nothing. He advises me to inform the indians of this fact, which I decline doing, as I am confident it will bring about an immediate war.

In my opinion the treaty is perfectly good and should be respected until it is either approved of or annulled at Washington. If this is not so, the whole affair between the Commissioner and the indians is a mere farce, which requires but the lifting of the curtain to turn into a grand tragedy.

Hoping that the Commander General will give due attention to a subject fraught alternately with so much gravity I have the honor to remain.

Your mo obdt Sevt
G. W. Tatten
Brvt. Maj. U. S. Army
Commanding

Asst. Adjutant General
Hd. Quarters Pacific Division
San Francisco, Ca.

P. S. Enclosed is a copy of the Governor's letter.

Sacramento City
Aug. 10, 1852

Major G. W. Tatten
Com. at Fort Miller

Sir,

Some days since I received a communication from Genl. Hitchcock, enclosing one from you advising the arrest of Major Harvey and requesting me to communicate directly with you at Fort Miller on the subject of his arrest etc.

I now comply with the request of Genl. Hitchcock and would have done so sooner if health had permitted.

If, as is charged, Major Harvey had violated the laws of the State, it is clearly the province of the civil authorities to act in the matter—to arrest and if found guilty, punish him in the manner and form prescribed by law. But, if you have reference to an arrest by Military authority, I must say that I am not aware of the existence of any law which confers upon the Executive the power to order an officer in command of United States troops to place a citizen under arrest.

It is proper that I should inform you that I know but little about the facts of the case, and have therefore addressed a communication to the District Attorney of Tulare County and enclosed him copies of your letters of July 26th and Aug. 3rd, 1852, so as to fully acquaint him with the charges made against Major Harvey and his command.

In your letters you refer to Indian Reservations, and say that "the Indians wish to know whether they are to be protected or not by the Government on their own Reserves." If you have reference to the Reservations set apart by the Board of Indian Commissioners, as I presume you have, it is proper for me to remind you of the fact that the Treaties by which districts of country were set apart for exclusive Indian occupation, have not received the approval of the Government, and recent information render it almost certain that they will all (eighteen in number, I believe) be rejected by the Senate of the United States.

It may be that the Indians misunderstand the subject, that they are still ignorant of the fact that the sanction of the Senate is necessary to give force and effect to the Treaties made with them by the Indian Commissioners. On this point correct information should be imparted to them. They should be told that the Senate of the United States has not as yet ratified the action of the Commissioners, and that until the Senate approves, the Government cannot be regarded as having given its assent to the Reservations, and, of course, will not attempt to enforce treaty stipulations which have not and probably will not receive their approval.

I trust the difficulties in the Tulare country will be settled without further conflict with the Indians, and our citizens rendered safe in the pursuit of their various avocations.

> I have the honor to be
> Your Obt. Servt.
> John Bigler

Mission of San Diego Cal
August 23, 1856

Sir,

Thomas, the principal Captain of the Santa Isabel Indians, together with thirteen of his Captains came into this post some two weeks since, and complained that Mr. J. J. Warner, (Sub Agent for these Indians) had informed them of his intention to take all animals, having no brands upon them, in the hands of the Indians, from them as his property.

As many of these Indians own mares, which have had colts, and which are not branded for the reason that they have no brands, this proceeding would be manifestly unjust. I therefore directed Thomas to bring the animals here in case any attempt was made to take them, and I would endeavor to secure his property for him.

This is one of the many cases of injustice practiced upon these Indians, and by the very men whose duty it is to protect them, and I presume my action will be reported as "an interference on the part of the military" with the duties of an Agent. I therefore have the honor to report the case, in order that the Commanding General may be made aware of the characters of the persons making such reports.

I am Sir,
Very respectfully
Your obt. Servt.
Wm. A. Winder
1st Lt. 3 Arty.
Comdg. Post

To
Bvt Major W. W. Mackall
Asst Adjt. General
No. 61. Dept. Pacific Div.
Benicia Cal.

Nome Lackee Reserve, Cala.
Maj. W. W. Mackall   Sept. 1st, 1857
Asst. Adjt. Genl. U. S. Army
San Francisco, Cala.

Sir,
Pursuant to instructions, I make this, my semi-monthly report.

The amount of wheat gathered and stored away by Indians under the direction of White men on the Reservation this year exceeds eight thousand bushels. Besides this the Indians have a great quantity in their cabins which has been gathered by the old women. There is an ample supply for the Winter. While there is water in the creeks, the mill belonging to the Reservation is kept busy grinding wheat for the Indians and making flour for the consumption of the employees on the place. For some months past the mill has not been worked owing to a want of water, but in the meanwhile the Agent has a contract with a Miller near Tehama to exchange one bushel of Indian flour for each bushel of wheat furnished by the Indian Department, so that the Agent is always able to furnish the Indians with flour.

The Indians from Yuba County are not satisfied. They every now and then run away in squads. Some are caught and brought back; others escape to their old homes. The reason of their discontent is plain, in the neighborhood of Oroville and on Feather River where they formerly lived some worked for farmers; others worked in the mines. They got money and found out its uses. They had an abundance of fish and other things that they have not here. On the Reservation at the present time they are furnished with flour and clothes— nothing more. If they want anything besides bread to eat they must go out and hunt for it as they did years ago. There is no water here and they are for this reason deprived of their most necessary recreation. Some work hard and live, others keep out of the way and they live, too. There is no inducement for them to work. White men and mankind in general only labor when they either know or fancy their labor will produce them some good. Brutes alone work without motive. These Indians have lived so long amongst Whites that they have imbibed a great many of their notions, particularly a knowledge of the value of money. If they were paid, no matter how small a sum, for their labor, I believe they would remain on the Reservations contentedly and work willingly provided these Reservations were suitably located. There could be enough grain and hay sold to pay for the additional expense.

The whole number of Indians on the Reservation at the present time is about eight hundred.

There is sickness in every Rancherie and almost in every cabin. There is a great deal of sickness even among the Whites. The Physician is at present sick and unable to go his rounds. Almost every farmer in the neighborhood is either now sick or has been so within a month. The farmers are moving off for more healthy "locations" being unable to live here. My Detachment has suffered a great deal from chills and fevers.

The Reservation is now being surveyed.

In June I made a Requisition of Capt. Cullender of the Ordnance Corps for Rifles and Ammunition with six Colt's Revolving pistols, and notified Col. Ripley of the fact. These arms I considered necessary for the use of the Detachment under my command at this place. As I have heard neither from Col. Ripley nor Capt. Callender, I presume that they considered the arms as unnecessary or else they were then absent from their posts and have still remained absent. The requisition was at least reasonable and certainly merited some reply.

I am, sir, very Respectfully
Your obdt. Servt.
M. R. Morgan
1st Lt. 3rd Arty., Comdg.

Nome Lackee Reserve, Cala.
Sept. 15th, 1857

Major W. W. Mackall
Asst. Adjt. Genl. U. S. Army
San Francisco, Cala.

Sir,

I have the honor to make my semi-monthly Report. There has very little transpired since the 1st Inst. which I deem necessary to report to the Head Quarters Dept.

On the 10th Inst. the Foreman of the Reservation returned from Oroville with 150 Indians, Yubas. Some of them had been on the Reservation but had run away; others had never been here. I do not know that they came willingly. It was found necessary to employ wagons for them and to hire some twelve or more White men to bring them here. This may have been done to keep off the worthless Whites who are always found in some way connected with the Indians when in the neighborhood of our Cities and towns. A great many of the Indians are now out in the mountains gathering Acorns for their Winter consumption.

There is still a great deal of sickness on the Reservation. The Trinity Indians, Wilackes, were taken from here to the farm on Thom's Creek, six miles from here, in hopes that the mortality amongst them might be diminished, but it would now seem that it was of no avail as they die quite as fast there as they did here.

Of the twenty two men that I have now here, fourteen have been sick. At present there are two men sick of intermittent fever.

I have now here two deserters, one, Elijah R. Moore from Company "D", 4th Infy., who deserted from Fort Jones in June last; the other, James Barry from Company "D" 3rd Artillery. He deserted from Fort Jones in May or June 1856. The constitution of the first seems to be broken from sickness and Barry has the appearance of a drunkard. They are an incumbrance to me.

I am, sir, very Respectfully
Your Obdt. Servt.
M. R. Morgan
1st. Lt. 3rd Atry., Comdg Detachment

Fort Terwaw, Calif.
December 25th 1857

Major [Mackall]:
I have the honor to acknowledge the receipt of your
letter of December 5th 1857 and to report the Indians perfectly peaceable and quiet here, the Smith River Indians
having left for their old homes on Smith River (with the
exceptions of 8 or 10) by permission of the Supt. of Indian
affairs. Had not this permission been given them, I feel confident that the majority of them would be here now, and
perfectly satisfied to remain as they were coming in daily and
evinced a disposition to remain which I had never seen
amongst them before. But even before this order was known
to the Agent, a certain set of whites around Crescent City
and vicinity knew of it, and communicated it to the Indians,
and by making them glowing promises and telling them they
were illtreated on the Reservation ect., they succeeded in
getting even the most contented of them to leave.
There is a party of bad, unprincipled whites about
Crescent City and vicinity who have been living with squaws
and subsisting off the Indians, and who with a few head men
of the Smith River tribe, have been at the bottom of all this
trouble. The Agent has positive that some of these men have
way laid the trail between Crescent City and this place, to
assassinate him for moving the Indians on the Reservation!
Also that a responsible man overheard a conversation between these men just before my arrival here, to persuade the
Indians all to leave the Reservation, get me to feed them, as
Lt. Garber had done, and then that they would get employment. It is a notorious fact that they are the same class if not
some of the same party who commenced the Rogue River
War in 1856, by going to a settler's garden after night in their
bare feet, destroying his vegetables, firing his house and then
the next day one of this same party was an officer in a

109

volunteer Company, who massacred a Rancheria of innocent Indians, for the alledged depredations! Also that during the War two of these very same men, now causing this trouble, slept with Indian women and the next morning beat their brains out! These very same men were beyond a doubt at the bottom of the conspiracy, which the Indians attempted to put into execution of the 17th ultimo! It is these men now who pretend to sympathize with the Indians and say that they were starved and illtreated on the Reservation, when to my positive knowledge there has been no just cause given them here for dissatisfaction since my arrival! And it will be these very same men now, if the Indians are let remain amongst them, who will cause a war, and at the close of which, bring in a large claim against Government for services never performed. The respectable portion of the community about Crescent City and vicinity, are anxious to have the Indians return to the reservation.

The Indians number now on Smith River between 6 and 700. They have not as here before laid up their winter supply of food, and without it they must either steal or starve. I feel satisfied that, should any attempt to bring back these Indians cause a war, it will not extend here, as all the Indians on the Reservation desire the return of the Smith River Indians and even express their willingness to assist in bringing them in.

But even in the extreme case, I have sufficient force to close the war and compell the return of the Indians to the reservation.

I enclose herewith the agent's views on the subject, with an extract of a letter from the Supt. of Indian affairs.

I am sir very Respectfully
Your obt. Servt.
George Crook
1st Lieut. 4th Infantry
Comdg. Post

To Major W. W. Mackall
Asst. Adjt Gen. USA
San Francisco, Cal
(via Humboldt)

Office Supt Indian Affairs
San Francisco, Cal
H. P. Heintzelman Esqr   Nov. 23, 1857
Sub Indn Agent
Klamath Reserve

Sir

I have received your report of the 23rd ulto. in regard to
the absconding of a portion of the Smith River Indians from
the Reservation. I know perfectly well the views of Genl.
Clarke to be adverse to the use of Soldiers, either in taking
Indians to the Reservation, or compelling them to remain
there. It is therefore useless to make any application to him
of the subject.

The foregoing is an extract of a letter of date as above,
and signed, Thos. J. Henley, Supt Ind. Affairs

Office Klamath Indian Reservation
Lieut. Geo. Crook   December 15th 1857
4th Infantry U. S. A.

Sir

In reply to your querie of what I deem the proper
course to pursue with the Smith River Indians who have
recently left the reservation to induce them to return to remain. To state that in my opinion the only method that will
ever have the least tendency towards effecting that object
will be to follow them to their old haunts and severely punish
them. Portions of them have been captured by citizens of
Crescent City at various times when difficulties would be
apprehended and retained until things would become quiet
and then would be turned loose to return to their old haunts.
At the close of the late Oregon War they were removed to
this Reservation by Col Buchanan where they remained for a
short time when they left for their old haunts. On the 19th
of October 1856 they were taken charge of by Lieut Garber

111

4th Infantry and for a number of months retained by him and fed at Smith's Island—and from this kind of treatment and what they are told by squaw men they are induced to believe that there is no power to compel them to remain. I finished removing them from their old haunts on the 5th of August last and built for them to reside in at this post 23 log houses 15 x 18 ft. I furnished them regularly their food and clothing. Many of those Indians were in the whole of the late Oregon War and are accustomed to the use of fire arms. They are closely allied to the Hosantas and Chet Coe Tribes, who are now in the mountains and from all the information that I can gather, are induced to believe will break out into open hostilities in the spring—and that the Tolowas will join them there can be no doubt. To attempt to bring them in by peaceable means I deem utterly futile—that has already been tried twice and with the same result. There must be some power to teach them that the Reservation is their home and that the Agent is there to protect them and see to their wants and that what they are told by Squaw men are lies. That power must be the Military. That the late attack upon myself was the prelude to an outbreak, there can be no doubt. It is but the history of all previous outbreaks in this northern country, to kill the agent first.

Very Respectfully your Obt Servant
H. D. Heintzelman
Sub Indian Agent

4:5   Letter, Browne to Mix

San Francisco, Cal.
Sept. 29th, 1858

Hon. Chas. E. Mix
Commissioner of Indian Affairs

Sir:

  I have the honor to enclose a printed copy of certain resolutions adopted by the citizens of Humboldt Bay in relation to Indian affairs in that vicinity at a recent meeting at the town of Union and to submit for your consideration the grave and important questions involved in the proposed action of the people of Humboldt.

From a perusal of these resolutions, you will perceive that, in consequence of Indian depredations and the murder of several white settlers in the vicinity of Humboldt, for which the federal authorities have failed to provide any remedy, the citizens, through the Board of Trustees of Union, have assumed the responsibility of declaring war against the Indians, and taken measures to carry it into effect. They have levied a tax upon property, the proceeds of which are to be devoted to the expenses of the war, "until provision shall be made for the payment of the same by the State or General Government."

When the war of 1855 broke out in the territories of Oregon and Washington, it was charged that it was a war of speculation gotten up by the citizens of these territories for the purpose of enriching themselves at the expense of the public Treasury. A debt of some five or six millions is now but a portion of the result. Another expensive war has broken out, originating, as I conceive, like the first, not in the aggressions of white settlers for speculative purposes, but in the failure of the General Government to pay the Indians West of the Cascades for their lands, and the apprehensions entertained by the more remote tribes that sooner or later they would be overrun and exterminated by the white race unless they concentrated their energies and made a vigorous resistance. They saw before them the examples furnished by the Yakimas and Klickitates, driven from the lower Columbia to the mountains without recompense for the possessory rights of which they had been deprived; and naturally became alarmed lest they should soon meet with the same fate.

Whilst this war is going on, another one, another on a smaller scale perhaps, but presenting equal claims to the consideration of the government, is now undertaken on the private responsibility of a few citizens in the northern portion of this State. It is entirely useless to indulge in charges and recriminations against a particular class of white settlers, whose misconduct towards the Indians has always been a prolific source of trouble. This class exists in all frontier

113

countries. It is not practicable to get rid of them by written complaints. They will be found on the outskirts of civilization wherever it goes.

The proceedings of the citizens of Mattole Valley, also enclosed, will show that the conduct of these renegade whites meets with the disapproval of the better class of settlers, and that even in the frontier parts of the country there is a strong feeling against them. A treaty of peace is here made with the Mattole Indians, some forty of whom it will be remembered were killed by the whites during the past summer for alleged murders of white settlers. A war of extermination has been declared against the Cascouse Creek, Bear River, Eel river and other neighboring Indians. Some twenty or thirty armed men are said to have been busily occupied during several months past in killing Indians South and East of the Mattole.

These difficulties both at Humboldt and the Mattole have been fully represented to the Superintendent of Indian Affairs. Complaints have been made in the public prints and by the people of the country from time to time during the past year; and the removal of the Indians to the reservations has been repeatedly demanded. The Indians East and South of the Mattole have been suffered to run wild, and with the exception of a remote Agency of little practical use, nothing has been done for their relief or benefit. In the extensive region lying along the banks of Eel river and the Trinity and to the Eastward and Southward of Cape Mendocino, are numerous hostile tribes with whom little or no communication has been had, and by whom many of the outrages complained of by the people of Humboldt have doubtless been committed.

The Commissioner of Indians Affairs, in August 1857, saw the policy of concentrating these Indians on the reservations—especially Mendocino. In a letter to the Superintendent, dated August 16th, he says, "The recent explorations between the reservation and Cape Mendocino tend to confirm the opinions expressed in connection with the eligibility of the position for Indian purposes. In consideration of the fact that the Klamath reservation is also situated on the Pacific coast, it is suggested as the third point of concentration for all the Indians north of Nome Lackee and west and north of the Sacramento. By thus bringing all the Indians of the State within the three reservations designated, on and near the coast, they would be further removed from the encroachments of white settlers, and would consequently be more secure from the attacks of hostile bands of their own races."

Not only did the Superintendent fail to carry out these suggestions, but during the past winter he suffered most of the Indians who were on the Mendocino reservation and who had been brought there at great expense, to go back to their original homes. The Sub-Agent at Klamath reported the escape of Indians from that reservation, and asked authority to bring all in who properly belonged to it; but he was told to turn his attention to agriculture. The settlers between the Mattole and Cape Mendocino complained of an attempt made to extend the reservation over their claims, but desired that the Indians should be brought in to the reservation proper and taken care of; in default of which and in consequence of several murders, they undertook the task of extermination and killed, as before stated, some forty or fifty Indians. At Nome Cult, a few miserable Indians were brought in from Eden Valley, twelve miles distant; but the main body there are those who have always frequented and occupied the Nome Cult valley. The Indians of Eel river valley, and between Nome Cult and the Cape are as wild and hostile as they have ever been.

I reiterate the opinion that no practical good has resulted so far from the reservations—not because the system of colonizing and subsisting the Indians by their own labor is impracticable, but because it has not been properly tested.

If the citizens of Humboldt carry their present purpose into effect and entail upon the government another expensive and disastrous war, it will be because they have applied for relief in vain, and the fault will be attributable to the manner in which the affairs of this Superintendency have been conducted.

Very respectfully, Your Obt Srvt.
J. Ross Browne
Special Agt of the Treas'y Dept.

San Francisco, Cal,
Hon. Chas. E. Mix,   October 8th, 1858
Commissioner of Indian Affairs

Sir:

I have the honor to transmit herewith certain affidavits and letters in relation to affairs at the Tejon reservation in 1855, which were duly forwarded to Washington in that year, but were never, as I am informed, submitted for official action.

No. 1 is the testimony of Saml. R. Dummer, clerk to E. T. Beale Esq. during his superintendency in relation to the sale of flour to a Spaniard by Wilmot Martin, Clerk to T. J. Henley Esq., the present Superintendent.

No. 2 is a letter from Mr. Henley to Mr. Dummer in which Mr. Henley expresses entire confidence in the integrity and business qualifications of Mr. Dummer, from which it would appear that the testimony of the latter is strictly reliable.

In relation to the cause assigned for the removal of Mr. Dummer, I have to remark that it is exactly in conformity with my views both then and now, and that I have invariably urged upon Mr. Henley the propriety of carrying that policy rigorously into effect in all cases. No reservation can prosper, where it is made a mere vantage ground for the benefit of the employees. Yet no sooner is Mr. Dummer dismissed from office for owning stock, than the employees on all the reservations commence keeping stock on their own account; and Mr. Henley approves their conduct by setting the example himself. At this very time, it is well known that Mr. J. R. Vineyard, the Agent at the Tejon, owns several thousand head of sheep on that reservation, which are herded by Indians; and I have already shown the nature and extent of Mr. Henley's speculations in stock. Messrs. White and Simpson, at Mendocino, have become wealthy by their stock speculations. Mr. Ford owns both stock and a stock ranch; S.

P. Storms owns stock at Nome Cult; and, indeed, it would be difficult to find an agent or employee who is not engaged to some extent in the stock business.

I consider the Tejon reservation little more than a private stock ranch.

No. 3 is the testimony of A. Godey, in relation to the sale of a blanket by Wm Sanins, Late Agent at the Tejon to an Indian woman. Mr. Sanins is now Post Master at Stockton, and can probably explain the nature of the transaction.

No. 4 is the testimony of Wm. H. Neal in regard to a mule trade, in which Mr. Neal alleges that he defrauded the government out of $350.00 and undertakes to show that Mr. Henley was a party to the fraud.

No. 5 is the testimony of the same Neal in regard to the purchase by him of reservation clothing. As there is no evidence that this money was not turned over, or otherwise properly accounted for, it can scarcely be considered a direct charge of fraud, though all such transactions are suspicious and improper.

No. 6 is a letter from Mr. Henley to T. A. Bishop, farmer at the Tejon under Mr. Beale. The above testimony was procured as I have understood, by Mr. Bishop, and additional testimony to the following effect, which, however, is lost or mislaid:

Clapp's affidavit in regard to the sale of blankets to the Indians, by persons in charge at Tejon.

Dummer's   do   lumber sold to A. Godey
Do   do   double and single trees "
Do   do   swapping a mule for a horse and putting the mule on returns as present.

Chas. Kinney's affidavit on sale of double-trees.

Kinney and Clapp's affidavit as to wastage of wheat, and number of bushels wasted and fed to teams.

In connection with the above, I have to remark that Mr. P. E. Connor, a highly respectable citizen of Stockton informs me that some time in '54 or '55 he was at the Tejon and was engaged in surveying; that being out of provisions for this party he borrowed some of the Indian Agent; afterwards

117

that he paid the said Agent in money, and that the money was taken and receipted for in payment of a private debt of the Superintendent to the Agent. Mr. Connor states that he reported this matter to the Commissioner of Indian Affairs, but that it never received any attention.

Very Respectfully,
Your Obt. Sevt.
J. Ross Browne
Special Agt. Treas'y. Dept.

Fort Tejon
County of Tulare
State of California

    On this twenty fifth day of June A. D. One thousand eight hundred and fifty five, personally appeared before me the undersigned a Notary Public duly commissioned as such for the County of Tulare California, Samuel R. Dummer who being first duly sworn according to law deposeth and saith, that on or about the 15th day of December A. D. One thousand eight hundred and fifty four, he saw Wilmot Martin Clerk of Thomas J. Henley Supt. Ind. Affairs on the Sebastian Indian Reserve sell to a spanish cattle driver one hundred pounds of flour belonging to the United States at the rate of Ten Dollars per hundred pounds.

Sworn and subscribed to   Saml. R. Dummer
before me the day and
date above mentioned
A. C. Wakeman
Notary Public

Fort Tejon
County of Tulare
State of California

    On this twenty fifth day of June A. D. One thousand eight hundred and fifty five, personally appeared before me the undersigned a Notary Public duly commissioned as such for the County of Tulare California Alex Godey who being first duly sworn according to law deposeth and saith, that on or about the twenty seventh day of January A. D. One thousand eight hundred and fifty five, he saw William Sanins the Sub. Agent in charge of the Sebastian Indian Reserve Tejon Valley California, sell to an Indian Woman Louisa One blue blanket for the sum of Three Dollars, which said blanket was taken from the public stores of goods which were purchased by the government for the use of the Indians residing upon the aforesaid Reserve: and I further state that I saw the said amount of Three Dollars paid for said blanket to the said Sub. Ind. Agent Wm. Sanins by the said Indian Woman aforenamed.

Sworn and subscribed to   Alex Godey
before me the day and
date above mentioned
A. C. Wakeman
Notary Public

This is to certify that on or about the 27th day of November 1854 I traded a sorrel horse for a gray mare mule on the Sebastian Military Reservation and received from Col. Thomas J. Henley fifty dollars boot as the difference in the trade. The said Reservation is in the southern portion of Tulare county California. I valued the horse at four hundred and fifty or five hundred dollars. The said mule was branded with the Sebastian Military Reserve brand and was on the said government Reservation under the control of Col. Henley, the Superintendent of Indian Affairs for this State. I was then employed in the capacity of Farmer to the said Reservation.

Wm. H. Neal

San Francisco, Cal.

Hon. Chas. E. Mix.   Nov. 1st 1858

Commissioner of Indian Affairs

Sir:

I have the honor to transmit herewith affidavits marked
A, B, & C, in relation to certain abuses connected with the
Indian service at Tule river and the Tejon; also a transcript
marked D, from the books of the Land Office at Visalia.

From these it would appear that Alonzo Ridley was
employed by the Superintendent of Indian Affairs to keep
possession of a tract of land on Tule river for the alleged
purposes of an Indian farm; that Ridley was paid for this
service as per vouchers signed by him, and remained there for
six or eight months after all the Indians were transferred to
the Tejon reservation; that he forbid persons from settling
there and informed them that it was reserved for Government
purposes. In pursuance of this object, the reservation teams,
provisions, agricultural implements, etc. under direction of
public employes were used to cultivate the land, build a large
adobe house upon it, and otherwise improve and render it
valuable. At or about the same time that this work commenced some two thousand acres of land, embracing this
entire tract were covered with school warrants by T. P. Madden, clerk at the Tejon, and John A. Benson, a person who
resides near Sacramento. After the warrants were located,
Messrs. Vineyard, Harp and Madden, alternately supervised
the progress of the work. The expenditures of public means
on this farm can scarcely be less than ten thousand dollars. I
understand the allegation of the parties interested to be that
if government desires to purchase the land, it can do so, and
that this was done to preserve it from the encroachments of
settlers.

It strikes me that if this policy is once admitted, there
can be no limit to speculations upon the public Treasury.

Any person charged with the transfer and disbursement of public money can settle upon and improve public lands on the plea that if government desires to avail itself of the result, it can do so. But suppose Government does not deem it expedient to pursue that course, who will pay back the money expended in improvements; what advantages will then result from this misapplication of means and to whom will they accrue?

In November 1856, I informed the Department of the bad condition of affairs at the Tejon reservation. The accompanying affidavits will show that the recommendations made in that report are still worthy of consideration.

Very respectfully,
Your Obt Servt.
J. Ross Browne
Special Agt Treas'y Dept.

Statement of J.L. Clapp

Have a claim about three miles below what is termed the Indian reserve on Tule River and one mile beyond Goodhue's on the stage road. An adobe house has been built on said reserve, under the supervision of Col. Vineyard, D. Harp and J. P. Madden. Was told by Dorsey that it was to be sold to Government if the government wanted it; if not it would be retained by the above parties for their private benefit; that they had secured the land by school warrants. Have seen two or three wagon loads of wheat, blankets, [illegible word], sugar, coffee and plows etc. which came from the Tejon reservation, brought there. The work was done principally by Indians, under the supervision of Dorsey, for a while; but I always understood that Vineyard and Madden were the principal parties interested. Last fall about fifteen beeves, receipted for from Ridley, were killed there and fed to the working hands; after which the Indians were nearly starved, and were forced to subsist chiefly by stealing from the settlers. From that time till the first of June, Dorsey told me

121

they had killed about one beef a month. Some wheat was put in by the same parties. They got out lumber for the house in the mountains by the aid of two white employes from the Tejon. Since July they killed about a beef a week, whilst they were at work putting up the adobe building. The Indians have been very badly managed, and the reservations have in my opinion been a curse to the settlers the way they have been conducted. Two thirds of the time the Indians have been starved and forced to steal. Only those who worked on the building were fed. The rest were left to shift for themselves, and no attention was paid them.

Saw some of the cattle purchased of Vincenhaler delivered at the Tule river. Understood from Dr. Jones [?] of Los Angeles, who stated that he was Agent of the Williams estate, and received the pay from Col. Henley for the cattle, that the price paid was $10, $15 and $22 for yearlings, two year old and three year old cattle. These cattle were averaged, as I understood, at 450 lbs at 8¢ per lb. Saw these cattle at Tule river, and know that they were so poor that they were not fit for beef even for Indians. Do not believe as they were then that they would have averaged over three hundred and fifty lbs. The balance of the cattle, about four or five hundred head, were afterwards driven up the San Joaquin Valley, as I was informed, to Col. Henley's ranch at San Matteo.

Alonzo Ridley was stationed at Tule river for about a year and a half, as an Indian Agent, and kept settlers away by telling them it was an Indian reserve, and forbidding them to settle upon it. He boarded at Goodhue's and received pay, during a period of six or eight months when there were no Indians there. Do not blame Ridley for this; he was acting under orders; but the Indians have been very much neglected all the time.

J. L. Clapp

Statement of H. A. Bostwick

On the 19th of October 1857, the undersigned, together with F. P. Johnson, John A. Bostwick and W. W. Poe, took up and commenced improvements upon four separate claims on the Tule river, about two miles and a half above Goodhue's. At that time Alonzo Riddley, a Special Agent of the Indian Department, occupied the land so settled upon as an Indian reserve, under alleged authority from Col. T. J. Henley, Superintendent of Indian Affairs; but told us he did not think they could hold it under the law. He did not interpose any obstacle to our settling there. I understood that he had forbidden others from settling, but that he had had some misunderstanding about his pay, and was not friendly to Col. Henley at the time we settled. He told us we were in range 27S, and we entered our declaratory statements accordingly. After the entry was made we found that range 27 threw us into another township, and in the mean time T. P. Madden located School warrants over our claims. As Madden came up to Visalia to find out the Sections, after we had located, I have no doubt his entry of warrants at the Land Office in San Francisco, was antedated in order to throw us out of our rightful claims. Great injury and injustice has been done to me and the other parties named by this extraordinary course on the part of public officers, who have prudently made an Indian Reservation there for their own private benefit. I have seen an adobe house built there, and know that supplies of provisions and implements were brought from the Tejon reservation to carry on the work.

Henry A. Bostwick

Statement of Henry G. Sears

On the 12th day of October 1857, myself and Henry W. Niles settled on the Tule river, about seven miles above Goodhue's. Alonzo Ridley, a Special Agent of the Indian Department forbid us from settling there, stating as a reason that he was ordered to preserve from settlement the tract of country lying along the Tule river, a distance of fifteen miles up river and two miles in width; that it was for an Indian reservation. We paid no attention to his notice, believing he had no right to hold any public lands, which by law were open to settlement. In August last, or thereabouts, Mr. Dorsey, an employee of the Indian reservation at Tejon, commenced building a large adobe house about two miles and a half above Goodhues'; was assisted by Indians. Doctor Hays and a carpenter came there from the Tejon soon after the house commenced, and Dorsey left. Doctor Hays continued there until about three weeks ago, superintending the place. I got lumber out in the mountains for my house, and at the same time two white men were at work there getting out lumber for the adobe house before mentioned. Their names are Robert McKee and Gray. They were both employees of the Indian reservation at Tejon, and McKee in the presence of Gray informed me that he was paid $75 a month wages. During the same time six mules and a wagon from the Tejon (the mules with the Tejon brand) were in constant use hauling lumber and material for the house; also two riding mules. The mules were to my knowledge badly used and poor, so that they are now nearly broken down. They were driven by the Indians, and whipped up the mountains till they could scarcely stand. Know that half a barrel of pork was brought from the Tejon, for the men at work in the mountains, and heard McKee say the rations were brought from the Tejon. Col. Vineyard made a contract with S. D. and Alfred Wilson for twelve head of beef, six of which were purchased from us. We sold our six for 8¢ a pound, averaging about 1 beef $32; 1 do 518 lbs $41.44; 1 do 467; $37.96; 1 do 628 $50.24 and two more, one 535 $42.80 and 1, 488 $39.04. Two of these were killed at home and hauled down to the adobe house; the rest were driven down there and killed. Dr. Hays did not desire us to kill any more because he wanted the offal for the Indians. These were fed to the white employees and to the

124

Indians who worked. The Indians who did not work got none. Some of the land has been plowed and some fruit trees and vines planted which I think were brought from the Tejon. A blacksmith shop has also been built there this year, and is now stocked with tools—think they were brought from the Tejon. They have been in constant communication with the Tejon and have brought various supplies from there.

H. D. Sears

San Francisco, Cal.
Hon. Chas. E. Mix,   Nov 1st 1858
Commissioner of Indian Affairs

Sir:
I have just returned from a tour of inspection through the San Joaquin valley, during which I visited Visalia, Millerton, Kings River and the *Fresno*. The Indians in the vicinity of Visalia work for themselves and receive no aid from Government. At Campbell's on Kings river, there are now twenty Indians, the remainder being "in the mountains gathering acorns." These employes are paid out of the Indian fund for improving this farm. I am entirely unable to perceive that it is of the slightest advantage to the Indians. Considerable dissatisfaction arose there recently from the fact that some of the Indians had gathered up some grain from neighboring farms (as a reward for labor and stored it in their rancherias) which was taken away from them and put in the public storehouse.

At Millerton, I examined the books of Hughes & Co. storekeepers and ascertained that they sell goods to the Indian department upon orders from the Fresno; which goods are delivered to the Indians at the discretion of Messrs Hughes & Co. These are put upon the property returns and abstracts of issues and duly sworn to, although the employees at the Fresno never see them, and have no positive knowledge that the goods are actually delivered.

The same is the case with goods delivered by Roane, by Hunt, and by Leach.

I consider the practice liable to great abuse. Neither the property returns nor the abstracts of issuees, as records of any actual transactions, are of the slightest practical value.

The Fresno farm costs government some twenty or twenty-five thousand dollars per annum. It has not been of the least benefit to the Indians for the last few years.

In my report of 1856 I informed the Department that this farm was a useless expense. If any further testimony than the regular annual failure of crops is desired, it can readily be procured.

Very respectfully,
Your Obt Servt.
J. Ross Browne
Special Agt. Treas'y Dept.

A. B. The number of Indians now actually on the Fresno farm is not over one hundred or one hundred and fifty. The remainder are "in the mountains gathering acorns."

4:8 Letters, Henley to Mix; Lewis to Henley; Lewis to Whitmore; Fresno and Tulare County Citizens to Lewis; Lewis to Henley

Office of Supt. Ind. Affs.
San Francisco
Dec 4th 1858

Char. E. Mix Esqr.
Commissioner Ind. Affs
Washington D. C.

Sir

I enclose copies of the correspondence in reference to the removal by the Citizens of Kings River of the Indians to the Fresno Ind. farm.

This circumstance is an embarrassing one, as there was not food enough raised there for the Indians previously on the farm.

And for the same reason (The Drouth) the surrounding country is in the same destitute condition, so that whatever subsistence is required for them must be purchased in this city, which will be expensive on account of the high rates of transportation at this season of the year. But I know of no other means of feeding these unfortunate people during the winter. The men who have escaped to the Tules will no doubt give considerable trouble to the Settlers, more, even than if they had allowed the entire tribe to remain until they could have been induced to remove willingly.

These movements on the part of the people can not be prevented and they must be met in the spirit of conciliation.

Very Respectfully your Obt Servant
Thomas J. Henley
Supt Ind Affs

Office Fresno Indian Agency Cal
November 14th 1858

Sir:

Among the strange and unexpected occurrences which sometimes happen in this section of country was the arrival at the farm on the 13th inst. under the escort of seven armed and equipped white men, of some two hundred nearly destitute Indians, consisting of nearly all of the Na-tu-ni-tas and We-mel-chy's whose former residence was on Kings River near the lake and are termed King's River Indians, and about one half of the Ta-chee's and Wo-wels who resided on the margins of Tulare Lake. By far the greater number are women and children, and among them are twenty or thirty invalids. The men of the Ta-chee's and Wo-wels said to number about seventy escaped into the Tules.

They were apprehended and brought here by the citizens of King's River for the reasons set forth in their communication herewith submitted.

I had no intimation of the troubles existing in Tulare Lake until three days prior to the arrival of this party: at which time Gregora came to the place and informed me that, during the absence of the men a party had seized the women and children of these two tribes and driven them to Whitmore, where he expected they would be detained until his return. He said they were captured on the charge that his men had been killing hogs and cattle, which he declared they were innocent of.

Gregora having rested three days I dispatched with a letter to Mr. Whitmore, a copy of which is herewith enclosed.

It is truly unfortunate for these suffering people that they should have been driven from their homes where they had a bountiful supply of subsistence for the season. It is however their fate, and they will not be permitted to return.

I shall so soon as they are able to travel send all except a few who are very ill to the San Joaquin River there to remain during the fish season: there they will be enabled to subsist themselves with a little help for some three weeks and have a few fish on hand. In the mean time I will send a wagon to the lake for a loan of their seeds thereby acertaining whether it well to continue hauling them or otherwise.

The men who had the Indians in charge treated them very kindly, and conducted themselves with propriety whilst here.

All of which is respectfully submitted by

Your Obt Servt.
M. B. Lewis
Sub Agent

To
Thomas J. Henley Esqr.
Supt Ind. Affairs
San Francisco
Cal

Office Fresno Indian Agency Cal

Mr. Whitmore

November 11th 1858

Dear Sir: Gregora has been here inquiring of me what to do, stating that the women of his tribe have been taken from their ranch by a party of white men and marched up to your place where they are bound to suffer unless they are fed. He also states that they had plenty of seeds and other feed at the ranch which he fears will be wasted. I have not been able to satisfy myself as to what the matter is, but would suggest in their present destitute condition that they be treated with humanity and moderation. It would seem a human calamity for those people to be forced to leave their homes and winter supplies at this time, where they have abundance of the natural products of the soil, and otherwise gifts of providence to subsist on when it is out of the question for me to feed them all on the Indian farms. I can help them some in the way of subsistence and clothing but have not the means to fully provide for them. I would visit your section of country and consult with the citizens as to what was best to do with those people were it not that I am daily awaiting instructions for the season not knowing what might be required immediately on their reception. It is hoped however that it will not be absolutely necessary to drive those people from the vicinity of the Lake this winter. I would be very thankful for any assistance in your power, and if found necessary communicate with me on the subject, sending a letter by an Indian whom I would pay well for his trouble on the delivery of the letter.

Very Respectfully
Your Most Obt.
M. B. Lewis
Sub Agt.

Judge M. B. Lewis
Ind Sub agent
Fresno

Dear Sir

We the undersigned citizens of Fresno and Tulare counties having removed a numerous body (say 200) of the Na-tu-nu-too, A-ta-chee, and We-mel-chy's Indians from their homes and hunting grounds of King's River and the margins of Tulare Lake to this reservation would respectfully state the reasons that have induced us to this course.

First: Ever since the settlement of that region by the whites these Indians have been in the habit of killing great numbers of hogs and cattle and stealing provisions and other articles of value from the houses and camps of the whites. And recently these depredations have been so frequent and of such agrevating character that further forebearence became impossible.

Second: The presence of these Indians in a region so densely populated by whites whose exclusive business is stock raising is prejudicial to their interests in many ways. These Indians and a community of stock growing people cannot inhabit the same country. No violence was used in capturing these Indians. They have been kindly treated, and have been subsisted at our expense from the place of capture. We would also state that this is the last time their peaceable removal will be attempted and that should they return they will surely be harshly dealt with. *As abide with us they shall not.* We have warned those who still remain in the vicinity from whence these came of the consequences that will fall upon them if they persist remaining where they now are. We have advised them to depart in peace. Among these, there are probably thirty mission Indians who are all daring and expert marauders and who will be summarily treated should they not peaceably retire, or be removed from their present haunts.

Respectfully submitted by yours etc.

Justin Esney
B. A. Andrews
W. G. M. Kinney
A. M. Net
B. J. Hickell
W. A. Tull

Office Fresno Indian Agency Cala.
November 21st 1858

Sir

As item of information showing the condition of things in this Agency I enclose herewith the letter of Mr. H. Morrison, whom I engaged a few days since to go with and look out for the welfare of the destitute women and children and a few men recently forced from their homes on Tulare Lake by a party of white men to this place as has been reported to the office by last mail. I have this night sent to the relief of those starving people 1,000 lbs of wheat and 400 lbs beans which will keep them [from] suffering for five or six days, and tomorrow morning I leave this place for Tulare Lake where there are some seventy (70) warriors secreted in the Tulas who solemnly avow that they now only live to avenge the wrongs done their mothers, wives and children. They have been in the Tulas some 15 or 20 [days] and it is the absence and influence of Gregora that keeps them from inflicting their threats, which is only known to myself and one other man. Three nights from tonight I expect to sleep with them in the Tulas, from whence I will bring them without the aid of a soldier or a white man, and without expence, and satisfy them for the time being; after which and during the trip I will compromise the trouble between the Indians and Whites in that section of the country.

131

A majority of these Indians in question I design taking back to Kings River near Whitmore; but those who lived immediately on the lake, it will not do to take back; their winter supply of seeds and acorns will be destroyed and they are bound to be fed.

I dare not haul them away as I intended lest the necessary means required to pay the freight might not be allowed. There is at this time no place to take these unfortunates where are acorns. The entire acorn region is occupied by Indians and Hog men.

There is yet as always has been a war going on between the White people in the neighborhood of Kings River Indian farm—about the Indians in that vicinity and it is only necessary for one party of the whites to be satisfied that they have the advantage and they will pitch into the Indians. The most of the acorns gathered by these Indians have been destroyed by the hogs of white men.

Very Respectfully your most obt

To Thos J. Henley　　　　　　　M. B. Lewis, Sub Agent
Supt Indian Affairs
San Francisco Cal.

4:9   Letter, Browne to Denver

San Francisco, Cal.

Hon. J. W. Denver,　　　　　　　　　　　Jan. 18th 1859
Commissioner of Indian Affairs

Sir:
Since the receipt of the recent orders from your Department, reducing the expenses of the Indian service in this State, repeated applications have been made to me by the

Superintendent and Agents for advice and assistance in the premises, although it is well known that under your instructions I have no authority to interfere in the administration of the affairs of this Superintendency.

A brief statement of the difficulties at present existing in the service will enable you to adopt some suitable remedy and relieve me from a very embarrassing position, without powers of any kind and yet solicitous of maintaining the public interest.

The order requiring an immediate reduction of the number of employees on the different reservations, was, as I am informed by the Superintendent, promptly carried into effect. It is represented, however, that there is an arrearage of pay for the last two quarters due to each person discharged, and that a large proportion of the forces so discharged are wholly without means to leave the reservations, and in debt to the neighboring storekeepers. No funds to pay these arrearages have been received, and it is not known how soon the payments can be made. In all cases where the appointments have been sanctioned by the Department and where service is supposed to have been actually rendered, as in the case of regular employees, it would seem but just and reasonable that their discharge should be accompanied by the prompt payment of their wages.

The Agents complain that they cannot, in justice, drive these men away from the reservations—that many of them are really unable to seek employment elsewhere without some ready means; that such a proceeding would engender great difficulty and probable retaliation against the action of the Department by creating desertion and disaffection among the Indians.

As it is presumed that the charges brought by me, showing the inefficiency of this force, had some influence in procuring its reduction, I am now requested to exonerate the Agents from any blame in taking care of the discharged employees until their wages are paid. This, as you must perceive, is a question of some difficulty—it being manifestly unjust to remove them forcibly without payment, and equally improper to keep a large number of idlers on the reservations at public expense.

Another subject of difficulty has recently been presented in the case of Humboldt prisoners taken by Genl. Kibbe. The Department will remember that several months ago I forwarded the printed proceedings of a public meeting at Humboldt, calling for the intervention of the Federal and State military authorities to protect the citizens of that region from the depredations of hostile Indians in the vicinity. In compliance with the call of the citizens, Governor Weller ordered out some of the State militia, under Genl. Kibbe, who has been for the past three months scouring the country with the forces under his command, attacking and routing the Indians wherever he met them. After several engagements, in which it is said he killed about forty Indians, he succeeded in capturing between a hundred and fifty and two hundred of the disaffected warriors, and marched them down to Humboldt with a view of turning them over to the Superintendent, for safe keeping on some of the reservations. Here again was another difficulty. They could not be delivered at the Klamath, because it is in the vicinity of their customary haunts to which they would have escaped and thus renew all the troubles of the past few months. Nome Lackee and Nome Cult could not be reached conveniently at this season by as large a body; and Mendocino seemed the only available point. The citizens of Humboldt had repeatedly avowed their intention to exterminate them if ever they were let loose upon them again. The force of employees at Mendocino have been reduced to four men, which would be amply sufficient with partially domesticated tribes, but might find some difficulty in controling and keeping within bounds a hundred and fifty or two hundred perfectly wild and hostile savages.

Under these circumstances, Superintendent Henley and Genl. Kibbe called upon me for advice and assistance in the premises. The former stated that he was adverse to taking any action without a recommendation from me sustaining him, and the latter stated that in turning these Indians over to the Superintendency his duties must cease. I thought it best, in view of all the difficulties of the case, to call upon Genl. Clarke and ask him to send up to Mendocino a small military force to aid the reduced force of employees in maintaining peace, which would relieve the Superintendent of the necessity of disobeying orders by enlarging the forces. It was necessary also to provide some means of conveyance for the prisoners from Humboldt Bay to Mendocino, and temporary provision for their subsistence whilst they might be compelled to remain there. Upon consultation with the Superintendent, I could see no other way of accomplishing the object than to charter a small vessel to take them down, and to ship up a sufficient quantity of beans to meet their present necessities. The cost of transportation will be about $1,200 and the beans purchased will amount to about $800. This was accordingly done by the Superintendent, and Genl. Kibbe has gone up to Humboldt to deliver up the Indians and put them on board. Genl. Clark has ordered up the small military force asked for, and the provisions have been shipped. The necessity for the latter shipment has been sufficiently explained in my various reports relative to Mendocino.

I trust the advice given under these circumstances with the full understanding that it was entirely unofficial and without authority, will meet your approval.

The next serious difficulty to which I would invite your attention is that existing at the Fresno in the San Joaquin Valley. During several years past, as the Department is aware, two Indian farms have been conducted by Sub Agents in the San Joaquin Valley—one at the Fresno under M. B. Lewis, and the other at Kings River in charge of Mr. Campbell.

The results at both of these places, as shown by me in official reports dating as far back as 1856, have been a continued and almost entire failure of crops—especially at the Fresno—and an absolute waste of public money, without the least practical benefit to the Indians in that vicinity. So far from any encouragement being given to them to come on these farms and work, they have been kept away by positive orders, on the plea that there was nothing there upon which to feed them; and during my last visit to the Fresno (a few months since) Judge Lewis alleged as a reason for the informality of certain vouchers for articles purchased at Roane's Store, 30 miles distant in the mountains, and at Fort Miller, 16 miles distant—all of which were certified to in the Abstracts of Issues as having been delivered on the reservation— that he was forced to let the Indians get the articles there upon written orders, sent up by the Chiefs, in order to prevent them from coming upon the reservation, where he had nothing to give them. Considering the amount of money expended at these points, and the entire absence of any beneficial results, the citizens of Kings River, who are mostly small rancheros and farmers, after repeated remonstrances against the petty depredations committed upon their property by the Indians who were constantly lounging about their places, assembled in a body about a month ago, gathered up a hundred and fifty of these destitute Indians, and took them to the Fresno, where they delivered them over to Judge Lewis, against his protest that they must starve. The last news received from that point is that there has been extreme suffering among them; that several, driven to the utmost extremity by the pangs of starvation, wandered out upon the plains and perished from hunger and cold.

These facts are well established, and the Department must perceive that they present a most pitiable condition of affairs. If, instead of the large and useless expenditure of means devoted to the payment of white employees at the places referred to, direct purchases of clothing and provisions had been made, or a better location chosen for a farm, where some return in the way of crops could have been obtained, much of this suffering might have been avoided. The facts are submitted for your consideration; but as everything now seems to be in an unsettled condition, as far as the future policy of the Department is concerned, I am unable to suggest a remedy.

Besides these isolated cases, there is much that requires

prompt attention at various other points. What is to be done with the Indians at Hoopa Valley? What is to become of the Eel River Indians? I would suggest that some speedy action is absolutely necessary. A proper understanding should be had with all these Indians. The policy of the Department, as laid down by the Secretary of the Interior and late Commissioner of Indian Affairs (Mr. Mix) can be carried into effect; but it can only be done by a hearty cooperation in the views expressed, and unremitting zeal and energy on the part of officers charged with its administration.

A thorough investigation of existing liabilities for goods, provisions and other supplies, should at once be made, and the indebtedness of the Department promptly discharged, so that the new organization of affairs can be put into immediate and successful operation.

If the Department should deem it expedient to favor me with instructions on this or any other subject connected with the service, under its present exigencies, I shall, with great pleasure, carry them into effect.

Very respectfully
Your Obt Servt
J. Ross Browne
Special Agt. Treas'y Dept.

4:10   Petition, Tehama County citizens to Secretary of the Interior

To the Honorable Secretary of the Interior

Greeting: The undersigned, being citizens of Tehama County, California, and residents of that portion of said county lying contiguous to the Nome Lackee Indian Reservation, beg leave to state to your Honor that we are aggrieved, in consequence of the location of said reservation in our immediate neighborhood, for the following reasons, to wit:

137

First—that the Indians on said Reservation are few in number and at peace with the whites, committing no further depredations than those of killing hogs and young calves.

Second—the lands occupied by said Reservation are among the best in our State and capable of subsisting a valuable community of settlers who would afford within themselves a much purer and better protection against such attacks than any that has heretofore or is likely hereafter to be extended to us by the General Government.

Third—In the establishment of the present system of reservations in California it was the intention and belief of its projectors that within three years the Indians would maintain themselves by their own labor, and that in our opinion are now and have been for years able to support themselves, had they been allowed the privilege of working for wages in the neighborhood, where employment would have been afforded them at remunerative prices, in the absence of such restraints.

Fourth—That by reference to a plat of said Reserve, it will be seen that it lies in such a shape as to extend its evil influences several miles further than it would if it all lay in a single body.

Fifth—That the Agent will not allow settlers to locate within one mile of the Reservation lines, which from the peculiarity of their location, enables him to virtually occupy several-fold the quantity of land designated in the survey, to the great detriment of all classes, and hindrance to the growth and prosperity of our county.

Sixth—That under the management of the present Agent, V. E. Geiger, and the worthless horde whom he employs, the establishment has become a disgrace and a nuisance.

Seventh—That Mr. Geiger, who from his position as Agent, we are obliged from force of circumstances to admit into our houses and into the presence of our families, has brought disgrace upon his office by habitually living in a state of open adultery with a white prostitute, while the menials whom he keeps hovering around him, instead of endeavoring

138

to elevate and improve the character and condition of the Indians, are dragging them down to a level with themselves by compelling the squaws, even in the presence of their Indian husbands, to submit to their lecherous and beastly desires; and further, that they have introduced among them diseases of the most loathsome character, with which the employees, hangers-on and Indians are and have for a long time been continually afflicted, and that much of the medicine furnished by Government for the use of the Indians has been used by the whites; and that by this disgraceful conduct on the part of the Agent and others, the establishment has been brought into bad repute and made a mockery and a by-word insomuch that it has earned and acquired the appelation of "the Government Whore House," exerting in the community a blighting influence against morality and good behaviour, and putting a frightful example before our children and young people.

In consideration of the above facts, and many more that we might enumerate, we earnestly ask that you will use the power vested in you, for the abatement of this moral leper, or at least, that it be removed beyond the pale of our thickly settled districts; or if such a course does not meet your approval, that you use means for the removal of the present incumbent, who, in addition to the vices above enumerated, is an habitual drunkard, and cause to be appointed in his stead a man of better habits and business capacity.

P.S.—If a petition be necessary to the furtherance of the above objects, we believe we can forward to you the name of every respectable citizen of Tehama County who is not pecuniarily interested, as well as a large portion of those of Colusa County, which borders upon ours on the south.

[Eleven petitioners' signatures]

Office Supt. Ind Affairs
San Francisco Cal
October

Hon A. B. Greenwood
Commissioner of Indian Affairs

Sir

I have the honor to acknowledge the receipt of your letter of September 3rd in relation to removals and appointments of Agents and Sub Agents in this Superintendency, and instructing me in all cases where a change is suggested to submit the reasons for your consideration.

In my general report dated September 4th ulto. on the condition of the reservations in California, I stated in reference to the Nome Lackee reservation "that during the past season there had been cultivated about eight hundred acres mostly in small grains out of which one hundred and fifty acres of which was almost totally destroyed by smut" also that "these eight hundred acres are divided into small farms some distance apart but all within the circumference of seven miles, the richest bottoms only being selected for cultivation, causing this separation."

On my late visit to Nome Lackee on the 30th Sept. I was surprised to learn that Mr. Geiger had disposed of a portion of this crop at private sale for his own benefit, and that he claimed to own a considerable portion of the wheat which was stored at Head Quarters, and contemplated selling it in the same manner. He admitted having sold a portion of the barley and hay, and claimed the right to sell the wheat on the ground that it became his property by purchase of the land—As this crop was planted at public expense under the supervision of Mr. Geiger and harvested for the use of the Indians with Government teams, and by Indian labor, I was unable to perceive upon what grounds of justice or propriety Mr. Geiger can lay claim to it. I have therefore instructed him by letter (a copy of which is enclosed) not to remove any grain or other public property from the reservation.

I have also to report that during my late visit to Nome Lackee I saw teams of oxen belonging to the reservation engaged in hauling timber from the mountains to the above claim of Mr. Geiger, at a time when their services were required for public purposes; that the garden and orchard were entirely neglected and the fences are now fallen down and the fruit trees destroyed by cattle; that there are living upon the reservation and apparently at public expense a number of white persons not in the employ of Government; that no effort has been made to gather up the cattle placed there by my predecessor, which cattle are now scattered down the Sacramento Valley a distance of fifty miles and that some thirty or forty horses, also public property, have strayed off and no effort has been made to recover them; that there are but few agricultural implements available out of the large purchases made; that in short nothing appears to have been done at the reservation during the past three months except upon private and adjoining claims. Most of the Indians who were present during my former visit to this reservation have been permitted to leave or no impediment has been placed in the way of their doing so, and most of the working hands are employed upon Mr. Geiger's claim.

The survey of the Nome Lackee reservation was made by Mr. Gray in September 1857 under instructions from my predecessor to Mr. Geiger—By what means a valuable portion of the then recognized limit of the reserve could be excluded, I am unable to say. Nor can I ascertain what reason there could be for the cutting off the mill and water ditch which I am informed cost the government a large amount of money—As the mill and water ditch however appear on the map, it would seem that some error must have occurred by means of which no approval of the survey has been obtained to which the department would not otherwise have given its assent had the facts of the case been known.

In consideration of these circumstances it must be obvious to the department that there can be no official cooperation between Mr. Geiger and myself—I have therefore to recommend his removal and the appointment in his place of

141

Judge Lt. P. Haun of Yuba County for whose capacity & qualifications to fill this position with credit to the department I respectfully refer you to the delegation in Congress from this State.

In reference to the other changes recommended by me viz the removal of Mr. B. Lewis & H. L. Ford Sub Agent. I have to say that they are unfit for their positions. I would be pleased to have them removed without the necessity of a protracted controversy involving personal charges. The only general objections to them which I can state from my own knowledge is that the [illegible] of the service in their charge have been grossly neglected and that I have no confidence that there will be any change for the better while they remain in public office. For the same reason I recommend the removal of J. R. Vineyard, Agent at the Tejon and the appointment of J. J. Kendrick of San Diego County.

Since the receipt of your remittance to defray the liabilities of the 1st & 2nd Qr. of 1859, I have examined all the bills presented to me & upon proper verification of the late Superintendent and the Agents have turned over corresponding sums for their payment.

This examination, however, satisfies me of the impracticability of my settling these accounts & doing full justice to all parties. Having had nothing to do with the contracting of these bills I, of course, cannot judge of the necessities demanding them & can assume no responsibility in their settlement. I am extremely desirous that the department will relieve me of all responsibility in the matter, and remit any further funds for the payment of debt incurred prior to my coming into office direct to the Agents. Many of these bills appear to me to be unnecessary & improper, but as I have stated above, I know nothing personally of the circumstances under which they were contracted. The Department will confer a favor upon me by charging some other person with this duty as it greatly embarasses the current operations of my Superintendency to have anything to do with the accounts of my predecessor.

Very Respectfully, Your obdt. Svt.

J. Y. McDuffie, Supt. Ind Affs for California

Hon. A. B. Greenwood   San Francisco Oct. 18, 1859
Commissioner of Indian Affairs

Sir
I have the honor to enclose herewith a communication
from V. E. Geiger Esq. Agent Nome Lackee Indian Reserva-
tion, in reply to a letter addressed to the Department by J.
Ross Brown, Special Agent of the Department of the
Interior, a copy of which was furnished him.

Very Respectfully
Your Obdt. Svt.
J. Y. McDuffie
Supt. Ind Affs for California

Nome Lackee Reserve
Oct. 12th 1859
Sir–
Mr. J. Ross Brown, special agent of the Interior Department, has furnished me with a copy of a communication,
addressed by him to you, dated Oct. 3rd, 1859, relative to
some grain claimed by me and as to the use of Government
oxen for my private purposes. By the courtesy of Mr. Brown
I am enabled by the same mail to make a statement of my
own relative to the matter.
When the proclamation of the President appeared
authorizing and directing the sale of the public lands in this
district, all the lands embraced in this reservation were offered, which necessarily attracted attention in this part of the
State. Many persons examined the line of the survey, and were
anxious to become purchasers, believing that the lands of this
place were properly reserved. I wrote to the then Supt. of
Indian Affairs on the subject, and also protested with the
Register of the land office against such sale. Persons, however, anxious to purchase continued their examinations, and
after investigating the survey of the Reservation, discovered
that a portion of the lands claimed to belong to this Reserve,
and which had been used for agricultural and other purposes,

were not included in the survey, and hence became subject to entry or purchase. Prior to this, however, and before I was aware of the fact that any of the lands claimed as belonging to this Reservation were outside of the survey line, a gentleman by the name of Greene, County Surveyor of the County of Colusi, ascertained that such was the fact, and by virtue of the law of this State, under which the 500,000 acres of land, donated by the general government, could be located under the school land warrants system of this State, located three hundred and twenty acres of the land in question. He made his location, and it was confirmed to him, as I understand, after the Register of the U. S. land office had communicated with Commissioner Hendricks at Washington. On a portion of this land grain was growing at the time, and shortly after the location, Mr. Greene visited this place for the purpose of taking possession of his land, to the end that he might put it into the market, he being a speculator in such property. He informed me that he had already several offers for it, and I knew personally that two gentlemen had been here to examine the land with a view of purchasing it. Mr. Greene contended that he was entitled to the land and everything growing on it, and consequently placed an additional value thereon, because of the then growing crops. After some delay, I made a bargain for the purchase and agreed in connection with another person, who was not then nor since under my employ, to pay him at ninety days (90) for the land, at the advanced sale of five dollars & twenty five cents per acre, he having paid $1.25. It may be proper for me to state here that I had no personal acquaintance with Mr. Greene prior to this transaction, and further that the first knowledge I had of his location was through the Register of the U. S. land office, responsive to some inquiries of mine relative to land locations in the vicinity of this reserve.

As Mr. Brown does not seem to object to my purchase of the land, I do not deem it necessary, unless asked for, to furnish copies of the warrant located, and of the certificate of the Receiver & Register of the U. S. Service office at Marysville for other lands purchased & entered by me. If the Department desires, I will furnish them on request.

In view then of the fact that I had purchased this land, a portion of it from Mr. Greene, after he had located it in conformity with the laws of this State and the United States, and the balance having been purchased at the public land sales, and entered in the land office, in pursuance of the law, I deemed that I was entitled to the land and the enoblements, at the time of the location and the purchase at the land sales. It was well known by all that there was a growing crop on portions of this land, and this fact being known induced bidders at the sale to bid up the land to $1.75 & 2.00 per acre. Having made all these purchases in good faith, without collusion, agreement, understanding or arrangement with any one, to conceal or misrepresent the condition of the land, I was satisfied in my own mind that *all* belonged to me, the grain as well as the grass and timber growing on it. It was sold without any reservation whatever, and I looked upon it throughout as a *bona fide* transaction. It is true that the grain was put in by the Government, with its teams & implements, but it was not harvested entirely by the "labor and rations furnished by Government, under the authority and supervision of the Agent." I furnished an equal amount of white help with the Government, not only to gather & thresh this grain but the entire crop belonging to the Government. The number of employees allowed by the Government was not sufficient to superintend the harvest week, & so while it furnished *one man* at the thresher, I furnished *another*, and while it furnished *one man* in the field to superintend the hauling, I furnished *another*, and had it not been done in this way, I feel assured that the Government would have been the sufferer. I am not disposed to prate about in detail the various steps that had to be taken during the troubles recently & at that time existing in the Indian Department by individuals to carry on the work of this place as it is well known to every one, at that time, the Department in this State was destitute of means furnished on the personal responsibility of those having it in charge. The implements used to harvest, as well as the very oil to put the machine in operation to thresh the grain were so furnished.

It is true also, that I have used some of the government

oxen recently to haul timber from the mountains—some to "the aforesaid claims of Mr. Geiger" and some along the dividing line of the reservation. This timber is now and will be used in making fences on the boundary line (between my purchases & the location of others) of the Government Reservation, thereby making a work as much for the benefit of the government as another. The great complaint by all has been the want of means to keep outside stock off the government lands & by this improvement the great inlet on the northern boundary through which stock mostly depredate, will be closed. It may not be out of place here to remark that the timber spoken of was cut, split and worked at private expense entirely, although, it was hauled by government oxen. I should not have given this detail of the full purposes of which this hauling was done, had been made known & such could have been done, had inquiry been made of me in reference thereto by the special agent.

Since the establishment of this place, I believe it has been customary with every one who had had it in charge, to give & receive neighborly favors to render aid to the settlers around, when it worked no detriment to the public interests, and when required receive in return friendly assistance. This has been more necessary in the last year as the impression has been growing that this place should be given up to white settlement, and hence without any aid but the four employees, it would be the worst of folly for the agent to incur by "unfriendly legislation" the displeasure of all around. Then while I have always extended favors to my neighbors, I could see no impropriety in doing the same to a gentleman who happened to be a part purchaser with myself in land. Indeed, I hardly think the government designed that a person by accepting a federal position should throw off all claim to friendly neighborhood accomodations, when it was productive of no injury to Government property. Under the late order of the Supt. Ind Affairs all such accomodations must cease. I believe it may be productive of ill will & ill feeling against Government interests, for disguise it as you may, their Indian reservations exist merely by the sufferance of those who live around them. Let the community become soured,

146

hostile, evil minded & neither the property, crops, buildings or the Indians would be secure from their depredations.

I have thus, sir, given you a "plain unvarnished" statement of the facts in this case, responsive to the letter of Mr. Brown. He, however, speaks of the survey in this reservation. Of it I know nothing, neither of the survey, except as it appears by the map, nor of the man who made it. Never to my recollection have I seen Mr. Nicholas Gray, nor would I know him now were I to meet him. This is mentioned to rebut the impression that the survey was made under my directions or at my suggestion. I disclaim and defy all such impretations. See note*.

The value of the grain I have taken and used as my own is of comparative small importance. I seek not to disguise or even up the transaction. It was as I believe, both proper & legal, and under such convictions I acted. As far as my *official* action in this matter is concerned, it is left to your province to decide. As to my *legal* rights of property, I suppose that I am entitled to the same judicial rights as any other citizen, because of the fact that by holding federal office I am not deprived of all the rights & immunities to buy or sell that attach to other citizens.

In a word, after thus submitting to you all the circumstances I deem necessary, you should determine to act upon at the present, I have no objections, if however you conclude to ask for or make a more minute examination. I am prepared for such action.

Respectfully
Your Obt. Srvt.
Vincent E. Geiger
Ind. Agent

Hon. A. B. Greenwood
Com. Indian Affrs
Washington D. C.

*Since my attention has been called to the fact, I find that the survey was made before I was placed in charge of this Reserve.

Vincent E. Geiger
Ind. Agt.

San Francisco, Cal.
Hon. A. B. Greenwood   November 5th, 1859
Commissioner of Indian Affairs

Sir:

I have examined in detail the vouchers of M. B. Lewis, Sub Indian Agent at the Fresno, for the 1st and 2nd Quarters of 1859, and beg leave to submit the following remarks.

The Fresno farm produced a fair average crop when it was first established in 1854, but since that date it has been a heavy expense to government without any corresponding benefit to the Indians. During the greater part of each year the number of Indians on the farm, deriving any actual aid from government has not exceeded from twenty to fifty. The occasional hands by whom it has been rented have procured their own subsistence as they did prior to the establishment of the farm. Compared with the enormous expenditures for hire of hands, implements of agriculture, supplies and clothing, these results are not only discouraging but manifest in my opinion, either negligence or incapacity on the part of the officers charged with the disbursement of the Indian fund. The expenses on this and the King's River farm during the year ending June 30th, 1859, exceeded $36,000. A brief review of the vouchers will present the best evidence of the purposes to which the fund has been applied.

By reference to Vouchers Nos. 4, 5, 6, 7, 8 it will be seen that the expenditures for beef alone during the 1st Q of 1859 were in the aggregate, $1,215.38, of which E. G. Campbell, acting overseer at King's river, received $373.59, and Wm. M. Lewis, son of the Sub Agent, received $109. During the same quarter, John H. Blair signs voucher No. 25, for 11,500 lbs. Acorns at 3 cts. per lb. $345 and for hauling the same $535, being $880; and Jeremiah Lewis signs voucher No. 21 for freighting Acorns and ferryage of teams ammounting to $322.00. The Indians gathered these Acorns on King's

River, and white men sold them for the use of the Indians. The "freighting" or more properly hauling, (it being a land route of forty miles from Kings river to the Fresno) was done at an expense of $815 by private agreement, when government had a wagon, two pair of oxen, and eight mules at Kings river, and two wagons, and thirty six mules, and horses at the Fresno, all of which were, or should have been available. Ira McCray, as per voucher No. 28, is paid $84.50 for the hire of a team. Jeremiah Lewis is allowed $42 for ferryage, but keeps no ferry and submits no sub vouchers. Under a standing contract C. P. Converse (Voucher 23) is allowed $50 a quarter for all the ferrying across the San Joaquin, which is the only river between King's River and the Fresno. The Abstract of articles issued as forage during this quarter shows an issue of 4,000 lbs of barley and 7,195 lbs of hay; but if this was "issued to the animals belonging to said Agency" for what purpose are teams hired from private individuals?

Vouchers Nos. 9, 22, 26, 29 show large expenditures for wheat and barley; and vouchers 1, 2, 9, 10, 11, 15, 17, 18, 20 for flour and other provisions—sufficient, it might be supposed, to obviate the necessity of hiring outside teams and purchasing acorns, especially when it is considered that the Sub Agent in his official report dated August 18th 1858 estimates the wheat raised on the two farms at "sixty-seven thousand and fifty pounds; in addition to which," he adds, "there has been raised on this farm a fair variety of vegetables in abundance, and on the two farms twenty acres of corn, which gave a fair yield." Mr. Lewis further informs the Department that by judicious management, aided by seemingly a good mast it is believed "the wheat and corn raised on the two farms can be made to suffice for Indian breadstuffs during the fall and winter season of the ensuing year" that is to say, the season of 1858-9. It seems almost incredible that so great a miscalculation should be made inadvertently from year to year, when the number of Indians, instead of increasing, is well known to be rapidly decreasing. Nor can it be alleged that the cause of the extraordinary expenses of the year ending June 30th 1859, was owing to the removal of the King's River Indians to the Fresno. When they were not fed and supported by the King's River farm, there was that much deduction to be made from the expenses of that establishment. Both farms are within the Fresno Agency, and it mattered nothing at which farm the Indians were. If they were not supported by either, but lived among the whites (as was really the case) there could have been no excuse for the enormous expenditures of the previous year, and of every year during which the farm has had an existence. In his letter of explanation dated March 31st 1859, Mr. Lewis says "there has been kept alive, but poorly fed and clad, on, and in the vicinity of the two farms within this Agency—including the subsistence and clothing of the permanent laborers—who have neither suffered for food or clothing, not less than (950) nine hundred and fifty Indians, at the expense of less than 14 cents a head per day, at a time too when there was none of the natural products of the country to be had for their subsistence, other than acorns hauled from Kings River at two & a half and three cents per pound." It will borne in mind that he has just shown from his official report of August 18th /58 that it was apparently a good mast year, that there was available 67,270 lbs. of wheat, and 37,450 lbs. of barley (the odd lbs. showing the accuracy with which the weight was taken) besides vegetables in abundance and twenty acres of corn. From the same report it would appear that up to August there had been a "concentration of from three to five hundred Indians on this farm (the Fresno) during the last nine months working season," and that all except 200 on both farms (say 100 in each) then went on their way "rejoicing into the mountains to take their annual manzanita feast, where they will remain until Salmon season, at which time a large majority of them will [illegible] repair to the San Joaquin river, there to remain until called for to commence the labors of another year, and the remainder to go into the mountains for the purpose of gathering the winter acorns and such other spontaneous means of subsistence as the seasons may afford."

It will be conceded, after a careful perusal of the above that the Sub Agent is good authority that there was no increase in the number of Indians and no scarcity of provisions to justify the extraordinary expenditures of the ensuing winter of 1858-9, as shown by the vouchers. But the fact is, when the citizens of King's river brought to the Fresno, late in winter, some two or three hundred Indians, they were informed by the Agent that he had not the means to support them, and prior to that time there were but two or three families on the farm, all the rest having "gone to the mountains."

The vouchers for the 2nd Quarter, ending June 30th/59, show a similar state of things. Mr. Wm. J. Campbell (whose brother E. G. Campbell signs the vouchers for beef) is owner of the Kings river farm for which he is allowed $500 a year (Voucher 28). By the use of Indian labor and government supplies he has this year erected a good brick house, built a barn, fenced in his farm with a substantial fence, gathered in a considerable supply of hay (upon which he keeps the stage horses of the Visalia and Hornitas stage) plowed up his land and put it in seed for his own use during the ensuing season, cut off the wheat and barley raised for the Indians; enjoying at the same time the advantage of an assistant or overseer Wm. Day (See vouchers 37 and 25 for 1st and 2nd Qr/59) his private business requiring his absence a large portion of the time for which he is paid. He is also favored with a beef contract to supply the necessities of his own farm, and sells to himself as manager of the farm beef for $275.85 (see voucher 15 signed by his brother) in addition to that shown in the previous quarter. Thomas Vinsonhaler receives $250 a quarter rent (voucher No. 26) and sells beef $215.37 (voucher No. 16) which beef is attended by Fresno Indians. See also beef voucher from M. Lewis, No. 17 for $256.95.

The payroll during the first quarter of /59 shows a list of seven employees including the Sub Agent, on the Fresno farm, and two at Kings river. There is 1 Sub Agent, whose duty it is to oversee the farm; but this being deemed insufficient there are three other overseers, one of whom is son of the Sub Agent. There is also a blacksmith and a Chinese Cook—all of which is not only in direct conflict with the instructions of the Department limiting the number of employees, but in my opinion wholly unwarranted by the condition of the place and the necessities of the service. Clark Hoxie is employed as blacksmith at a salary of $75 a month (voucher No. 33) when the accounts of the P. O. Department show that he is and was at that time Post Master at Millerton; and the Sub Agent's own reports show that the wagons and mule teams belonging to the Agency were not available to do the necessary hauling from Millerton and Kings River. Of what use was it to have mules shod and wagons mended if they could not be used? See Vouchers 13 and 14 for 2nd Qr/59. Al Sing, a Chinese, is cook at $150 pr quarter for 1st & 2nd Qrs. of 1859, (vouchers No. 22 & 38) as well as for previous quarters. Why employ a Chinese Cook, when according to the report of the Sub Agent dated August 18, 1859, he could have had a selection from 2,555 Indians, upon whose services he could at any time rely, and in whom he has been equally disappointed in their ability to acquire a knowledge of civilized life." But it is useless to particularise. All of these employees were equally a burden upon the service, without any corresponding benefit, either to government or the Indians.

Vouchers for the 2nd Qr of 1859 (see 1, 2, 3, 4, 5, 6, 7, 8 & 19) of Hughes, Evans, Hunt and others, for supplies of flour, bacon, beef, pork and even tobacco, show such a remarkable recklessness of expenditure as scarcely to need comment. The price for barley is 5 cents pr lb, when it was worth but 2 cents; bacon 30 cents, when hogs on King's River (the great hog country of California) were worth about six or eight cents; beans 8 cents, worth in San Francisco 2 1/2, and other articles, in the same proportion.

I have thus briefly, and somewhat irregularly glanced at a few of the principal items in the accounts before me. Doubtless the vouchers for preceeding quarters are of a similar tenor, but they are not in the office of the Superintendent, and I am unable now to refer to them. By reference to reports made by me in 1858, however, it will be found that other serious abuses are enumerated, which have failed to attract the attention of the Superintendent. In 1856 I reported the waste of public money upon this Agency, and recommended that it should be abolished.

The question now arises what is Mr. McDuffie, the new Superintendent, to do with the Indians of the San Joaquin? At present most of them are hired to white settlers on King's River and at Visalia; and so long as these settlers can obtain their labor at a small cost, they will probably not suffer. But a few mischievious white men are liable at any time to cause difficulty, when further scenes of murder and outrage may occur. I submit, if it is possible for the new Superintendent to carry on farming in either the King's River or Fresno Farms, by confiding the management to the present Sub Agent, whose efforts have so signally failed during the past four years. Nor do I believe any other Sub Agent can now be successful in that locality, so utterly and entirely has the public service fallen into discredit, and so various are the conflicting interests of the settlers and Indians.

I am clearly of opinion these Indians should be moved over to Owens Lake Valley which offers an open field for a fair trial of the reservation system; but it is now too late in the season to attempt the experiment. Nothing can be done till spring. Meantime, the Indians must do as they have always done—depend chiefly upon natural products gathered by themselves, and upon the aid and charity of the better class of white settlers.

Very Respectfully
Your Obt Servt.
J. Ross Browne
Special Agent

153

Fort Humboldt, Cala.
April 30th, 1860

Sir:
I find it my duty to report the fact that Indian Agent D.
E. Buel without authority apparently in direct violation of
Section 2nd of Chapter 33, Laws of the State of California,
for the Government and protection of the Indians passed
April 22nd, 1850, forcibly removed the Indians from their
homes on lower Mad River as per inclosed, which rendered it
necessary for me, to prevent a repetition of the late horrid
massacres, immediately to induce the Indians in this vicinity
and on Eel river to immigrate to the Klamath Reservation,
which happily accomplished by persuasion only, some 322
leaving this post in charge of an Officer, U.S.A. and an escort
of soldiers for their protection, April 21st, 1860, with a suitable supply of provision (see inclosed print [reproduced following next letter]), as the letter of Agent Buel under the
head of correspondence dated Eureka, April 11th, 1865,
would materially lead to a wrong inference. I beg leave to
state that previously to writing it, he had been repeatedly at
this post conversing with the Indians here, where these poor
creatures temporarily found an asylum from the assassins,
who had murdered 150 of their wives and children *for no
crime whatever*, and I had already informed him that I turned
over the Indians to him, and would persuade, but, declined
using force to get them away, as his letter appeared designed
to afford a paragraph to a news paper sheet called the Humboldt *Times*, devoted to the interest of the assassins (where it
afterwards appeared). I did not reply except as stated.

P. S. It may not be amiss, in a post script to state what
perhaps has already been notified in detail to the Hon. Commissioner of Indian Affairs, a synopsis of facts connected

154

with the late events upon this (Humboldt Bay). About 2 years since July 1858, a squaw was stolen by a packer some 25 miles back of Union Town, brought into town and sold for $50 to a Mr. Dankin for a servant. The Indians demanded their squaw, but the man who had taken the woman, it is said, told the Indians it was his partner, Ross, who had done it, whereupon they shot Ross. Their intention was good to kill him doubtless, yet satisfied with the revenge taken, they looked on, suffered the partner to take care of the wounded man, and send word to Union for medical assistance, and ultimately Ross was removed to that town and I believe still surviving. A Capt. Bell, as he is called, immediately gathered some 30 volunteers with the pecuniary and otherwise active assistance of a Mr. Wiley (Editor of the newspaper called the Humboldt *Times*), but without sanction of civil or military power, and going out fired into every "Indian Ranch" they could find, killing indiscriminately all ages and sexes. The U. S. Troops were not called for until after Bell's party were driven in, losing one of their number killed and another wounded. The call was then made, but the troops except 13 men had been sent away some 150 miles distant into the field by order of Genl. Clark Comdg. Dept. On learning this fact, application was made by the above volunteers to the Governor of the State, and Adjt. Gen'l. Kibbe mustered into State service some 80 volunteers who killed untold numbers of Indians, but finally changing their tactics made provisions and shipped to Mendocino Reservation some 350 Indians or more, Kibbe having attained the glory as was said of finishing the war, and ridding the country of the Indians on Mad River, Redwood and van Dusins fork.

A petition was soon after sent to me for troops for protection signed by some of Kibbe's late volunteers, saying that the worst Indians had been left and troops were sent as required. Reports afterwards reached me that the Indians carried away to Mendocino had returned in a starving condition and were killing cattle belonging to citizens living on Eel River and elsewhere, for their subsistence, and having received a petition from the citizens for aid, I sent Capt. Lovell and Company to van Dusins fork where he was during the past summer. But volunteering was considered a good business, as it was thought that those under Kibbe had been well paid, so as they were already in the field before the call was made and Capt. Lovell's Company sent, it is questionable if not other motives were at the bottom, of the application. Capt. Lovell's Company in the winter was decided to be called in by Gen'l. Clark and retained at the fort for awhile, the volunteers having abandoned the field previously after killing some few squaws and children.

Efforts were now made in Jany. last to get up another volunteer Company under a Capt. Wright as the fishing season was over and many men out of employ. Their supplies were furnished on credit of future idemnification by persons on Eel River, and they took the field perhaps some 20 or 30 in number or more, and after killing 40 Indians on South Fork of Eel River applied to be mustered into service to the Governor of the State, who did not consider it necessary, especially as another Company of U. S. Troops were under orders by the Dept. Commander for the protection of citizens and property here. The Legislature of the State had before them at the same time the reports of a Committee adverse to payments to murderers of women and children in Jarboe's case and others analagous to what already had been perpetrated in this region. So I learned a portion of Capt. Wright's Company held a meeting at Eel River on getting the news of failure and resolved to kill every peaceable Indian man, woman and child in this part of the country.

On the night of 25th Feby. last some 15 or 20 of these arrived on horseback at Humboldt point, took Capt. Buhners's boats, surreptitiously crossed the bay and murdered 9 men and 47 women and children. Then the same party returned, rode to Eureka while yet dark on the morning of the Sabbath, 26th, took a ship's boats, proceeded to Indian Island, and after firing and killing 3 men and thus scaring away the rest of the men (except 2 they shot afterward) they entered the Indian Lodges, and five of them having been found sufficiently cruel, barbariously murdered with axes, hatchets and knives, 51 women and children. They afterwards returned, went to Eagle prairie and there murdered some 30 or 35 more.

These Indians were the most inoffensive I ever saw, killed nobody, troubled nobody, and nobody's cattle, were useful, furnishing fish and clams to the whites after finding them in their fantastic corners, living apart by themselves, orderly, never drank liquor, and were in hostility with the Mountain tribes, whom they were accused of supplying with ammunition and getting beef from, until it became known that these later killed the cattle with bows and arrows only, and the former neither man, woman nor child would eat beef through some superstitious prejudices. So their wives and children were murdered for no crime whatever, but they were victims only to a military prestige or resentment falsely located. And this forcible ejection of the Indians in this country from their homes and firesides, has been got up and accomplished by the aiders and abettors of the murderous villains to pander for their votes for office, and after some 115 had been forcibly removed from Mad River, acting upon the fears of many good people in a petition to me to aid in their removal but they all but murdered, and making strangers believe there must be some great objection to this population and some occult cause for dissatisfaction, their withdrawal or destruction.

Very Respectfully, Your Mo. Obedt. Servt.
G. J. Raines, Major 4th Infy.
Comdg.
To   Actg. Ind. Agent
Hon. Thos. J. Hendricks
Commissioner of Indian Affairs
Washington City
D. C.

Removal of the Lower Mad River Indians

In our issue of last week, we suggested that as the agent having charge of the Klamath reserve was present, and ready to take charge of such Indians as could be gathered in, it would be well for our citizens to devote some time to the matter, and render such aid as circumstances should require. Upon consultation, C. M. Buel found the people of this town anxious for the removal of the Indians, and ready to assist him by any and all means necessary to that effect.

The first step taken in the matter was to bring a few of the most important Indians into town, tell them what was to be done, and by truthful statements and arguments to endeavor to convince them that it was for their interest that they should go, and that they should go willingly; but willing or not, they were told that go they must, and that immediately. After urging countless objections against leaving their old homes, and fears for their welfare on the reservation, they said they thought they would go, but wanted a little time—two or three days—to make ready. To all this they were answered by the agent and citizens, that if they did not consent to remove, force would be used to compel them; that should any of them succeed in eluding the agent and his assistants at this time, they would henceforth be treated as enemies; that before sunset every Lower-Mad River Indian must be in town ready to start the next morning for the Klamath; that some of the party present were to remain in town while the others would accompany white men to the different camps and rancherias to bring in the balance of the Indians, and that there was to be no more talk on the subject.

These few plain words had the desired effect, and was no doubt what the Indians had expected would have been said to them long before. They had talked the matter over among themselves many times, and concluded to go peaceably and quietly when there was no longer a chance for argument; when they should find that protestations and promises would no longer pass earnest, and that the white men were united in the determination to remove them.

As soon as this matter was settled, there was no further hesitation, but all set to with a will to prepare for the journey. Such property as they could carry with them was collected, and the balance—including houses, boats, and provisions—destroyed by the Indians themselves, for they were determined, they said, that no other Indians should profit by them after they were gone. By four o'clock in the afternoon they were all gathered—one hundred and thirty in number—according to directions.

The Indian Department and Major Raines

After the massacre at Indian Island and South Beach, Maj. Raines gave orders that the survivors should be provided for and protected at Fort Humboldt until some other disposition could be made of them. This was a judicious movement at the time, and one that the circumstances required. A few weeks ago the agent in charge of the Klamath reserve sent word to the Major to the effect that he was prepared to receive the Indians and ready to remove them. Maj. Raines replied to the messenger that he was "truly glad to hear it, and that it would afford him great pleasure to co-operate with the agent, to the extent of his ability."

Immediately upon his arrival in the country—Monday of last week—Mr. Buel waited upon the Major and received assurances of his desire to be relieved of the Indians, and that he would do all in his power to assist the agent in their removal. The Major then had the Indians removed, and said to them that Mr. Buel had "provided safe homes for them at the Klamath, that he was their friend, and would talk nothing but the truth, and that it was for their own good that he wished them to go with him." &c., &c. So far it was all plain sailing with our officials; but at an interview the next morning Maj. Raines gave the agent to understand that it would be necessary first to obtain the consent of the Indians, and that he would use his influence to induce them to agree to go, but that he had no authority to compel them. To this Mr. Buel objected that it was "immaterial whether the Indians wished to go or not; that he was there to remove them and willing to use force to compel them to obey him, if requisite." Mr. Buel then left the Fort and subsequently sent

159

the letter—published in another column—to which the Major declined making any reply.

Without pretending to know whether Major Raines is acting in accordance with orders or not, we submit that Fort Humboldt is not a proper place for these Indians. The question of employing force in the removal of the Indians at the Fort is a mere abstraction. There are but about seventy of them all told, men, women and children, as we are informed, and it requires nothing but moral force to make them obey. But whether this should prove sufficient or not, we maintain that it is of no importance whatever, except as a matter of convenience, what the Indians think or wish in the premises. They must be made to understand that henceforth they are to be taken care of by government, and that they must yield implicit obedience to the officers appointed to take charge of them.

Note From Indian Agent Buel to Major Raines:

Eureka, Cal., April 11, 1860

Sir: I learn that you have in your possession and under your protection, a number of Indians. I am here for the purpose of removing those Indians to the Klamath Reservation, at which place I am prepared to subsist and protect them. I desire that you will deliver those Indians to me outside of Fort Humboldt Military Reservation, with an escort to protect them from here to the Klamath Indian Reservation.

An immediate answer is respectfully requested.

Very respectfully, &c.
D. E. Buel,
Indian Agent, in charge Klamath Indian Reservation
Maj. G. J. Raines
Commanding Fort Humboldt

To this Maj. Raines made no reply; the people of Eureka, supposing that he did not wish the Indians to go to the Reserve, addressed a letter to the Major requesting the removal of the Indians under his immediate charge, and the following answer was returned:

Fort Humboldt, Cal., April 14, 1860

GENTLEMEN: Your request for the removal of the Indians, handed to me yesterday, will be acceded to, as far as my authority goes.

Very respectfully, &c.
G. J. Raines,
To Messrs. B. Van Nest,   Maj. U. S. A., Com'dg
A. W. Hanna,
J. H. Kimball,
C. S. Ricks,
Jonathan Clark, and others.

The undersigned begs leave to return his sincere thanks to the citizens of Arcata and vicinity, for their assistance in collecting the Indians for removal to the reservation. The Indians that I am now removing will be taken to the Klamath reserve, and properly cared for. I do not think any of them will return to this county; but should a few of them become discontented and succeed in making their escape, I hope they will be arrested and word sent me.

Again thanking the gentlemen who so generously and materially aided me in carrying out the policy of the Indian Department, I remain, very respectfully,

Your Obedient servant
D. E. Buel,
Indian Agent, in charge Klamath Indian Reservation
Arcata, April 12th, 1860

161

Grief of Indians upon Entering the Reservation

A writer in the Butte *Record* describes the removal, a few days ago, of a tribe of Indians from Butte creek, Butte county, to the Nome Lackee Reservation, in Tehama county. It is certainly better for the whites that the Indians should be collected in one place, where there may be some sort of supervision over their movements, and it is probably better for the Indians themselves that they should be removed from the careless and cruel assaults of white men, and a reasonable means of support assured to them. Yet the rudest savages have the common sentiments of humanity, and they cannot but feel that "there is no place like *home*, be it never so homely." This feeling was strongly manifested on the present occasion. The writer in the *Record* mentions that on the journey to the Reservation the guard was doubled, "on account of six Indians who had joined us during the day with the avowed purpose of rescuing their squaws." When the white walls of the Reservations buildings were seen "the poor Indians began to show some signs that they had a regret in leaving the place of their birth. The women in the wagons set up that peculiar plaintive cry used by them at their funerals, while the men walked behind the wagons in mournful silence." Here, one of the Indians, who spoke good English, demanded that his people should all have their arms, "which", says the writer, "was refused them, and I think prudently." It is a painful necessity of advancing civilization that the Indians should gradually disappear; yet it is some consolation to think that their physical wants are somewhat better supplied, and that the memory of their old homes and hunting places does not lie very long or heavily upon their minds.

The same writer says of the Indians' new home:

The Reservation consists of over twenty five thousand acres, the greater portion being fine valley land, well adapted to grain-growing. Indeed it must be so, since, according to Captain Martin, the secretary, the crop of wheat was over twelve thousand bushels. The buildings are very neat, and resemble in their style the old California missions. They are built of adobe and whitewashed. The most perfect order prevails around the establishment, and in order to enforce obedience, Lieut. Morgan is stationed there, with twenty men, who appear well pleased with their quarters and their office. The Indians whom I observed round the place, were well clothed, fat and healthy looking. They followed Mr. Titus around the barns, storerooms and buildings, taking him by the hand and playing with him as a child would its father. And indeed he well deserves the title, for throughout the journey, he was either walking while some of them rode his horse, or he had one of them up behind him, and often in the night, would he go around and cover their limbs with even his own blankets, remaining all night on guard, and making fires to keep them warm. Mr. Titus resides in their midst with his lady and two daughters, whose presence there seemed like ministering angels to soothe and cheer the poor exiled Indians. Every good citizen should do his utmost to keep those removed to Nome Lackee, who are elsewhere dying with hunger and loathsome diseases.

4:15   Newspaper article, Sacramento, 1857

Indians Up North

From a Crescent City correspondent we learn that Indian matters are going badly. Heintzelman induced the Smith River Indians to go on the Reservation, partly by threats and the promises of kind treatment and subsistence. Now he tells them to "go to work or I won't feed you." This is a harsh way; the consequence is many have left and are back on the river. He has announced his intention, should they not return to the Reserve, so soon as the troops arrive there from Fort Jones, he will proceed to have them shot. If the Agent starves the Indians, after robbing them of their lands, I am in hopes no U. S. officer would lend himself to murder them, simply because they go back on their own land to obtain food.

4:16   Newspaper article, San Francisco, 1861

Indian Affairs in the Northern District
The Reservation System

The Marysville *Appeal* of the 24th July says: G. M. Hanson, Superintendent of Indian Affairs for the Northern District of California, has just returned from a hasty tour to the different Reservations within his jurisdiction, which are known respectively as the Mendocino, Klamath, Nome Lackee and Round Valley. During his absence a droll story obtained circulation, to the effect that he was pursuing his predecessor, Major Driebelois, who studiously eluded him. The truth is, both gentlemen were seeking one another, and under a misapprehension the Major traveled north while Mr. Hanson followed close in his rear, always coming up a little too late. In this way the Superintendent in esse and in posse raced from Reservation to Reservation, Hanson on one occasion taking a 60 mile ride in a canoe down the Trinity river and having finally to return to San Francisco ere he could meet Driebelois. Certainly there never was such a chase for office before, and doubtless friend Hanson thinks possession far better than pursuit, whatever debating schools may decide to the contrary.

The following appointments have been made by the new Superintendent at the different Reservations, in his jurisdiction: At Mendocino—D. W. Smith, Superintendent; Stanley

Wiley and Frank K. Upham, Overseers. Klamath—W. W. Cradock, Superintendent; Roark, Thomas Linder and Nathan Hanson, Overseers. Nome Lackee—John G. Alender, left in charge of the property pro tem, the Indians having fled. Round Valley—James Short, Superintendent; John Clark and Mr. Cloud and son, Overseers. The salary of the Superintendents is $1,500 per annum; that of the Overseers but $50 per month.

Mr. Hanson finds that the Reservations have been very poorly managed, and have generally been in charge of persons who failed utterly to appreciate and assist the humane designs of Government. Too often the object of employees has been one of self-aggrandizement, rather than to render the Indians comfortable and contented. Frequently they have associated with the Indian women on terms of demoralizing familiarity, thus weakening their authority over the men, and making themselves a curse instead of a benefit to the simple race that Government would protect and civilize. To remedy this particular evil, Mr. Hanson proposes that as many of his employees as possible shall be married men. The salary of the overseers is not enough to enable them to support families, so they will have an opportunity given them to make up clothing and other articles for the Indians, which have heretofore been purchased at extortionate rates.

The superintendents' and overseers' wives and daughters will also be induced to educate the younger and more tractable Indians and to teach them the household arts. He thinks if the poor savages, who are commonly of a gentle and susceptible nature, can be made to believe that the officers of the Reservations are their friends, and desirous of benefitting them, they can soon be reconciled to remain at the Reservations, and after experiencing a year or two of plenty and good treatment will not care to resume their nomadic habits. He finds that their desertion of the Reservations is generally traceable to neglect or unkindness. They have not always been fed and clothed as they should have been or as they expected to be. The interference with their women, and the apprenticing of their children have also been causes of dis-

165

content. The presence of soldiers, too, has been demoralizing and provocative of ill temper. In a majority of instances the only use of the soldiers would seem to be to protect the Indians against the whites.

We understand Mr. Hanson to say that General Sumner will withdraw the troops stationed at the Reservations, except, from localities where it can be proved they are of actual service in preventing escapades and depredations. Mr. Hanson thinks there are more Reservations than are necessary, any way; and believes that at Round Valley is amply sufficient, both in extent and natural advantages, to be made the home of all the northern Indians who can be gathered upon it. He does not despair of making the Reservation system nearly what it was intended to be—a benefaction and salvation to the red man, and we are rejoiced to know that he brings to his responsible position feelings of humanity, and an intention to perform his duty honestly towards the Government and the simple people confided to his care.

4:17   Newspaper article, San Francisco, 1862

A Cry for Indian Agent Hanson

The Colusa *Sun* of 1st November says:

The citizens in the neighborhood of Nome Lackee Reservation, Tehama county, held a meeting lately and passed resolutions expressive of the sense of the people in regard to the large number of Indians that had lately been congregated there by the military authorities. They say that the Con Cow and Hat Creek Indians shall leave there, and can do so without molestation, and that they will furnish them subsistence for their journey. The cause of the difficulty is this stated by Col. E. A. Stevenson: Some 300 Indians who had left Nome Cult had been overtaken by the United States authorities, and concentrated at Nome Lackee. They were absolutely destitute of all means of subsistence, and were left at the Reservation in that condition, there being no Government agent, civil or military, to look after them supply them or control them. They were loose there, without constraint of any kind, and must therefore depredate upon the property of citizens. Where is Hanson, Indian Agent for this District? He seems to have entirely neglected his duties. Is the Government paying him a salary of $3,000 per annum, and perquisites, for doing nothing?

4:18 Newspaper article, Sacramento, 1862

MENDOCINO COUNTY—The following order has been published by General Wright:

Headquarters Department of the Pacific
San Francisco, October 13, 1862

Major G. M. Hanson, Superintendent Indian Affairs, Northern District of California—Sir: I have the honor to acknowledge the receipt of your communication of the 9th and 16th, with copies of the letters addressed to you from the Round Valley Reservation.

To prevent any farther molestation of the Indians remaining on the Reservation, I have directed Colonel Lippitt to declare martial law over the whole valley, and to station a sufficient number of troops there to insure peace and quiet, as well as protection of the public property.

After a careful consideration of the subject, I fully concur with you as to the best disposition of the Indians, viz: Let there be but two Reservations, one embracing the Round Valley, for all interior Indians, and one at Smith's River valley, for the coast Indians.

Should you deem it advisable, you are at liberty to submit this communication to the Commissioner of Indian Affairs.

With great respect, I have the honor to be your obedient servant.

G. Wright
Brigadier General U. S. Army, Commanding

It is said the order has been issued at the request of the Indian Agent, Hanson, who represented to General Wright that the settlers have turned their stock upon the Round Valley Reservation, and committed other outrages and trespasses which have finally resulted in a general stampede of the Indians. He found it impossible to keep them under existing circumstances.

4:19   Newspaper article, San Francisco, 1865

Daily Evening Bulletin, January 9, 1865

Indian Affairs in California

Congress passed at its last session an Act reorganizing the Indian Department of California, making the State constitute one superintendency under the general management of one Superintendent at a salary of $3,600, with a clerk at a salary of $1,800 per annum—payable in greenbacks, of course. The Act limits the number of Reservations to four; authorizes the Secretary of the Interior to compromise with settlers on Reservation lands, subject to the approval of Congress; requires abandoned Reservations to be surveyed and sold at auction at an appraised valuation, or held subject to sale at private entry; and authorizes the President to appoint a resident Agent for each Reservation, at a salary of $1,800. This Act greatly simplified and economized the administration of Indian affairs in this State. Under the new system the appropriations have been at the rate of only

$75,000 per annum, while instead of spending money to obtain pork and beans via Cape Horn, the Indians are fed on the products of their own labor on the Reservations, the chief expenditures being for salaries and clothing, and no opportunity being afforded for repeating those extensive cattle operations by which private ranches used to be stocked and the Government diddled.

There are four Reservations—or four parcels of land being used for Reservation purposes—in the State, situated as described below, and under the general superintendency of Austin Wiley. At Smith River Valley, in Del Norte county, there are about 700 Indians, under charge of William Bryson. They are well provided for, and apparently contented. It was thought at one time that it would be impossible to keep the Northern Indians upon the Reservation in that region, and it was in contemplation to remove them to Catalina Island. This project has apparently been abandoned, and there is now reason to believe that the late hostile savages can be retained under guard in the neighborhood of their old haunts, if they are only well fed and treated. Many of them have voluntarily given themselves up, beseeching the protection of the Super-intendent and Agent; and for the first time in many years there is peace between the two races in the Northern counties, as throughout California.

A Reservation was located at Hoopa Valley, Klamath county, last summer, and the location has been approved by the Secretary of the Interior. On this Reservation, all the Indians surviving of the tribes that have been engaged in the ruinous hostilities that have afflicted Humboldt and Klamath counties during the past five years, are collected. They have surrendered their arms, and seem anxious to live at peace with the whites in future. Notwithstanding there are local objections urged to the selection of this site for a Reserva-tion, a sense of security seems to have followed its establish-ment, and the settlers do not fear any more outbreaks, if the Indians are cared for and protected. The Reservation is in charge of R. L. Stockten.

At the Round Valley Reservation, situated in the

Northern portion of Mendocino county, there are about 1,200 Indians of various tribes. Many of the Indians from the head waters of Eel river have recently come to the valley of their own accord, and appear perfectly contented to remain there when assured of food and protection. This valley contains 30,000 acres of arable land, all of which has been reserved for Government purposes, though there are a considerable number of settlers thereon whose improvements will have to be purchased before full possession can be had. All the Indians in Northern California, it is said, could be subsisted in this valley by their own labor. The labor of those already there has produced enough grain for all the tribes of the North, if it could be got to them. This Reservation is in charge of G. W. B. Yocom.

The old Mendocino Reservation was broken up on the 31st day of December last, but the Indians will remain there in charge of an employee until next fall. They are said to be well provided for.

The only Reservation in the Southern portion of the State is on Tule river, in Tulare county. This is on rented land, and will be abandoned after this year, for a Reservation located on Government land. There are about 800 Indians on this farm, who are in charge of G. Hoffman, Special Agent. They have food enough to subsist them until the new crops come in. There are many Indians in both sections of the State, not upon reservations, who need looking after, and who, we are informed, will be cared for as soon as arrangements can be made for their maintanance. Indians employed on ranches or in the towns will be left where they are, as they are doing well enough for themselves; but some of those roaming at large, deprived of their old fishing privileges to a great extent, might be tempted by hunger to steal beef—an offense which is sure to be visited upon their heads with murderous vengeance, leading to a repetition of the so-called "Indian hostilities" which have disturbed and injured the northern counties so greatly. It will, therefore, be wise as well as benevolent to gather them as soon as convenient where they can be fed and saved from slaughter. Their race is fast

170

passing away, and the least we can do for them is to prevent their ending from being hurried and violent.

4:20   Newspaper article, San Francisco, 1865

Condition of the California Indians—Superintendent Wiley on the Late Sympathy Meeting

Office of Indian Affairs
San Francisco, Cal., January 6, 1865

EDITORS BULLETIN. Some three weeks since, you published proceedings of a meeting held at the church of Zion, in this city, the object of which was said to be for the amelioration of the condition of the Indians of California. In the preamble to the resolutions passed at the meeting, and published in your paper, the assertion was made that "It is reported that the Indians are destitute of food," etc.

A committee of correspondence was appointed to ascertain the facts in the matter, and after sufficient time had elapsed for them to make the investigation, I addressed the committee the following note:

Office of Indian Affairs, December 31, 1865

GENTLEMEN: Not long since a meeting was held at the Church of Zion, on Stockton Street, the object of which was said to be for the benefit of the Indians of California. At that meeting, Nathaniel Gray, William Shew, Dr. Henry Gibbons and John Beeson were appointed a committee of correspondence to ascertain the facts in relation to the true condition of the Indians in this State. As the preamble to the resolution asserts that "It is reported the Indians in this State are destitute of food," I beg to inquire of your committee whether or not you have ascertained the truth or falsity of the assertion. As a sufficient time has elapsed to enable you to make the necessary inquiries, justice to the public as well as myself demands that the facts should be made known. Very respectfully, your obedient servant.

Austin Wiley
Superintendent of Indian Affairs, California

N. Gray, W. Shew, H. Gibbons and J. Beeson, Committee

To this the committee replied as follows:

Sir: In answer to your letter of December 31st, we inform you that we were not present at the meeting referred to and that our names were used on that occasion without our knowledge or comment. Consequently we have made no inquiries such as are referred to in the published proceedings of that meeting, nor do we regard ourselves as in the least degree accountable for anything done or published in connection with it. Very respectfully yours.

Nathaniel Gray, William Shew, H. Gibbons.

San Francisco, January 2, 1865

While I would not detract by any word or deed from any legitimate effort that might be made in the direction of benefitting the Indians, I deem it a duty to the Government as well as myself to state that both the people and the press have been imposed upon through the action of John Beeson, who is the prime-mover in this project, and whose name appeared as one of the Committee.

I was one of the eleven or twelve men that composed that meeting. Mr. Beeson had the resolutions and memorial in his pocket when he came there. He nominated the three gentlemen whose names are signed above, and afterwards

172

succeeded in having himself placed upon the Committee. The respectability of these gentlemen is such as to attach more importance to the movement than it deserves, and if no denial were made by them of their complicity in the matter, it would be taken for granted that the Indians were in a starving condition. In conclusion, I beg leave to state that the Indians on all of the Reservations in my charge are well provided with food and have an abundance to last them through the winter.

That they are in want of clothing is true, as the annual shipment from New York did not arrive here until too late for them to receive it before the beginning of the late severe storm. I did all in my power to provide for their wants by purchasing a limited supply of blankets which were forwarded before winter set in. A portion of the shipment lately received has been sent to the Indians this week, and the remainder will be forwarded by the first opportunity.

If Mr. Beeson had manifested the same anxiety to ascertain the condition of the Indians in this State, that he has to give publicity to his personal efforts in their behalf, he would have saved me from resting under an unjust imputation, and himself from a public exposition.

In regard to the $100,000 which he so knowingly spoke of in his speech as having been squandered by the Indian Department in this State, I have only to say that the employees and myself are as anxious to know what became of it as Mr. Beeson, and would be greatly obliged to that gentleman or any other man who can enlighten the public on that point, if he will do so.

Yours respectfully,
Austin Wiley
Superintendent of Indian Affairs, California

Courtesy SM

Chemehuevi girl

5

PROPOSALS FOR INDIAN PROTECTION AND WELFARE

Here is presented a series of recommendations, both official and unofficial, for a solution to the problem of what to do with the Indians. While some of these proposals were made for humanitarian reasons, the majority of them seem to have been based on a desire to get the Indians out of the way. Note in Document 5:16 dating from 1864 that the reservation system instituted in 1853 was not yet effective.

Chico, California
July 6th 1850

Sir:

Difficulties of somewhat a serious character have recently taken place between some of the Indian Tribes and the white population on the head waters of the Sacramento, which was originally included within the bounds of my Agency. The more recent occurred on the waters of Bear River and Wolf Creek where several white men were killed and some property destroyed by fire. At the time of these difficulties I was South of San Francisco and did not know of them for several days. Indeed, I was not sure, after the appointment of Captain Sutter, Agent for that region, and my own Agency having been designated for the Valley of the San Joaquin, that the scenes of those difficulties came properly under my notice. Being aware, however, that Capt. Sutter had declined accepting the appointment and that no other Agent had been appointed, it occurred to me that some good might result from the presence of a Government Indian Agent in that region of country. I accordingly set out for "Camp Far West" situated on Bear river. I reached Sacramento City on the morning of the 27th of May when I met with Maj. Genl. Thomas J. Green of the California Militia, who informed me that he had just returned from above, and not only chastised the Indians who committed the crimes attached to them but had also entered into an amnesty or treaty with them. Genl. Green and his Excellency Governor Burnett were about leaving for San Francisco on the steamer. The Genl. expecting to leave for the States soon after arriving in that city, desired me to examine his treaty and to approve or recommend its adoption to the Department, if on examination I thought it such as to warrant me in doing so. I thereupon concluded to return to the city with them. On my way down and after reaching San Francisco I gave to this document a careful examination, but could not give it my approval or recommend its adoption to the Government.

On the 3rd day of June I again left the city of San Francisco for the scene of those difficulties and on the 7th reached "Camp Far West", a Government Military post under the command of Capt. Day of the 2nd Infantry, an accomplished officer, to whom I am indebted for his hospitality and friendship during my stay in that region of country. It was not far distant from this cantonment that the Indian depredations were committed. On inquiry, I found the people of that vicinity did not view the transaction of the 25th as of very great importance or vitality in controling or restraining the Indians. Such transactions sometimes receive much of their magnitude from being reduced to paper. From all that I could learn in the vicinity of the difficulty, and from my knowledge of the Indian character in this country and their present condition, I am of the opinion it would be miserable policy on the part of the Government to adopt the Treaty as it stands. My reasons for coming to this conclusion are the following:

First. The occasion was isolated, having been committed by but few individual Indians and perhaps provoked on the part of the whites, and under no circumstances was it of sufficient magnitude to call for a Treaty.

Second. The Chiefs present were but few in number and without power to bind the balance of the numerous surrounding Tribes.

Third. The object of the Treaty seems to have been the purchase of Peace and Friendship from the most stupid wretches of the country. That kind of consideration does not seem to me such as should enter into any arrangement the Government might be disposed to make with them.

Fourth. The payment of one thousand Dollars as a semi-annual annuity to the several Tribes represented in the Treaty by the Government of the United States for the purpose of obtaining peace and friendship for the most degraded and [?]-like beings on the Continent would not only be unnecessarily expensive to the Government but wholly useless to the Indians. They have not the least conception of the value of money, and the consequence would be it would fall into the hands of a few avaricious whites without benefiting the Indians.

With due respect for those connected with the formulation of the Treaty, I must for the above reasons dissent from their opinions in regard to its adoption by the Government of the United States. I visited the region of country in which the Treaty was concluded principally to meet the several Chiefs whose names appeared upon the Treaty and to ascertain whether they fully understood its import and the contingency of its adoption or rejection on the part of the Government. I was, however, disappointed as I did not get to see any of the intelligent Chiefs, they having gone to one of their annual festivals or councils on the head waters of the Feather River.

After remaining a few days at and in the neighborhood of Nevada [City], I returned to the Mouth-of-the-Yuba and from thence continued up the Feather river. On my way I visited the several Tribes inhabiting the shores of that stream, the "Hock", near to the residence of Capt. Sutter and from whom the celebrated Hock Farm takes its name, the "Yubas", the "O-lip-as", the "Boga", the Nolilla-pas (properly spelled [illegible]), the "Lorskins" and the "Ma-chuc-na" and have had some talk with most of the Chiefs of these Tribes. they reside in Valleys at some distance from each other and number from 70 to one hundred and fifty in each family or Tribe. They are independent of each other but possess much the same characteristics, live in the same manner and speak almost the identical same language. Like all Indians west of the Sierra Nevada, they are the least war like or savage of any Indians on the face of the globe. They possess no weapons of war except their bows and arrows, no war clubs, scalping knives or savage tomahawk. They are a wild and ignorant people as yet, and though not warlike they will steal and commit murders on individuals, but in my opinion it requires but little time to remedy these evils.

178

They seem to have some sagacity in locating their villages on the most beautiful spot to be found on the banks of the streams. The whites have generally in locating their Ranchos, built their houses near to those of the Indians, not only on account of the beauty of the situation, but that they can the more readily command the services of the Indians. Some of them are used as domestics by the Ranchores while others work at some of the more simple arts of husbandry such as [illegible] and cleaning barley, wheat, etc. In some instances the whites have not only built their own houses close to those of the Indian villages but have laid out towns around and over them which must eventually drive them from such homes.

Their means of subsistance, which have heretofore been limited, are now greatly diminished on account of the immigration overrunning their country. The miners have destroyed their fish dams on the streams and the majority of the tribes are kept in constant fear on account of the indiscriminate and inhumane massacre of their people in many places, for real or supposed injuries. They have not any particular boundaries or fixed homes for any great length of time together, but change their locations as taste or their necessities may require. Yet they all have an undistinct and undefined idea of their right in the soil, the trees and the streams. From these they have heretofore obtained their subsistence, which consists of grass seeds and roots from the earth, acorns, pine seeds and berries from the trees and bushes and fish from the streams. They become alarmed at the immence flood of immigration which spread over their country. It was quite incomprehensible to them. I have been told of several acts of depredation which were instigated by the Chiefs of certain Tribes through the apprehension that their people must die of starvation in consequence of the strangers overrunning their country, feeding their grass, burning their timber and destroying their dams on the streams. For these inovations they claim some compensation, not in money for they know nothing of its value, but clothing, blankets and something to sustain life upon. So far as I have yet been able to ascertain all the Tribes in the Valley of the Sacramento would not only be satisfied but greatly gratified with an arrangement for a small annuity to be paid in clothing, blankets and food, at stated periods. That they have some cause for complaint, no one familiar with their mode of life, their present condition and in some instances the cruel treatment by a few of the whites, can doubt.

I have seldom heard of a single difficulty between the whites and the Indians of the Valley or Mountains in which the original cause could not readily be traced to some rash or reckless act of the former. In some instances it has happened that innocent Indians have been shot down for immaginary offences which did not in fact exist. For instance, on one occasion when cattle were missing, it was quickly supposed that they had been stolen by the Indians, and the lives of several Indians taken on this supposition. Again when a man was absent a few days longer than he was expected to be, his death was imagined and attributed to the Indians in the neighborhood and the lives of several paid the penalty of the supposed murder. In the one case, the cattle were found in the course of a few days and in the other the man also returned, but the innocent Indians were no more.

Several similar instances have been related to me where the lives of Indians have been taken for supposed injuries. The consequence of such acts inflicted on Indians knowing themselves innocent has been revenge on their part. They possess a principle similar to the Old Jewish law, which required "an eye for an eye and a tooth for a tooth". If one of their number be killed by a white man, they require the blood of a white man, and it seems to matter little whether or not he be the guilty person—the blood of one is required for the blood of the other. This kind of retribution is a matter of religion with most of the Tribes of this country.

As the Indians of California have been undoubtedly disturbed in their possessions and the means by which they have theretofore sustained life rendered more difficult to obtain, I beg leave to suggest a plan for their management which I think would not only ameliorate their present condition and gradually bring them into a civilization, but be the least expensive to the Government.

It is to stipulate with the various Tribes in the Valley of the Sacramento to pay them semi annually a certain amount in clothing, blankets and provisions. The climate is mild and they would require but little clothing, although I find they readily adopt the apparel of the whites when they can by any means obtain it, and this seems as much to cover their nakedness as for comfort. It seems to me this course would be less expensive to the Government than any other plan for managing the Indians of this country and it certainly would be more beneficial to the Indians themselves. To pay them money would only be individually to put it into the hands of a few unscrupulous whites without benefiting the Indians, as they know nothing whatever of the value of money. They will readily give all they may have for any article they may fancy.

In order to carry out this plan it might be necessary to establish two or three depo[t]s in the Valley of the Sacramento. Say, one at Plumas near the present residence of Captain Sutter, one about two hundred miles up Feather river, and one about the same distance up the Sacramento river. These would be sufficient to supply the whole of the Tribes in the Valley of the Sacramento and adjacent country. It would be well if some means could be adopted by which to insure those who labor for the whites a reasonable compensation. Heretofore those living near to the Ranchos have labored for little or no compensation. A calico shirt worth perhaps fifty cents would be given for a weeks labor. Captain Day of the 2nd Infantry, who has resided some time in this country kindly furnished me with his observations regarding the present condition of the Indians of the Mountains wholly which agree with my own. They are as [illegible]. "These Indians, unlike any heretofore treated with have no nationality, but are divided into small bands, each under Subchiefs and wander independent of each other. Inhabiting by nondisputed possession the hills and mountains of the Sierra Nevada, most of the year subsisting on vegetable products but occasionally on wild game and principally on the fish of the streams, both of which are debarred them now by the mining population. It becomes a question, how are they to be provided for in mere charity, to say nothing of their native right in the soil? Remove them further West unless it be beyond the West and into the Pacific, is out of the question. To the East of the Sierra Nevada into the Desert would be more certain than utter extermination. [Illegible line] farms or settlements in the valley with a liberal allowance of subsistance in kind from the United States. Of money they have no idea, and therefore an annuity in coin would only fall into the hands of avaricious white men. One half of the bread and meat rations of a Soldier might, together with such items of vegetable kingdom as are to be found, and to which they are accustomed, would form ample subsistance for them."

H Day, Capt. 2nd Infantry
June 9, 1850

These observations agree in general with my own, although made in regard to the Indians inhabiting the Mountains.

Under some such regulation as I have recommended herein, I am convinced it would require [illegible line] and mountains to abandon their present mode of living and adopt a civilized life.

During the last few months I have been engaged in collecting such statistical information as is required by the Department. I find it tedious and not infrequently difficult on account of not being able to obtain proficient interpreters. In many cases the Indians have no words in their language to express the ideas I would wish to impress them with, and I have not found either a white man or native of California who could speak the full extent of even their limited language. There are many who have been acquainted with the most common terms and are able to make themselves understood in ordinary matters, but this is about the amount they ever agree on. So with some of the Indians, they have acquired a few words of the Spanish but not sufficient to make themselves understood to any extent or to understand more than a few ideas. This applies to the Indians of the Sacramento Valley. Those on the San Joaquin and Southern part of the State have become more proficient in the Spanish language.

In order that my agency be of efficiency it is necessary that the salary be increased considerably, as it is immensely costly to travel or to live in any position in this country. There should also be more facilities afforded me in cases of necessity. I should, when necessary, have authority to call upon the Military Posts and to cooperate with them under certain circumstances.

On my return I shall be able to furnish the Department with such statistics as I have collected.

I have the honor to be
Very respectfully Your Obt. Servt.
Adam Johnston

5:2   Petition, Woodbridge to Taylor

To General Zachary Taylor
President of the United States

Memorial in Behalf of the Indians of California

General:
Your high character as a just man and an upright magistrate and your personal politeness when I had the honor of an interview with you at your residence in Baton Rouge, embolden me to address you.

Respectfully, I would represent,

That the Indians in the Sierra Nevada are driven in large numbers from their usual haunts, are consequently deprived of their customary food—acorns, and hence are exposed to starvation.

That they are often killed, because when urged by hunger, they have attempted to seize the horses or cattle of the American emigrants.

That Indian women and children, guilty of no offence, are frequently put to death, and sometimes in cool blood, in these onslaughts.

That the system of serfdom still continues on the Spanish ranches in this country.

Respectfully I would venture to suggest

That the powerful and benevolent influence of *the Great Father* of the Indian nations be employed to collect those most exposed in California, into ranches of their own, separate from the presence of the white community.

That good men, farmers, teachers, etc, be placed at the head of these ranches, for the Indians though docile are as children, without judgement or foresight.

That on the ground of benevolence and economy the Missionary Societies be encouraged to assist in carrying out this project.

The following sites are respectfully suggested as appropriate.

San Juan Mission is unoccupied and already stocked at least partially with wild cattle.

Valley of Rio de los Reyes is a fertile country, not in a gold region.

Beriessa Valley is a very secluded spot from 30 to 40 miles north of Benicia, occupied at present by a Spanish ranch.

Valley of Clear Lake is full of wild Indians and therefore is unoccupied by the whites.

The advantages of this plan are

Practicability of immediate adoption.

Economy, for after the farms are once stocked, and occupied, small additional expences need be incurred.

Efficiency, for every Indian would at once have a home.

National credit and *noble benevolence.*

No wish to interfere with the arrangements of the bureaux of Indian affairs, but a deep sense of the necessity of prompt and effectual aid being rendered to the poor outcast houseless helpless savages thrown upon American protection has led me, a clergyman by profession, and the Pastor of the Presbyterian Church in Benicia, to address you in this appeal.

With profound respect
I am, General,
Your most obedient
and humble servant
Sylvester Woodbridge, jr.

Benicia California
January 23rd 1851

5:3 Letter, Campbell to Commissioner of Indian Affairs

California, Sonoma, June 1st, 1851

Sir

The laws of California making it imperative on the Magistrates in the different townships to visit and superintend the indians, occasionally to instruct them, adjudicate and punish them for any crimes they may commit either against Indians or White people, as well as to protect them from oppression, has given me an opportunity these two years past whilst acting in that capacity to become well acquainted with their habits and disposition, and not aware of an Indian Agent ever having been sent to this northern Section of the State, stimulate me to write these lines for the general information of the Indian department at Washington.

The California Indian commonly called the digger Indians are the most abject poor, stupid and filthy tribe I have ever been acquainted with. Their chief food consists of roots, seeds, insects and vermin. Sometimes they hunt the deer, elk and antelope which are very abundant here, but they are slothful and indolent, seldom hunting till forced by hunger. Nevertheless they are docile enough and will converse with good reason and judgement and when taught husbandry are very ingenious as many of them have been on the Ranches and in the Missions before 1836 at which point the Missions were being sacked by the Mexican authorities and the Indians banished to the mountains, where they became vagrant, thieves and idlers, and vowed continued warfare against the White population. And those who have lived in the missions are the most licentious, particularly if they drink liquor, of which they are very fond. There are many of them living on the Ranches in this country and work very well, but they are all inclined to theft. The working or mission Indians, as well as the wild tribes, will lie and cheat and are very fond of gambling. Nevertheless, with kindness they can be taught and subjugated with more facility than any that I have been acquainted with, and as far as I can learn, the three Commissioners now on duty in the mining districts have little difficulty in accomplishing a treaty with such as can be pre-vailed on to venture among them. But still many tribes and scattering Indians owing to their being better mounted and prepared for hostile and thieving purposes and who have these times past obtained considerable booty from the miners and rancheras so numerous in their vicinity. Horses, mules and oxen ect. being so abundant that those wild tribes prefer keeping the mountains till they are compelled to submit. In the northern Section we experienced but trifling difficulty with them, and even what we did originated from reckless-ness, wantonness and unnecessary cruelty towards them in the beginning. The principal difficulty experienced here originated in cruelty and terminated fatally. Some farmers in this vicinity who had several Indians on their farms, as was customary, went to the clear lake distant from here about sixty miles and compelled about one hundred of the Indians to go with them to the Sacramento Mines. In the Sickly Season most of them took the intermittent fever and died, and of the whole scarcely ten returned alive. Those on arriv-ing with their friends complained of the usage they received, and it is probable vowed revenge. Some time after about January 1850 the wife of one of these men [Kelsey] in

186

Sonoma was threatened by a young Indian and for which he received 100 lashes by order of the alcalde and in about an hour after was shot through the head by her husband. Next night all the Indians in the vicinity fled to the lake and in a short time they in return murdered the brother of the man who shot the Indian, and his partner and drove off large numbers of their cattle, for which the brother of the murdered man collected a strong force and on pretence of going to the lake and punishing the murderers but instead of which they commenced an indiscriminate slaughter of the Indians who reside on farms working for Americans and in one night slew twenty. They were prevented by the citizens from utterly annihilating them, and most of them were arrested by order of the Government, but no further proceedings instituted. Since this the Indians were severely punished at the lake by the expedition sent to chastise them, commanded by Capt. Lyons, of which you are already in possession, and through dread they have kept to the mountains, till lately that they are becoming friendly. But if there were proper persons in whom they could impose confidence placed over them or among them who would teach them husbandry etc. and teach them civilization they would become very docile and useful. Servants in a country where labor is at such a maximum as the immense influx of immigration requires the agricultural resources of the State to be husbanded and which will amply repay the labor in the valleys. Last week I was called on to go up Russian River some 50 miles to settle a dispute between some Spaniards on a Ranchero and a tribe of Indians. The Mexicans believing they had a right to exercise dominion over them as usual, but they learning that our government did not permit such tyranny appealed to me as Magistrate by the State law [with?] jurisdiction over the Indians and after hearing both parties I gave them a locality of a League of land on the N. E. side of the river where their rancheria stands. There are about one hundred in the Rancheria. They were very well satisfied and requested I would live on their land to instruct them, and they would work for me. The chiefs promised to obey my orders, and that should any of their youths steal or injure the white men, they would bring them to me to be punished and entreated much that I would come to live with or near them or send some one I could recommend to teach them how to procure and raise food as they say the herbs, roots, insects vermin &c. on which they subsisted is getting scarce on account of the white population occupying so much of the land they formerly occupied.

I therefore believe that the department at Washington was not in sufficient information regarding the Indians in the Northern Section of our State, as men here generally care more for the obtaining ore than furnishing any accurate information that might tend to benefit the Indians as there seems a marked hostility towards them more especially by the western population and those from Oregon and Washington I am at a loss to account for. I am therefore of opinion if a man accustomed to their habits, one in whom they would place confidence was located among them with sufficient power over the different tribes between here and Trinity or Humboldt Bay (and the expense would be merely nominal) would result in much good and prevent serious consequences if Government will act speedily therein as at present they are a dread of the Americans and in want of food &c.

I have the honor to be your most obt. Servant

Peter Campbell

The Hon. Commissioner of Indian Affairs
Washington D. C.

5:4 Letter, Bigler to Hitchcock; petition, northern county senators and representatives to Bigler

Executive Department
To Gen. E. Hitchcock   Sacramento City, April 8, 1852

Sir:
I have the honor to submit for your examination a letter addressed to me to-day by the Senators and Representatives

from the Counties of Trinity, Klamath, Shasta and Siskiyou. You will learn, from a perusal of this communication, that there has been a resumption of hostilities in the North, and that our fellow citizens residing in the northern Counties are suffering the horrors of a predatory war. You are also presented with an aggregate statement of the number of citizens ruthlessly murdered in these counties by Savages within a "very few months" past. Annexed to this melancholy narrative is an aggregate statement of the value of property destroyed by Indians during the same period.

The history of these troubles, as recounted in this despatch, and in other papers before me, show that the acts of these Savages are sometimes signalized by a ferocity worthy of the cannibals of the South Sea. They seem to cherish an instinctive hatred toward the white race, and this is a principle of their nature which neither time nor vicissitude can impair. This principle of hatred is hereditary, and it is transmitted from the live to the Son by example and by injunction. Another infirmity of the Indian character of which we have incontestible evidence is that their respect for treaty stipulations ceases at the moment when the inciting causes—self-interest or apprehensions of punishment—are removed. The character and conduct of these Indians presents an additional illustration of the accuracy of observations repeatedly made—that Whites and Indians cannot live in close proximity in peace; and it seems to confirm the opinion expressed in the inclosed despatch, that an ultimate evacuation of the Northern Counties by Whites or the Indians will be unavoidable.

In contingencies like these a simple but imperative duty is imposed upon the Executive: to place the State in the hands of the General Government, and to demand from it that aid and protection which the guaranties of the Federal Constitution assure us we are entitled to receive. If the General Government is neglectful of the demand which we make upon it—if it is unmindful of the duty which it owes to us—we have one other alternative—to fight our own battles—to maintain our independence as a sovereign but isolated State, and to protect ourselves from intestine troubles, as well as from the incursions of merciless and Savage enemies. Although we have found it necessary to embrace this alternative hitherto, we have not forgotten our allegiance to the General Government, nor have I forgotten that devoted citizens, who respect their private and political obligations, possess the most sacred and binding claims upon the fostering protection of Government. The interests of a Government and a people are mutually dependent, and there is a line of reciprocal duty upon which a continuance of their mutual relations and interests depends. The citizen cannot absolve himself from this allegiance so long as he claims the protection of the Government, nor can the Government disregard the interests of the citizen in whatever quarter of the globe they may lie.

But, sir, it is my duty, however unpleasant it may be, to express conviction that adequate protection has not been extended by the Government in Washington to American citizens residing in the State of California. I refer particularly to the fact that the number of regular troops detailed for service in California and on the borders of Oregon, have not been proportionate to the demand of the service. The mountain Indians, whose activity, sagacity, and courage has never been surpassed by Indians on the continent of America, are untamed and unconquered. Collissons [sic] between them and American citizens have been frequent, and the number of victims sacrificed to this neglect of the General Government is being augmented every day. The strong and decisive interposition of that Government is now asked: if this reasonable petition is not granted, I am apprehensive that results will ensue which every true friend of the Government must deplore.

I deem it my duty to assure you that unless prompt protection is afforded to the citizens of this State by the General Government I shall feel constrained to resort to the only means left me to defend the frontiers and to conquer a lasting peace. A resort to these means will increase the debt of the State, and add to the burden of taxation imposed upon our citizens. To dispense with such a necessity I indulge the earnest hope that you, as the military representative of the General Government in California will exercise your authority to arrest hostilities and to secure to us the blessings of a permanent peace.

In conclusion, permit me to suggest that if you have not at your immediate disposal a sufficient number of troops to detail for this service, and if you are authorized to state that the General Government will assume and pay expenses incident to a call of volunteers in to the Service; I will promptly issue a call for them whenever you may indicate a desire to have it done.

I have the honor to be, Sir, Your obt. servant
John Bigler
[Governor]

Sacramento City, Cal.
April 6, 1852

To His Excellency
John Bigler, Governor of California

The undersigned Senators and Representatives from the Counties of Trinity, Klamath, Shasta and Siskiyou, most respectfully represent to your Excellency that the constant and continued depredations committed by the various tribes of Indians on the lives and property of our citizens demand your prompt, efficient, and constant resistance than the citizens of this district are longer able to make, as a short review of the past history of this Section of our State and the present alarming situation of our citizens will demonstrate. Since the winter of 1848-50 the Pitt river Indians have been constantly hostile, and their incessant depredations and murders have been only occasionally checked by expeditions of the whites made into their country. All the other tribes, to wit: the Cottonwood, Trinity, Klamath and Shasta Indians, have, in turn, been hostile since the first settlement by the whites; but it has only been within the last few months that there appears to have been a general combination among them of hostility to the whites.

From our own personal knowledge, and from information obtained from reliable sources, we feel satisfied that the following statement of losses, both in life and property, that have occured in our Section of the State from Indian depredations are considerably below the reality:

Shasta County
　　No. of whites murdered　　　　　　　　40
　　Amount of property destroyed
　　and stolen　　　　　　　　　　　$100,000

Trinity County
　　No. of whites murdered　　　　　　　　20
　　Amount of property destroyed
　　and stolen　　　　　　　　　　　$50,000

Klamath County
　　No. of whites murdered　　　　　　　　50
　　Amount of property destroyed
　　and stolen　　　　　　　　　　　$50,000

Siskiyou County
　　No. of whites murdered　　　　　　　　20
　　Amount of property destroyed
　　and stolen　　　　　　　　　　　$40,000

These enormous losses have all been sustained by the people of a small portion of this State, within a very few months. The evil is increasing every day as a more intimate knowledge of the whites makes the Indians more bold and reckless in their attacks. Already they enter our towns and villages at night and steal or set fire to property. The habitations of the industrious miners, while they are at their labors, are entered with impunity and robbed of their contents. The pack animals on which the miners must depend for their provisions, are either killed on the spot where found, or driven away to be roasted and eaten by the depredators. The people are compelled to travel from one portion of the country to another in companies, well armed to repel attacks.

It has been charged that the hostility of the Indians was superinduced by acts of injustice committed by the whites. As a general thing, we can state, from our own knowledge, that this has not been the case; and have no hesitation in saying that it emanates from the known character of the Indians—a mischievous disposition and desire for plunder. In but few instances have the first offences been committed by the whites.

[Illegible] . . . order out the militia for that purpose. Eighty or one hundred men, in addition to those proposed to be located at Cow Creek, properly distributed in bands of ten to twenty, along Trinity and Klamath rivers, and always in readiness for service, would probably be sufficient; for the Indians now generally act in small parties, although, there has not often been much difficulty in repelling them yet, it has been almost impossible to follow them to their haunts to chastise them. Instances have occurred where miners have attempted this, and returned only to find their habitations despoiled of every thing valuable.

For these reasons we now ask of you protection for the people of that portion of the State that has never yet received any thing at the hands of the Government, confidently expecting your speedy attention to the same.

We remain very Respectfully
Your obt Servants
Signed Thomas H. Coats of Klamath County,
ʼamuel Fleming, E.D. Pierce of Shasta County,
Geo. O. McMullin of Trinity County,
J.W. Denver, Senator from Klamath & Trinity Counties,
R.J. Sprague, Senator from Shasta.

Woodville, Tulare County, August 28th, 1852

Brig. Gen. E. A. Hitchcock
Commanding Pacific Division U. S. A.

Sir:

We the undersigned citizens of Tulare County beg leave respectfully to represent that in their immediate vicinity are located numerous tribes of Indians, many of whom have very little acquaintance with the whites, and whom they have every reason to believe will on the first favorable opportunity which presents itself for plunder, commence hostilities.

They would respectfully call your attention to the fact, that some of these are the same Indians who about two years ago murdered at this place 14 of our fellow countrymen settled here at that time.

They would further represent that recently these Indians have expressed dissatisfaction at the non-fulfillment of the treaty stipulations entered into with them by the Indian Commissioners to furnish them with provisions and sundry other articles, and some of their principle men have (after we had given them provisions to the extent of our means) demanded it as a right, and given unmistakable evidence of dissatisfaction when such demands were not complied with.

And further that they are thrown into daily contact with these Indians and liable at any time to fall into petty quarrels with them which without a day's notice might result in general hostilities, and more particularly so as they know we are but few, and they feel their great numerical superiority, and know that from our very isolated position that they could affect the extermination of our settlement before succour could possibly be had.

And they would further represent that their county would at this time have been entirely unprotected but for the patriotic offer of the gallant Maj. Fitzgerald, who seeing the necessity of the case, voluntarily proposed to Maj. Patten that he would remain here until such time as you could make arrangements for our permanent protection.

It is to us a matter of regret that the friendly professions of the Indians when in the presence of a display of military force should have any weight in forming the opinion of men who have *perhaps* our fate in their hands, but it is nevertheless feared that such has been the case.

The object of this petition is to ask at your hands such aid as you may deem expedient and necessary, and we most earnestly request that you take our condition under serious consideration and have no doubt that you will coincide with us in the opinion that the establishment of a post at or near this place is necessary to the existence of our settlement.

Your position warrants us in a high opinion of your knowledge of Indian character and we feel confident that this appeal to you for protection will not be in vain.

[25 citizens' signatures; not listed here]

5:6 Letter, May to Henley

Hon. T. J. Henley   Oct. 11th 1854

Sir

Having learned that you have succeeded to the general Indian agency for the State of California, beg leave to present the following state of facts for your consideration, and upon which we most earnestly solicit some effectual action on your part. That the Indians in and immediately in the vicinity of the afore said place number at least one thousand, and that winter is now fast approaching, and that they are in an entire state of destitution, and that by the recent accumulation of miners and by their operations in mining in the Riverbeds have entirely destroyed the fishing facilities which has heretofore been the source of support of the Indians, and also the fact that there is an entire failure of the acorns, the two being the only resources by which life has heretofore been preserved to these poor specimins of humanity. The result of which is starvation and death to them, or some aid and relief from the Government through your kind interposition. The valley of Weaver is now settled with miners whose claims can only be worked in the winter for want of water, and without some aid from you one of three things is indispensable: abandon their claims entirely, suffer themselves to be robbed of their own means of subsistence, or an indiscriminate slaughter of the Indians. The former they will not do, the second is insufferable and the latter insulting to all the natural kind impulses of the heart. We are of the opinion that with kind treatment, with a bare pittance of the cheapest of food to sustain life these miserable creatures will be content, and the lives and property of our citizens made secure, and without which the result necessarily will be first, stealing and robbery of the property of the whites, and unnatural and disgraceful murder and indiscriminant slaughter of the wretched Indians in turn.

In view of the premises we most sincerely entreat you to use all efforts on your part to avert the evils above alluded to.

We are very respectfully
Your Obdt servt.
W. B. May Senator of 12th Senatorial
District
Isaac Farwell

Office Superintendent
Indian Affairs
Hon. G. W. Manypenny   San Francisco Dec. 22, 1854
Commr. Indian Affairs
Washington D. C.

Sir
The enclosed is a copy of a communication from a respectable gentleman in the N. East portion of the State in the Pitt River country. As it is utterly impracticable to afford any relief to the Indians he alludes to, I have taken the ground in my reply that my power under the law does not extend to feeding the Indians in their present locations, but is confined to their removal and subsistence upon reservations selected for that purpose.

Though it must be admitted that the Indians suffer immensely, and hundreds die every winter from actual starvation, I am still of the opinion that any attempt to feed them in their rancherias would be attended with a heavy expense and would result in little benefit to them.

I send but a portion of the communications I received on this subject, that the Department may have some idea of the current of public sentiment which I have to meet in inforcing what I believe to be the only policy which can ultimately result in the welfare of the Indians.

Very Respectfully
Your obt. Servt.
Thos. J. Henley
Sup. Indn. Affairs

Sir
The only apology I can offer for addressing you is the importance of the subject and the deep interest felt in it by

the people at least of this region. It should be but I believe is not generally known that the people of this section have been far more annoyed by Indian depredations than those of any other in the State.

Every winter since the first settlements were made on the East side of Sac[ramento] River the Rancheries have lost more or less stock. Last winter was particularly hard on us. They not only stole our animals by the drove, but murdered some thirteen persons for their provisions and animals.

They grow more troublesome in proportion that their natural means of subsistence diminishes. The country inhabited by the most mischevious and daring is north of Pitt River, whose course here is east and west, uniting with the Sacramento nearly at right angle. McCloud Fork about seven miles east of Sacramento and Squaw Creek about same distance east of McCloud Fork, the two later empty into Pitt River and head in the same direction of the Sacramento River, the two running parallel with each other through an exceedingly rough mountainous country producing little or nothing of the vegetable of such kind that the Indians require and is chiefly inhabited for the great quantities of Salmon with which these streams formerly abounded. It also afforded them a safe retreat for stolen stock as they could not well be pursued until the discovery of mines on Squaw Creek made about 18 months ago and the consequent establishment of Ferries across Pitt River, which gave access to their country. Last winter for the first time they were severely chastised for robberies and murders they committed. It is believed they are impelled to stealing by hunger. This I cannot for a moment doubt, brought about by the failure of salmon and deer both of which are rapidly disappearing owing of course to the improvement of the country by the whiteman. During this season they have barely been enabled to take sufficient salmon for their present use, and as for deer they are hunted so much by the whites that they have become so shy that with their imperfect impliments they find it useless and have long since abandoned hunting them at all.

From these causes they are reduced to the utmost destitution. Even at this early season their chiefs or Shaktoos are much alarmed. They begin to understand the whiteman's power and of course dread it.

The principle one called "Bull por mah" with all his family has lately removed from McCloud Fork to north Crow Creek to escape from the fate that hangs over these poor and unfortunate people. He says he knows his Indians will soon begin to steal and that it would have been out of his power to have prevented it had he remained among them.

A circumference of ninety miles almost would embrace nearly if not all troublesome Indians within reach of the settlements. From the best information these would not exceed fifteen hundred souls, perhaps not much above a thousand. Two bushells of barley or wheat to each individual [should be] issued to them as soon as possible at or near some point on Pitt River. Should this not be convenient Fort Reading would do, though it is some 25 or 30 miles distant. This would be a god send and be perfectly satisfactory to them and they would feel grateful. They would perhaps be willing to remove by another season. It would prove to them that their great Father would not permit them to starve whenever removed.

It would, too, most effectually protect the property of the settlers as well as preserve the lives of many of these wretched people.

It would be satisfactory to the community and would be most hastily approved by all good men. Nothing short of this or their immediate removal will be satisfactory; neither will it be just. It is earnestly hoped that you have the means and authority to give them such relief as their impoverished condition requires. It is nearly certain should they get no help that from starvation and punishment for theft one half their present number will have perished by next spring. Humanity and justice as well as the policy of the general government on other occasions towards this unfortunate class of human beings forbid that such event should be allowed to take place, at least if there is any possible way to avert it.

Please answer this communication as soon as convenient that we may know in time whether they are to have relief or not. If not, it will stand us in hand to adopt other means for the protection of life and property, either to raise by contributions means to partly feed them, or should this be impracticable then the only alternative will be to petition the Governor of the State to accept the service of a Volunteer Company during the winter, and force them to starvation with the swords.

Enclosed I send you the proceedings of a meeting held at Pittsburgh in February of last year, I was appointed to bear a copy to Col Wright at Fort Reading and to receive his answer which you will find at the bottom of proceedings to enable you to judge how far this establishment deserves to be relied on for the protection of life, to say nothing about property. I have undertaken this task with a good deal of diffidence at the earnest request of my neighbors who will bear evidence to the truth of the statement herein made. I will refer you to some of the first settlers, men of respectability and standing.

D. C. Johnson, Littleton Dryden, W. Houston, George Woodman, William Johnson, I. Douglass, W. Harris, all farmers. To Judge Daingerfield, R. T. Sprague or any other persons you may be acquainted with residing in this county. Permit me to assure you that in making these statements I am actuated by no personal or selfish motives. Could you witness their utter destitution and the extremities to which it drives them, the selling of their children, their wives and their daughters, you would pronounce on it as I do, and as any just and humane man who is opposed to immorality must, as disgraceful to our people, our Government and to those in whose hands their welfare is placed.

I do not mean any disrespect to you. I have known you many years, not personally but publicly, and have always approved your political sentiments, believing it to be for want of honest information on your part, that they have been thus far neglected.

Very Respectfully
Your obt. Servt.
John A. Dreibellis

Hon. T. H. Henley
Supt. Indn. Affrs.
San Francisco

Hon. Geo. W. Manypenny
Commissioner of Indian Affairs
Washington City

The undersigned Captains or Chiefs of the various tribes composing the Nation of Coweello [Cahuilla] Indians of California desire to present the following history of their grievances and statement of their wants in order that the United States Government being informed of their condition and necessities may adopt some measures for their assistance and relief.

The population of our nation is about 5000 of which about 1200 are men the rest women and children. From time immemorial we have lived upon and occupied the lands of and adjacent to the Pass of San Gorgonia bounded on the North by the Cajon de los Negros and on the South and West by the Coast Range of mountains. Since the occupation of California by the Americans and particularly within the last two or three years we have been encroached upon by the white settlers who have taken possession of a large portion of our best farming and grazing lands and by diverting the water from our lands deprive us to a great extent of the means of irrigation. In some instances the water privileges have been wholly monopolized by the white settlers thereby depriving us of the most essential means for the successful cultivation of our crops consisting of corn wheat beans etc. etc. We have thus been frequently obliged to abandon portions of our improved lands greatly to the detriment and distress of our people.

While most if not all the other tribes of Indians of California have received material aid and have protection from the Government we have been wholly neglected. In the year 1850 a treaty was entered into with us by O. U. Wozencraft an Agent of the Government but the said agent failed to comply with any of its conditions.

What we particularly desire and ask of the Government is that certain public lands may be set apart for our use exclusively (which lands we have long occupied and improved) and from which we may not be forced by white settlers. We would, also, ask that a reasonable amount of farming implements and oxen may be furnished us, in accordance with a uniform custom of the Government, together with such amount of means as may be necessary to improve our means of irrigation.

We further desire to represent that we have received from time to time during a series of years past a limited supply of Beef Cattle and other important aids from Isaac Williams of Rancho del Chino all of which has been furnished us gratuitously. But for his timely assistance many of our people must have been driven to starvation and others have suffered great distress until our crops were properly matured and gathered.

In conclusion while hoping that this our petition may receive just and reasonable attention from the Government of the United States, we particularly desire that any action had for our relief and assistance may be communicated to us through Isaac Williams of the Rancho del Chino, California.

Rancho del Chino
California 15th May 1856

			Juan Antoino–Principal Chief	(x)	his mark
Aperra			Juan Chappo	(x)	his mark
Juan Bautista	(x)	his mark	Tavo	(x)	his mark
Francisco	(x)	his mark	Cholo	(x)	his mark
Ignacio	(x)	his mark	Blass	(x)	his mark
Pantalion	(x)	his mark	Victor	(x)	his mark
Cigno	(x)	his mark	Miterio	(x)	his mark
Lourio	(x)	his mark	Padro	(x)	his mark
Francisco	(x)	his mark	Capitancio	(x)	his mark
Martine	(x)	his mark	Josa Antonio	(x)	his mark
Cabason	(x)	his mark	Tenio	(x)	his mark
Juan Apasio	(x)	his mark	Juan Josa	(x)	his mark
Antonio	(x)	his mark	Victoriano	(x)	his mark
			Josa	(x)	his mark

The above being duly interpreted and explained to the Captains whose names are attached above the same was affirmed in our presence

I. F. Stephens
F. I. Murray

5:9 Letter, Henley to Manypenny; petition, Siskiyou County citizens to McClelland

Office Supt Indian Affairs
San Francisco Cal.
August 7, 1856

Hon. G. W. Manypenny
Comm. of Ind. Affairs
Washington D. C.

Sir:

In conformity with the request of the petitioners, the accompanying memorial is herewith enclosed.

A portion of the Indians alluded to reside at Scotts Valley, Fort Jones, and have heretofore been the subject of correspondence between this office and Genl. Wool, Comdg. Pacific Division, a copy of which has already been furnished you.

These Indians have already been offered subsistence at the Nome Lackee Reservation, if they would consent to remove there, but they declined to do so; and are well aware of the position of Genl. Wool, that no force will be used by the United States troops to compel them to remove.

There is therefore but little hope of their being induced to remove at present.

There is no necessity for the appointment of an Agent in that County, unless on condition of their consenting to removal.

Very respectfully
Your Obt Svt
Thos. J. Henley
Supt Ind Affrs

To the Hon Robert McClelland, Secretary of the Interior

The undersigned citizens of Siskiyou County, State of California, would respectfully represent that within the extensive limits of this County there are a great many natives who from the settlement of the country by our white population are deprived of nearly all their means of subsistence, and that they are reduced to the necessity either of begging or committing thieving depredations upon the cattle, grain fields and property of our citizens to avoid starvation. Some adopt the first alternative, being chiefly old men, women & children and reside at or near Fort Jones in Scotts Valley and live upon the charity of the officers of that post and that of the citizens of the Valley; others and most of the young men of a more independent nature considering themselves grossly wronged in our thus usurping their soil prefer to assert what they deem their right by appropriating to their own use whatever they find necessary to their comfort or desires thus constantly creating difficulty and is the immediate cause of our indian wars which have cost so much life and property to our community. That we firmly believe that should there be a reservation established for their use in some proper place in this upper country and an equivalent be granted them in blankets, clothing, implements of husbandry, etc. for the land which we now occupy and a suitable person who is acquainted with them, their language and habits as also entitled to the respect of our citizens be appointed to reside with and superintend their affairs, all cause of difficulty and dissentions would be removed and that the Indians would readily come in and reside thereon and become quiet, orderly and peaceable and thus relieve us of heavy burdens and much inquietude.

That we have for a long time past been acquainted with Mr. Edward Wicks and can sincerely and cheerfully recommend him as a suitable person to receive the appointment of Sub Agent, he being one of the oldest settlers in this portion of the State and every way qualified for the station.

[21 signatures of citizens]

204

5:10 Newspaper article, San Francisco, 1856

Indian Affairs on the Pacific

For a long time past, and indeed throughout the whole of the continuance of the war with the Indians that has existed in Washington Territory, Oregon, and the northern part of this State, the papers published in those neighborhoods have teemed with strictures upon the course pursued by the officers in command of the U. S. troops, and strong condemnation of the policy by which they appear to have been governed. The Executive officers of each of those Territories have echoed the sentiments expressed in the papers, and have made severe charges against the government officers who were sent against the Indians. When the Regulars and the Volunteers were in the field together, it seemed almost impossible to get them to act in concert, and indeed they were occasionally almost opposed to each other. This state of things is the natural result of the pursuance by the officers of the U. S. Government, and the settlers and frontiersmen, of two lines of policy which are directly opposed to each other—the one, the policy of protection; the other, that of extermination. Indian affairs upon the Pacific coast have come to such a pass, that for the maintainance of peace in our borders, one policy or the other must be at once adopted and adhered to. Extermination is the quickest and cheapest remedy, and effectually prevents all after difficulty when an outbreak occurs. But that civilized men, and Americans at that, can be found to openly propose and advocate such a remedy, is disgraceful to our nation, whether we look only to the barbarity of the measure, or the neglect of the general government, which has permitted matters to get into such a state as even apparently to justify such a recommendation, or the adoption of such measures as would carry it into effect.

The policy of the government of the United States when sincerely acted upon and carried out is really benevolent, and the desire of those having the direction of Indian affairs at

Washington, is ostensibly to protect the Indians, and assist and encourage them while accustoming themselves to the new habits and modes of living which are forced upon them by the continual and rapid encroachments of their white neighbors upon their ancient hunting grounds. But while such feelings may influence the authorities at Washington, and even govern the actions of all honest agents of the government who deal directly with the Indians, a very different sort of desires appear to influence a large portion of the inhabitants of our border districts. With them every inconvenience the result of the contact of the two races is to be remedied only by driving the red men back or by their extermination.

We are told that the Indians are treacherous, that it is impossible for white men to live in safety while Indians remain in the neighborhood; that the whites are continually exposed to sudden and unexpected outbreaks on the part of the Indians, for which it is impossible to be prepared and fully to run the risk of. Therefore, it is necessary for the whites to rid themselves of the presence of the Indians. If they refuse to move upon the demand of the settlers, a relentless course of punishment for the most trivial offences is adopted, which is putting into operation without a declaration of war, the policy of extermination. A single instance in point, that occurred several years ago, in one of the northern counties of this State, may be given to illustrate the utter disregard of the lives of these human beings that exists in the breasts in many of the class of whom we speak. The Indians near a small mining camp, having discovered that one of the miners left his bowl of sugar upon a shelf directly under the canvass roof of his cabin, cut a hole in it and helped themselves to a pound or so of sugar, two or three times. The miner, who had a medicine chest with him, took an ounce of strychnine that was in it, and, mixing it with a larger quantity of sugar than usual, filled the bowl with it, and placing it in its former position went to his work. The Indians taking it again, as before, and, making somewhat of a feast with it, the result was that some eight or ten were killed outright, and as many more only recovered after suffering severely. What plea

206

can be urged to justify such an act as that? And yet though this act alone is enough to inspire horror, it is but one of many equally atrocious. The same principle has been and is yet carried out in nearly all the dealings of the white men with Indians. It is the cruel and extreme punishment of small offences, when committed by Indians, death being made to follow the slightest transgression, when light or trifling penalties only would have been visited upon the culprit had he been an American or other white man.

When life is taken in this way, is it wonderful if savages, the relatives of those who are killed, endeavor to revenge themselves? And is it surprising if the Indians, feeling their inability to cope with the white man openly, yet burning for revenge, seek it stealthily, and by assassination of single individuals? Is it wonderful that in seeking it thus they frequently take, by accident or purposely, the life of persons who have not injured them? In revenging injuries upon them have the whites always been particular in finding the precise culprit and punished him only? He is little conversant with the history of Indian affairs in this State who cannot call to mind instances where, when one or two white men had been found killed by Indians, (whether in defence of life itself, or their dearest rights, inquiry never being made) to revenge them, all the inhabitants of a rancheria or village, young and old—men, women and children, were put to death.

If one white man, no matter how worthless he may be, nor how deserving of death, be killed by Indians, it is published in every paper in the State, and revenge is loudly called for. But the Indians have no newspapers. They may suffer every wrong it is possible to heap upon an injured and oppressed people, and if it is done out of our cities or villages, and out of the sight of any save the wrong doers, the world may never hear of it. They have no newspapers, and few indeed are their friends and those who are willing to speak for them.

The facts bear us out in asserting, and it is apparent to every one who has ever lived in the mountains of the State, that white men by their oppression of, and injustice to, the

Indians, have been the means of bringing upon their fellows, and upon the innocent wives and children of unoffending settlers, all the horrors of Indian hostilities in almost every instance in which they have broken out on the Pacific border.

We shall consider the subject further and speak of the remedy.

5:11 Newspaper article, San Francisco, 1858

Indians of Shasta and Scott Valleys

George W. Taylor writes a letter to the Yreka *Union*, complaining of the manner in which the remnant of the Shasta and Scott Indians has been treated by the Government. He says that these Indians some time ago assembled at Fort Jones, Scott Valley, and gave up their arms on a promise of the United States of protection and support. From that time till about three months ago, these Indians have remained peaceable and quiet; and have been regularly supplied with food from the fort; as per agreement. About three months ago, this fort was abandoned; and some sixty or seventy Indians are thus left entirely destitute of adequate means of subsistence. They have no resource except hunting, picking berries, fishing and stealing. Mr. Tayler thus exposes the meagre nature of these resources:

As to hunting, if they had arms and ammunition they could obtain but a meagre supply, as nearly all the game has been driven off their hunting grounds by the whites, and they are too weak to trespass with impunity upon the hunting grounds of their neighbors. As to fishing, owing to the obstructions in the river, for which the Indians are not accountable, but few fish have made their appearance this high up the stream; and as for berries suitable for the food of man, they are like "angel's visits" as far as this region is concerned. The winter is at hand, and then the poor Indian has no other resource than to beg, steal or starve; and who doubts or can blame them for the result, if driven to extremities. We all know they will steal, and murder too, if necessary, to supply the wants of nature; and will they not be justified in so doing? Necessity knows no law, and was a maxim in jurisprudence, as long ago as the days of Solon and Lycurgus, and it is one of the few rules to which there is no exception.

I am informed that the U. S. officers at Fort Crook, in Pitt river valley, are issuing four hundred rations daily to the Pitt river Indians, and they certainly have far less claims upon the government for aid and support, than have the Indians of Shasta and Scott valleys.

It is suggested to call a meeting of the citizens of Yreka to petition the Indian Agent to extend some kind of relief to these starving savages.

5:12   Newspaper article, Sacramento, 1860

Indian Affairs

The bill introduced by Mr. Warner, to give to the State the control of the Indians within her limits, proposes to devolve the direct management of the Indians in each county to the Board of Supervisors. Wherever Reservations exist, they would come under the supervision of the Supervisors and the Sheriff. The latter would be, in each county, the civil and military executive officer. When he, with the power conferred upon him by the Board of Supervisors and the law, found himself unable to control the Indians in his county, a call to be made to the State for aid. In order to compensate the State for her guardianship in the matter, the bill provides that a contract be made with the General Government, under which the State should be paid $50,000 per annum for ten years. But that sum a Californian, who is well informed on Indian affairs, thinks is too small. In his opinion, the State should not undertake the job for less than $100,000 per annum.

This Indian question is likely to become a leading one in our State. The Indians within her borders are estimated at some 70,000; they are now professedly under the charge of the General Government, and their Agents and soldiers are scattered over the State, in Forts and on Reservations, to protect both citizens and Indians. Experience, however, has demonstrated that United States Infantry soldiers are of little use as a protecting shield against warlike Indians. They are too slow and too systematic. When Indians are to be punished for murder and robbery, volunteers are always relied upon.

In no State in the Union has the General Government so extensive an Indian establishment as in California, and unless some plan is devised by which the Indians can be confined to specific limits, the State, before ten more years pass, will be forced to demand that the General Government remove them from the State. This policy the National Government was compelled to adopt in the States of Georgia, Alabama and Mississippi. In Georgia and Alabama, the Governors ordered out troops with the avowed determination to drive the Indians beyond their limits. But the course of the United States rendered it unnecessary for the troops to act. In Alabama, General Scott carried out the orders of the Government in removing the Creek Indians. There is danger of a similar issue arising in California.

5:13　　Newspaper article, San Francisco, 1860

Calaveras Asking That Its Indians Be Slaughtered?
No––Fed!

Senator Bradley of Calaveras county, presented a petition from some of his constituents, complaining of annoyances from a feeble remnant of the Alvino tribe of Indians remaining in the neighborhood of Clay's Bar. The memorial did not ask for a company of volunteers, nor for Kibbe, nor Jarboe, nor a war; but asked that the Indians might be fed! All honor to the men of Calaveras. This is said to be the first ray of humanity, in respect to the native Americans of this State, which ever illuminated a California Legislature.

The Expatriation of Guiltless Indians at Humboldt Bay
Eureka, Cal., April 23, 1860

To the Editor of the San Francisco *Bulletin*: — The last act in the tragic drama of murder and oppression, which began on Humboldt Bay on the 26th of February last, has just been performed. The friendly aborigines, in number of 450, have been removed from Humboldt county. Those on Mad river, about 120 in number, were first forcibly expelled from their residences, herded like cattle, and all, under the fear of death, had to leave their homes, as dear to them as ours are to us. These Indians are not of the bands of Diggers roving from hill to hill, to whom it would be but a matter of indifference on which they were, as the Humboldt *Times* might lead people at a distance to think, but are measurably civilized. Some of them speak our language, they have mingled with the whites, and are accustomed to aid in their domestic concerns. Printed accounts show plainly a violation of section 2d, chapter 133, of the statutes of the State of California, in the removal of the Indians from Mad river, which reads: "*Nor shall they (the Indians) be forced to abandon their homes in villages where they have resided for a number of years.*" This act was passed on April 22, 1850. It would have moved a heart of stone, to have seen these poor creatures grieving, burning up their boats and houses, and then driven from their homes—their "sacred hearths"—from the graves of their murdered relatives—from the land of their forefathers—a land still their own, for it has never been purchased, nor have they received one iota as *quid pro quo* for all this country.

It becomes us now to correct false impressions which have gone abroad (mainly propagated by a mendacious print here—probably pandering for votes,) by giving a statement easily verified by any disinterested person, proving that the objections to this population were without foundation. In many cases these Indians were useful. They were divers and hands at the fisheries; they were harvesters, aiding the whites in getting in their grain, and bringing them berries, fish and clams; they were packers and guides to the mountain trains; while their wives were of much service to the ladies of Eureka on their washdays and in other household duties.

Now to consider the objections: They were "Indians". Well, that is true and God forbid that color should be a criterion of merit in this country. They killed nobody— neither women, children nor cattle; they troubled nobody, and nobody's property; they never were drunk nor drank liquor, and really were the most inoffensive and harmless Indians, perhaps, the world ever saw. But, says the newspaper, they had *beef*—it was seen at Eel river, and on Indian Island; and they supplied the mountain tribes with 'ammunition' to kill men and cattle. Now the beef seen on Eel river was part of a seal. In its smoked condition it looked like beef, but it was not. And for what purpose they had beef on Indian Island, it is strange, for there neither man woman nor child would touch beef. It is well known to families in Eureka that they have a superstitious antipathy to eating that kind of food, and are known to have thrown away meat given them. Well, the "ammunition"? Now who should have been punished for the supply, if furnished to the mountain tribes? But we hear nothing of that now, since it has been ascertained that these latter killed the cattle with bows and arrows. A man whose business gives him the opportunity to know, says that the last cow shot with a gun was nine months ago; and poor Ellison, the last man killed, (a year since,) was rashly following up some twenty Indians—seen carrying off beef—with his party of about four men, firing into them, and had actually killed two Indians before, in a return of arrows, one wounded him in the groin, from which he died a few days subsequently.

Facts also disprove all friendship between those poor creatures of the bay and the mountain tribes, for not one of them fled to them for succor, but took to the bush and elsewhere, when their wives and children were butchered, and they hunted for their precious lives. Some six years past a party of them went to the mountains to pick acorns, and carried fish to purchase the privilege; but the mountain Indians scattered their fish along the road, and killed two of them. They have never been there since. These mountain tribes would murder them all if they could, and I blush for my color when remembering their allies. These unhappy Indians were killed for no crime whatever. They were slain on account of a false military *prestige*, or resentment to higher powers for not mustering a band of restless whites into service; and the survivors have been driven from their homes to convey a false impression.

Individuals constitute a community, and the acts of each member make up the common character of the whole body. It must be expected that villians will grumble and snarl; but it is the duty of the Press, the Bench, the Pulpit and of every honest man, to denounce crime. This is a duty which we owe to Heaven and the society in which we live— not merely a passive duty, for their villainies must go unpunished, and each good citizen will be victimized in his turn—but an active, zealous duty, bringing to justice especially those who out-savage the savage. We must not lay the flattering unction to our souls that in the great day of account and retribution, when the catalogue of human frailties and crimes is read out, we have disapproved sufficiently by our silence alone, lest the Mine Tekel—"thou art weighed in the balance and found wanting"—be pronounced against us, and "thou shouldst not follow a multitude to do evil."Exodus

5:15   Newspaper article, San Francisco, 1861

The Case of Our Northern Indians

The *Bulletin* has so often expressed its abhorrence of the indiscriminate slaughter of Indians in California, that it is not easy to intensify its position on that subject. Yet the constant repetition, on a large scale, of the same kind of outrages against humanity, renders it impossible to abstain from frequent reference to this crying evil. We published on Wednesday a letter for a gentleman who has long held a position connected with one of the Indian agencies in the northern part of the State, giving an account of a "battle" with the Wylackies, which took place in the neighborhood of Eel river on or about the 12th instant. The party attacking was composed of 10 white men and 50 picked Indians, of the Pitt river, Hat Creek and Concow tribes, while the Wylackies numbered from 400 to 500. The "battle" lasted from 10 to 15 minutes. More than 100 of Wylackies were killed, and one of the assailing party was dangerously wounded with an arrow. This account of the loss on the respective sides will give a pretty fair idea of the dangers of Indian fighting in California. The account continues: "There are thousands of these Wylackies yet left, and if this summary punishment does not intimidate them, it is feared that there will be many bloody massacres during the approaching winter."

Today we publish a communication from a prominent citizen of Humboldt county, containing a comprehensive description of the evils which the people of the northern part of the State suffer from Indian depredations. While we believe the manner in which the Indians are being exterminated is perfectly horrible, we are disposed to make every possible allowance for our own people. Throughout the region of the State referred to by our correspondent, the Indians are undoubtedly very annoying. They are becoming more and more accustomed to live on what they can steal, and it is almost impossible to settle the country and bring it under cultivation in consequence of the constant depredations of these natural enemies to civilization. The sentiment is steadily gaining among the people who have repeatedly had friends slain, or suffered loss of property, by Indians, that extermination of the aborigines is the only safety of the whites. This will certainly become the prevailing sentiment, and the Indians between Clear Lake and the Oregon boundary, on both sides of the Coast Range, numbering probably several thousands, will

214

all be killed within a short time unless Government assumes the task of saving their lives. In a few weeks the accumulation of snow on the mountains will again force them into the villages on both slopes of the Coast Range. Of course, they will depredate on the whites—drive off cattle, steal anything that will make food, and occasionally burn the houses of the settlers and commit murder. And, on the other hand, they will suffer fearful retaliation, as we have seen, until they are swept from the face of the earth.

The only remedy for this unhappy state of things must come from Government. Our correspondent suggests that Col. Wright send 200 of the mounted cavalry now being enlisted, to spend the winter along the Oregon mail route, which extends through the heart of the country inhabited by these troublesome Indians. It seems reasonable that this request should be granted, considering that the regular troops on this coast are being ordered East. Under good management it is at least possible for an efficient body of cavalry, during the winter, to compel most of the Indians now at large in the part of the State referred to, to congregate on the various reservations. There is an alternative before them that cannot be avoided: either they will be killed by the enraged settlers as speedily as possible, or else they must be gathered from the wilderness to learn the rudiments of civilization, to the end that they may continue to live without provoking constant aggression. If Government fails to act in putting into operation its humane policy of reclaiming the savages, its inactivity must be regarded as constructive license to the horrible butchery which is rapidly becoming an organized system.

5:16   Newspaper article, San Francisco, 1864

A New Policy Suggested Towards the California Indian

The Mendocino *Herald* of 22d April says:
Humboldt and Mendocino counties have suffered severe-

ly in times past, from the depredations of the wild roving tribes that infest this section of the country. Almost every system of treatment adopted heretofore by the Department at Washington has proved abortive, and we feel convinced that there is but one course to be pursued towards these treacherous red skins. We have long since thought they should be collected together and removed to some remote district of country, away from the settlements, or to an island in the sea, and there protected by the Government. The Indians are not so numerous now but what this would be feasible. Those of them that cannot be brought upon a reservation should be considered as guerrilas, and treated accordingly. This latter might seem harsh treatment, but those who have spent a number of years in an Indian country know full well that this is the only policy to be adopted for the protection and safety of the whites.

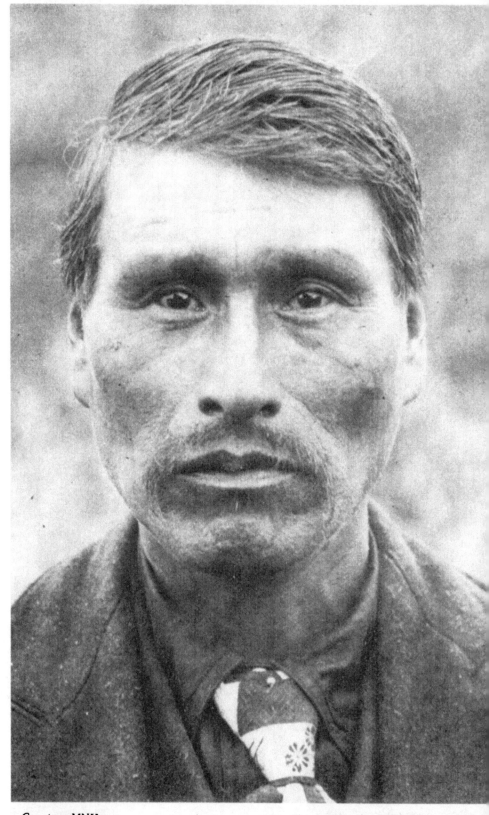

Courtesy MNH

Shasta man, Klamath Billy. *Photo 190*

INDENTURE, KIDNAPPING AND SALE OF INDIANS

The Act for the Government and Protection of Indians was passed in the first session of the California State legislature. It was amended in 1860. Securing Indian children for indenture or outright sale was common in California from 1850 to 1863, when the Act was repealed in conformity with federal emancipation procedures. The capturing and disposal of Indian children was, of course, not a matter of record, and the letters and newspaper accounts presented here (see also 2:7, 2:8, 2:10) attest to existence in California of what can only be classed as a particular and local form of slavery. It has been estimated that about 10,000 Indians may have been indentured or sold between 1850 and 1863.

An Act for the Government and Protection of Indians
April 22, 1850

The People of the State of California, represented in Senate and Assembly, do enact as follows:

1. Justices of the Peace shall have jurisdiction in all cases of complaints by, for, or against Indians, in their respective Townships in this State.

2. Persons and proprietors of land on which Indians are residing, shall permit such Indians peaceably to reside on such lands, unmolested in the pursuit of their usual avocations for the maintenance of themselves and families: *Provided*, the white person or proprietor in possession of lands may apply to a Justice of the Peace in the Township where the Indians reside, to set off to such Indians a certain amount of land, and, on such application, the Justice shall set off a sufficient amount of land for the necessary wants of such Indians, including the site of their village or residence, if they so prefer it; and in no case shall such selection be made to the prejudice of such Indians, nor shall they be forced to abandon their homes or villages where they have resided for a number of years; and either party feeling themselves aggrieved, can appeal to the County Court from the decision of the Justice: and then divided, a record shall be made of the lands so set off in the Court so dividing them and the Indians shall be permitted to remain thereon until otherwise provided for.

3. Any person having or hereafter obtaining a minor Indian, male or female, from the parents or relations of such Indian minor, and wishing to keep it, such person shall go before a Justice of the Peace in his Township, with the parents or friends of the child, and if the Justice of the Peace becomes satisfied that no compulsory means have been used to obtain the child from its parents or friends, shall enter on record, in a book kept for that purpose, the sex and probable age of the child, and shall give to such person a certificate,

authorizing him or her to have the care, custody, control, and earnings of such minor, until he or she obtain the age of majority. Every male Indian shall be deemed to have attained his majority at eighteen, and the female at fifteen years.

4. Any person having a minor Indian in his care, as described in the foregoing Section of this Act, who shall neglect to clothe and suitably feed such minor Indian, or shall inhumanly treat him or her, on conviction thereof shall be subject to a fine not less than ten dollars, at the discretion of a Court or Jury; and the Justice of the Peace, in his discretion, may place the minor Indian in the care of some other person, giving him the same rights and liabilities that the former master of said minor was entitled and subject to.

5. Any person wishing to hire an Indian, shall go before a Justice of the Peace with the Indian, and make such contract as the Justice may approve, and the Justice shall file such contract in writing in his office, and all contracts so made shall be binding between the parties; but no contract between a white man and an Indian, for labor, shall otherwise be obligatory on the part of the Indian.

6. Complaints may be made before a Justice of the Peace, by white persons or Indians; but in no case shall a white man be convicted of any offence upon the testimony of an Indian.

7. If any person forcibly conveys an Indian from his home, or compels him to work, or perform any service against his will, in this State, except as provided in this Act, he or they shall, on conviction, be fined in any sum not less than fifty dollars, at the discretion of the Court or jury.

8. It shall be the duty of the Justices of the Peace, once in six months in every year, to make a full and correct statement to the Court of Sessions of their county, of all moneys received for fines imposed on Indians, and all fees allowed for services rendered under the provisions of this Act; and said Justices shall pay over to the County Treasurer of their respective counties, all money they may have received for fines and not appropriated, or fees for services rendered under this Act; and the Treasurer shall keep a correct statement of all money so received, which shall be

termed the "Indian Fund" of the county. The Treasurer shall pay out any money of said funds in his hands, on a certificate of a Justice of the Peace of his county, for fees and expenditures incurred in carrying out the provisions of this law.

9. It shall be the duty of Justices of the Peace, in their respective townships, as well as all other peace officers in this State, to instruct the Indians in their neighborhood in the laws which relate to them, giving them such advice as they may deem necessary and proper; and if any tribe or village of Indians refuse or neglect to obey the laws, the Justice of the Peace may punish the guilty chiefs or principal men by reprimand or fine, or otherwise reasonably chastise them.

10. If any person or persons shall set the prairie on fire, or refuse to use proper exertions to extinguish the fire when the prairies are burning, such person or persons shall be subject to fine or punishment, as a Court may adjudge proper.

11. If any Indian shall commit an unlawful offence against a white person, such person shall not inflict punishment for such offence, but may, without process, take the Indian before a Justice of the Peace, and on conviction, the Indian shall be punished according to the provisions of this Act.

12. In all cases of trial between a white man and an Indian, either party may require a jury.

13. Justices may require the chiefs and influential men of any village to apprehend and bring before them or him any Indian charged or suspected of an offence.

14. When an Indian is convicted of an offence before a Justice of the Peace punishable by fine, any white may, by consent of the Justice, give bond for said Indian, conditioned for the payment of said fine and costs, and in such case the Indian shall be compelled to work for the person so bailing, until he has discharged or cancelled the fine assessed against him: Provided, the person bailing shall treat the Indian humanely, and clothe and feed him properly; the allowance given for such labor shall be fixed by the Court, when the bond is taken.

15. If any person in this State shall sell, give, or furnish

to any Indian, male or female, any intoxicating liquors (except when administered in sickness), for good cause shown, he, she, or they so offending shall, on conviction thereof, be fined not less than twenty dollars for each offence, or be imprisoned not less than five days, or fined and imprisoned, as the Court may determine.

16. An Indian convictied of stealing horses, mules, cattle, or any valuable thing, shall be subject to receive any number of lashes not exceeding twenty-five, or shall be subject to a fine not exceeding two hundred dollars, at the discretion of the Court or Jury.

17. When an Indian is sentenced to be whipped, the Justice may appoint a white man, or an Indian at his discretion, to execute the sentence in his presence, and shall not permit unnecessary cruelty in the execution of the sentence.

18. All fines, forfeitures, penalties recovered under or by this Act, shall be paid into the treasury of the county, to the credit of the Indian Fund as provided in Section Eight.

19. All white persons making application to a Justice of the Peace, for confirmation of a contract with or in relation to an Indian, shall pay the fee, which shall not exceed two dollars for each contract determined and filed as provided in this Act, and for all other services, such fees as are allowed for similar services under other laws of this State. *Provided*, the application fee for hiring Indians, or keeping minors, and fees and expenses for setting off lands to Indians, shall be paid by the white person applying.

20. Any Indian able to work and support himself in some honest calling, not having wherewithal to maintain himself, who shall be found loitering and strolling about, or frequenting public places were liquors are sold, begging, or leading an immoral or profligate course of life, shall be liable to be arrested on the complaint of any resident citizen of the county, and brought before any Justice of the Peace of the proper county, Mayor or Recorder of any incorporated town or city, who shall examine said accused Indian, and hear the testimony in relation thereto, and if said Justice, Mayor or Recorder shall be satisfied that he is a vagrant, as above set forth, he shall make out a warrant under his hand and seal,

authorizing and requiring the officer having him in charge or custody, to hire out such vagrant within twenty-four hours to the best bidder, by public notice given as he shall direct, for the highest price that can be had, for any term not exceeding four months; and such vagrant shall be subject to and governed by the provisions of this Act, regulating guardians and minors, during the time which he has been so hired. The money received for his hire, shall, after deducting the costs, and the necessary expense for clothing for said Indian, which may have been purchased by his employer, be, if he be without a family, paid into the County Treasury, to the credit of the Indian fund. But if he have a family, the same shall be appropriated for their use and benefit: *Provided*, that any such vagrant, when arrested, and before judgment, may relieve himself by giving to such Justice, Mayor or Recorder, a bond, with good security, conditioned that he will, for the next twelve months, conduct himself with good behavior, and betake to some honest employment for support.

Amendments in 1860 to the Act of April 1850

Chap. CCXXXI—An Act amendatory of an Act entitled "An Act for the Government and Protection of Indians," passed April twenty-second, one thousand eight hundred and fifty. [Approved April 18, 1860.]

The People of the State of California, represented in Senate and Assembly, do enact as follows:

SECTION 1. Section third of said act, is hereby amended so as to read as follows:

Sec. 3. County and District Judges in the respective counties of this State, shall, by virtue of this act, have full power and authority, at the instance and request of any person having or hereafter obtaining an Indian child or children, male or female, under the age of fifteen years, from the parents or person or persons having the care or charge of such child or children, with the consent of such parents or person or persons having the care or charge of any such child or children, or at the instance and request of any person desirous of obtaining any Indian or Indians, whether children or grown persons, that may be held as prisoners of war, or at the instance and request of any person desirous of obtaining any vagrant Indian or Indians, as have no settled habitation or means of livelihood, and have not placed themselves under the protection of any white person, to bind and put out such Indians as apprentices, to trades, husbandry, or other employments, as shall to them appear proper, and for this purpose shall execute duplicate articles of indenture of apprenticeship on behalf of such Indians, which indentures shall also be executed by the person to whom such Indian or Indians are to be indentured; one copy of which shall be filed by the County Judge, in the Recorder's office of the county, and one copy retained by the person to whom such Indian or Indians may be indentured; such indentures shall authorize such person to have the care, custody, control, and earnings, of such Indian or Indians, as shall require such person to clothe and suitably provide the necessaries of life for such Indian or Indians, for and during the term for which such Indian or Indians shall be apprenticed, and shall contain the sex, name, and probable age, of such Indian or Indians; such indentures may be for the following terms of years: Such children as are under fourteen years of age, if males, until they attain the age of twenty-five years; if females, until they attain the age of twenty-one years; such as are over fourteen and under twenty years of age, if males, until they attain the age of thirty years; if females, until they attain the age of twenty-five years; and such Indians as may be over the age of twenty years, then next following the date of such indentures, for and during the term of ten years, at the discretion of such Judge; such Indians as may be indentured under the provision of this section, shall be deemed within such provisions of this act, as are applicable to minor Indians.

SEC. 2. Section seventh of said act is hereby amended so as to read as follows:

Sec. 7. If any person shall forcibly convey any Indian from any place without this State, to any place within this State, or from his or her home within this State, or compel him or her to work or perform any service, against his or her

225

will, except as provided in this act, he or they shall, upon conviction thereof, be fined in any sum not less than one hundred dollars, nor more than five hundred dollars, before any court having jurisdiction, at the discretion of the court, and the collection of such fine shall be enforced as provided by law in other criminal cases, one-half to be paid to the prosecutor, and one-half to the county in which such conviction is had.

6:2   Letter, White to Henley

T. J. Henley Esq.   Mendocino, May 13th 1855
Supt. Ind. Affrs.

Dr. Sir: I expected to have heard from you, or to have seen you here, in person, and consequently delayed writing to you for some time, but now the clamors of the people here are so great and the cause so just that it is actually necessary to do something with the Indians. I forward you a letter on the subject written to me by the inhabitants settled on this coast, and would suggest that their requests be complied with, if possible, and also that you give me authority to hunt for them (the Indians) and employ a couple or three men to help me as game is abundant, and a few men could feed several thousand, and thereby prevent them from coming down to the Coast for fish, and the Coast being the cultivated part of this country, would thereby be in a great measure rid of the evil. I wrote to you about three months ago. I should like an answer to this letter as soon as possible.

With respect, Yours and etc.
Robt. White

P. S. May 17th, 1855. Since writing the foregoing (May 13) I have just learned that a man named McDonald, with others who live on Cache Creek, has stolen three Indians, a woman and two boys, and started for home with them by a by-road and intends to sell them or trade them for cattle, which has been much practiced of late by parties from a distance. If you wish me to follow them and recover the Indians, let me know when you write, and also give me some general directions.

I remain Yours, with respect,
Robt. White

6:3   Letter, White to Henley

Col. T. J. Henley   Mendocino Aug. 9, 1855

Sir

I have just returned after a twenty day hunt amongst the mountain Indians with the intention of hunting for those on the Coast, but I am compelled to return on account of some Spaniards that have been kidnapping some Indians belonging to the Metomas tribe which live about 25 miles from the Coast. According to the Indian reports they say the Spaniards stole twenty or twenty five young women and killed one. They say they know where the Spaniards live and want me to go with them and get their people back. They were taken to Belloncki Valley which is about 20 miles East of (Metom Ki) or Big Valley. I intend starting in the morning after them and will use every exertion to get them back, and if possible, have the offenders brought to justice.

I remain yours with respect
Robert White

6:4   Letters, White to Henley (2)

Mah-to Valley

Col. T. J. Henley   Aug 20th 1855

Your letter of July 23rd came to Camp on the 17th Inst. in which you informed me that you expected to pay us a visit this month, and I am anxiously looking for your arrival.

I informed you in my last that I was going to start in pursuit of some kidnapers, but when I visited the tribe the children were stolen from, I learned that they had made their escape, and returned to their tribe. On the 17th inst. an Indian came to our Camp and reported that two white men and a party of Indians had stolen from their tribe a lot of Squaws and children and were taking them away. I immediately started in pursuit and succeeded in getting them all back, which was thirteen in number, all females. The two white men said that they were from Clear Lake and was on an Elk hunt, and pretended not to have anything to do with the prisoners. The Indians with them numbered between fifty and sixty, and were all well armed, some having guns. After they had left, I learned that they had killed one old Squaw and shot a little boy with an arrow, which I think will kill him. After learning the above, I immediately started in pursuit of the two white men, but they had too much the start, and I could not overtake them.

I remain Yr. Obt. Servt.

Robt. White

Col. T. J. Henley   Mendocino Sept. 1st 1855
    Sir
    Since writing my last I have been busily engaged among the Indians in hunting and looking after them. I have heard nothing more about kidnappers, and the Indians have become quiet again. Since my commencement of hunting for the Indians, they have been very peaceable and have committed no depredations worth speaking of. I have visited and hunted for 15 different tribes of Indians numbering, as near as I can ascertain, from four to five thousand. Since June 4th (which was the day I commenced hunting) I have killed twenty three Elks, two hundred and sixteen deer, and seven Bears, which I distributed as equally as I could among the above number of Indians.

Very Respectfully, Your Obt. Servt.

Robert White

Fort Bragg Cal.
May 31st 1861

Captain

I have the honor to report that there are several parties of citizens now engaged in stealing or taking by force Indian children from the district in which I have been ordered to operate against the Indians.

I am reliably informed that as many as forty or fifty Indian children have been taken through Long Valley within the last few months and sold both in and out of the county.

The parties, I am told, at least some of them, make no secret of it; but boldly assert that they will continue to do so and that the law cannot reach them. It is pretended I believe that the children are purchased from their parents; but all who know these Indians can fully appreciate the value of this assertion. It is needless to say that this brutal trade is calculated to produce retaliatory depredations on the part of the Indians and exasperate them to a high degree; as how as to interfere materially with our efforts to find and chasten those Indians that deserve punishment, for these men keep the Indians constantly on the alert, attacking and chasing them before us and following in our wake for the purpose of obtaining children.

Very respectfully your most obt servt
Edward Dillon 2d. Lt., 6th Inf.

Capt. C. S. Lovell   Comdg. Detachment in the Field
Comdg. Sixth Infy., USA
Fort Humboldt, Cal.

Office of Ind. Affairs
Northern Dis. California
Hon Chas. E. Mix   Yuba City July 23rd 1861

Sir

In answer to your letter of June 1st, 1861 concerning the present laws and regulations connected with your department, and the changes that are deemed necessary, I beg leave to say,

Not being in possession of any of the laws (which I would be pleased to have sent me) I cannot give you an answer based upon my personal knowledge, of the defects or changes therein necessary. But upon information otherwise obtained, I am of the opinion that it is of first importance to the interest of the Indian work in California that the following changes be made, viz.

2nd   The laws should be so changed or made as to protect the Indians against kidnapers. There is a Statute in California providing for the indenturing of Indians to white people for a term of years. Hence under cover of this law (as I think unconstitutional) many persons are engaged in hunting Indians (see my report of this month). Even regular organized companies with their Pres., Sec. and Treas. are now in the mountains and while the troops are engaged in killing the men for alleged offences, the kidnapers follow in close pursuit, seize the younger Indians and bear them off to the white settlements in every part of the country filling the orders of those who have applied for them at rates, varying from $50 to $200 a piece, and all this is being done under a plea of "Kindness to the poor Indians". Such acts of injustice and violence are now tolerated by an unconstitutional law (as I believe) of this state (see my last report).

3rd   The law should provide that in the selection and permanent establishment of reservations for Indian purposes, they be made in districts of country shut out by mountains and other natural barriers from the white population entirely.

Demonstrations abound in California that in the contact of the two races the Indian soon falls a prey to the demoralizing vices of the unprincipled white man: disease and death following in the train.

4th   As an antidote for such evils, I beg leave to suggest that all the troops stationed on those reservations be removed and their stations turned over to the use of the reservation, and in lieu of said troops, to increase the laboring force, providing them with fire arms and other means of defence, and that no other officers or laborers shall be employed hereafter on said reservations except such as have a wife along with them.

The example and influence of unarmed white men cannot but have a happy effect among the indian women and their rising posterity, and they can be made very useful in the instruction of the women in the cutting and making up clothes for themselves and families, and also by teaching their children the rudimentary branches of an English education.

From my personal observations I know the effect produced by a contact between the two races is anything but desirable, honorable or profitable, as demonstrations abound in the shape of half breeds, jealousies, disease and death on every hand.

In connection with this, allow me to say, an increase of the wages of the laborers is indispencible in order to procure competent married men and their wives. $75 per month will be necessary.

5th   That no provisions or supplies be furnished to the employees by the Government, except that which they produce on the reservations.

6th   A special act enlarging the Round Valley and Klamath reservations (see report of this month and the enclosed memoranda of boundaries) also the selling out of the Nome Lackee and Mendocino reserves together with an appropriation sufficient to pay the settlers in Round Valley for their improvements and removing them who now cultivate their farms with indian labor, and many of them use squaws for housekeepers, and this state of things cannot be prevented if they are allowed to remain, and I am told they made those

231

settlements at the instance and by the permission of one of the first agents of Government.

The laws should be so changed as to give efficiency to the efforts of the men superintending agents of California and a sufficient appropriation at once made to place the institution in a respectable light before the Country, and make it a desirable and happy home for the poor indians. As hitherto conducted, the indians have looked upon the reservations rather as a hell than a home, and when they talk about their future Spirit land where deer and fish abound, among other blessings of that land, they aver that the white man can never get there.

7th A Clerk, black smith and physician is indispensable on each Reservation. Should any thing else occur to my mind of importance, I will advise you of the same.

I have the honor to be etc.

Geo. M. Hanson
Supt. Ind. Affrs N. Dist. Cal.

6:7   Letters, Henley to Manypenny; Wood to Henley

Hon Geo W Manypenny   Washington April 14th 1856
Comm of Indian Affairs

Sir: I have the honor to enclose herewith a communication of the Hon R. N. Wood, Judge of the Court of Sessions of Contra Costa County Cal, in relation to the compensation which ought to be allowed to Maj. Wm. McDaniel for conducting certain prosecutions in that state for the offence of kidnapping Indians and selling them into servitude. It was agreed between Maj. McDaniel and myself at the time he was employed in that service, that he should receive for his services in bringing to trial, persons guilty of this offence, one hundred dollars per month and such fee for conducting the prosecutions as should be approved by the Commissioner of

Indian Affairs. It was deemed by me absolutely imperative upon the Department to take such decisive steps as would speedily put an end to this infamous practice. The traffic was conducted by Mexicans desperate in their character and difficult to arrest. They reside at remote points in the vicinity of the Indians, and were strongly banded together by the prospects of gain in this inhuman trade. Their character for desperation, recklessness and revenge being so well known, there was but few men who were willing to risk their lives in prosecuting them. It would have been utterly useless to depend for one moment on the district attorney of each county to conduct these prosecutions. Being liable to the midnight assaults of these desperadoes, they shrank from the duty of executing the laws and there was no alternative but to employ counsel or fail entirely in the object of suppressing this crime. It is proper to say that the practice had been carried to an extraordinary extent. I have undoubted evidence that hundreds of Indians have been stolen and carried into the settlements and sold; in some instances entire tribes were taken en masse, driven to a convenient point, and such as were suitable for servants, selected from among them, generally the children and young women, while the old men and the infirm were left to starve or make their way back to their mountain homes, as best they could. In many other cases it has come to my knowledge that the fathers and mothers have been brutally killed when they refused assistance to the taking away of their children. One instance of this kind came under my own observation.

I recommended that in the cases alluded to by Judge Wood, as they had been tried twice in Solano county where the jury failed to agree on account of Mexican influence on them by change of venue and Judge Wood. That Maj. McDaniel be allowed a fee of five hundred dollars and one hundred dollars each for other causes tried by him in Nappa and other counties, not to exceed in all, the sum of eight hundred dollars.

Very Respectfully, Thos. J. Henley
Supt Ind Affairs, Cal

Thos. J. Henley Esq.   Washington City, March 18, 1856

Sir
     Your favor making inquiries of me relative to the
professional services rendered by Wm McDaniel as attorney in
certain causes wherein the U. S. were prosecutors of various
persons for kidnapping Indians in California. In reply it affords me pleasure to state that Mr. M.D. appeared before the
Court of Sessions of Contra Costa County, of which I was
presiding Judge and successfully prosecuted to conviction
several persons who violated the laws of U. S. and of California in kidnapping Indians, that those causes were tried before
me on a change of venue, and that Mr. M. D.'s services were
well worth five hundred Dollars, that those prosecutions were
the immediate and direct means by which the kidnapping of
Indians in that section of California was broken up, and that
Mr. M. D. is not only entitled to fair compensation but the
thanks of all good citizens. I am pleased to add from actual
knowledge that his efforts were held in high estimation by
the people. The sum I indicate for professional services is but
of a minimum amount and should be paid him at once.

                              Very truly
                              R. N. Wood

6:8   Letters, Whiting to Commissioner of
        Indian Affairs; Davis to McClelland

                              Department of the Interior
                              Washington, May 20th 1855

Sir
     For your information I enclose herewith a copy of a
communication from the Secretary of War of the 23 instant,
addressed to this Department, on the subject of the application of the Superintendent of Indian Affairs in California

to General Wool for a detachment of Soldiers to capture certain Spaniards under indictment for kidnapping Indians, which application was not granted.

I am, Sir, very respectfully
Your Obt. Servant
Geo. A. Whiting
Commissioner of Indian Affairs   Acting Secretary

War Department
Washington May 23, 1855

Sir:

I have the honor to acknowledge the receipt of your letter of the 17th instant with enclosures from the commissioner of Indian Affairs, and the Superintendent of Indian Affairs in California, in regard to an application made by the latter to General Wool for a detachment of Soldiers to capture certain Spaniards under indictment for kidnapping Indians, which application was not granted.

The commissioner asks that Genl. Wool may be authorized to detail a Military force whenever called on by the Superintendent to enable him to carry out in good faith the provisions of law, and the obligations of the Government to afford protection to the Indians, etc.

In the particular case mentioned by the Superintendent it would seem to be the appropriate duty of the civil officers to arrest the persons under indictment, and if aid be necessary, the *posse comitatus* is their proper reliance.

On being assigned to the command of the Department of the Pacific, General Wool was instructed to confer freely with the Indian Agents and to give them all needful aid in the execution of their duties, affording them the countenance and support of the Military power, which are so essential in the negotiation of treaties and in all dealings with Savage tribes.

These instructions would seem to be sufficient for all ordinary cases that may arise, and I cannot consent to enlarge the scope of them to the extent requested by the commissioner of Indian Affairs.

Very respectfully Your obt. Servt.
Jeffn. Davis
Hon. R. M. Clelland   Secretary of War
Secretary of the Interior

6:9   Newspaper article, Marysville, 1861

Child Stealing

A day or two ago a couple of gentlemen of this city, were out near the tules in Colusa county, when they came across a party of men, who had in charge five Indian children about three or four years old, three of them being girls, and two were boys:— The Marysville gentlemen were asked if they could not provide homes for these young heathen, their holders saying that their parents had been killed in battle and they were without anyone to care for them. The parties referred to said that they would see what could be done and went out again yesterday, having found homes for two, but the men who had them said that they must have some pay *for their trouble* and put the amount at which they would part with the children at $50, or such a matter. This, of course, showed that these men were *selling* the children, and the gentlemen, who would have placed the young ones where they would be taken care of, came over to town and lodged information with the Supt. of Indian Affairs, for the district, and he went out in pursuit of the party with an officer. The men were arrested and brought to Yuba City, with the children, who were taken in charge by Mr. Hanson. Subsequently it was found that these fellows had been in possession of nine children, of various ages, a day or two before, and were seen coming out of the Coast Range with them, and one of three, which had been disposed of to a Mr. Carmen, who lives eight or ten miles below Yuba City, was found in his possession, driving a lot of hogs to Washoe. The older two were on his

236

ranch, and he testifies that that he had contracted to pay $80 for the hog-driving boy, eight or ten years old, and $55 for a younger one. The third was left in his possession until a purchaser could be found. The men arrested for this crime, gave their names as Laurie Johnson, *alias* Lewis, formerly of Texas; Jas. Wood, of Green county, Illinois, and James Freak, of New York State, born in Canada. They gave a confused and contradictory account of themselves, and claim to have brought the children from Humboldt county. They were brought before Judge Keyser of Humboldt county, and on the affidavit of Mr. Hanson were sent to Humboldt county, where the offence was committed, for trial. The children, having been kidnapped, as is supposed, in the vicinity of Spruce Grove, Eel river country, it is likely some persons in that section may be able to furnish some information respecting them, or kindred matters, to the Superintendent; if so, they are requested to do so. And parties who are engaged in this nefarious business may as well understand that the present Superintendent is bound to put a stop to their trade, and they will be prosecuted and pursued to the uttermost. Parties who have propositions made to them by these kidnappers, or their agents, will do well to reject them and give information to the Superintendent. We have not space at this time to comment upon this matter, but it is enough to chill the heart of man to know that these vile kidnappers in human flesh are making a regular business of killing the Indians in the mountains, or running them off, and kidnapping their children, packing them about the country, like so many sheep or swine to sell, at retail or wholesale. We shall refer to this matter again.

6:10   Newspaper article, Marysville, 1861

The Little Indians in Court

Johnson, Wood and Freak, charged with kidnapping Indian children, were brought over from Sutter county day before yesterday, and lodged in Yuba county jail, for safe-keeping, there being none in Sutter, and yesterday, John A. McQuaid, counsel for the defendants, brought an application for the discharge of the prisoners, under the habeas corpus act, and the case was heard yesterday afternoon by Judge Bliss at chambers. General Rowe appeared, after some delay, for the complainant, Mr. Hanson, and the young sprigs of heathendom, eight in number, varying from two to twelve years old, were brought into Court, for what purpose, does not appear, as the poor brats could not understand a word of what was going on, but sat in a huddle of helpless silence, stolidly eyeing the tonguey lawyers, gazing in undisguised admiration at the inexhaustible *repertoire* of McQuaid's gesti-culation. The poor little creatures were clad in four sacks, open at each end, with their arms thrust through holes in the sides, and though these flowers of the forest were shrivelled-legged, pot-bellied and dirty, one could see that they had intelligence and were susceptible to education. After a wordy explication from the lawyers, and sundry bitches, the Judge decided that the prisoners were not legally held by the Sheriff of Yuba county, and ordered their discharge, no evidence appearing in the return made that any charge was brought against them. Their counsel told them that they were at liberty, but the Deputy Sheriff of Sutter said that he had a claim upon them; whereupon McQuaid said that he had no right to arrest them in Yuba county; Deputy didn't care, and McQuaid defied him to do it, and told his clients to "git", but they were not willing to take his word for their freedom and reluctantly and slowly went out, followed by the deputies, lawyers and eight little Indian boys—and girls. After much parleying, the culprits looking on sheepishly, McQuaid trying to urge them off, the aborigines hustled together on the Court House steps, the Deputy Sheriff of Yuba arrested the men, as though the affair was begun *de novo*, and so the matter rests until their counsel takes further steps in the case.

The Last of the Little Indian Case

When we last left our three heroes—as the New York *Ledger* would say—they were in the safe keeping of the sheriff of Yuba county; subsequently they were rearrested by the sheriff of Sutter, and an application for their discharge was heard yesterday before Judge Bliss, Mr. McQuaid arguing that the papers were incomplete and informal, and that the statute of 1850, under which they had been arrested, was repealed by the statute of 1860. The objections were overrated and Johnson, alias Lewis, and Wood, were held to bail in the amount of $500 each, to appear before a magistrate in Humboldt county, to answer. The bail was forthcoming, and the prisoners allowed to "git," in a legal way, Freak was discharged, and so Yuba county has done with the case.

6:12   Newspaper article, Marysville, 1861

Provided For

The nine little Indians lately recaptured by Superintendent Hanson from the kidnappers, have all been provided with comfortable homes by the Superintendent, who has assured himself that the poor little heathens will be cared for and well used by their guardians, most of whom reside in the city.

6:13   Newspaper article, Marysville, 1861

Wholesale Kidnapping

Under the caption a correspondent of the Red Bluff *Independent*, charges that certain parties, recently connected with the Nome-Lackee Reservation, have lately procured the services of the County Judge of Tehama to indenture to them, for a term varying from ten to twenty years, all of the "most valuable" (that smacks of cottondom) Indians on the Reservation. The writer very properly contends that the Indian Apprentice law, which was passed last winter, did not contemplate the taking of friendly, industrious Indians from the home provided for them by the Federal Government, but those that might be properly described by the term "vagrant," or such others as might be under the special care of Government. The Act relating to this subject is amendatory to one passed so long ago as 1850. It gives to county and district judges full power and authority, at the instance and request of any persons having rightful charge of Indian children under the age of fifteen, or at the instance and request of any person desirous of obtaining any Indians, whether children or grown persons, that may be held as prisoners of war, or at the instance and request of any person desirous of obtaining any vagrant Indians who have no settled habitation or means of livelihood, and have not placed themselves under the protection of any white person, to bind and put out such Indians as apprentices to trades, husbandry, etc. This condensed quotation from the law, embracing its whole substance, certainly does not warrant a conclusion that Indians who are under the protection of Government were meant to be apprenticed, and if such a practice is allowed or contemplated in Tehama county, the authorities should put a stop to it at once.

6:14   Newspaper article, San Francisco, 1861

Apprenticing Indians

This law works beautifully. A few days ago V. E. Geiger, formerly Indian Agent, had some eighty apprenticed to him, and proposed to emigrate to Washoe with them as soon as he

can cross the mountains. We hear of many others who are
having them bound in numbers to suit. What a pity the provisions of the law are not extended to greasers, Kanakas, and
Asiatics. It would be so convenient to carry on a farm or
mine, when all the hard and dirty work is performed by
apprentices!

6:15   Newspaper article, San Francisco, 1861

Kidnapping Indian Children in Mendocino County

A report has been abroad that some of the settlers in
Long Valley, Mendocino county, have kidnapped and disposed of Indian children to parties in the lower valley.
Among others, G. H. Woodman, formerly of Napa, has been
charged with being implicated in such transactions. Mr.
Woodman writes to us that he did, in fact, take some Indian
children, of the Rispoiner tribe, from Long Valley to the
lower valleys, but that it was done by request and consent of
their relatives. He further states that he took down one of the
head men of the tribe, to see for himself the homes provided
for the children, and that he returned highly pleased with
their situations. Mr. Woodman's statement is further corroborated by a certificate signed by 44 of the residents of Long
Valley. They deny that there was any kidnapping in the case,
and state that the children were taken by the consent of their
kindred, and that no stock has been killed on their account,
as has been reported. They say that the children are much
better off where they are, and that their removal has been
beneficial to the community, since if they had remained they
must have starved, unless the Indians had killed stock for
them to live upon. The certificate closes by saying that the
more of them that can find homes in the lower valleys, the
less stock the Indians will destroy to feed their children.

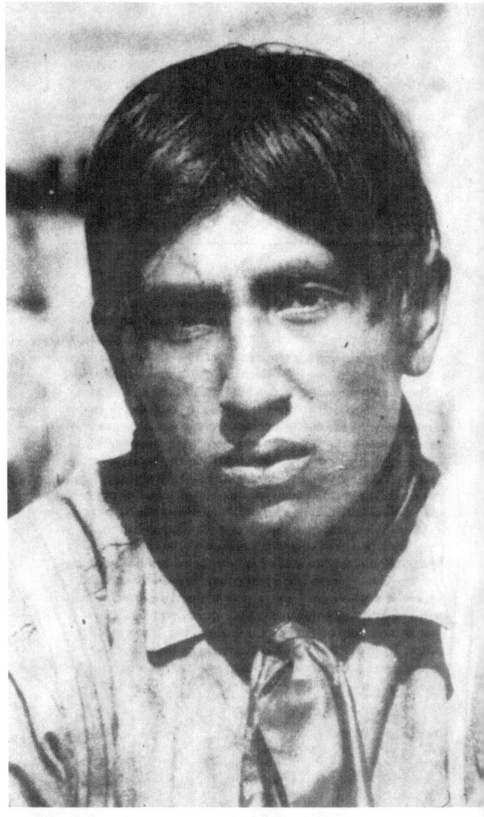

Courtesy LMA   Young Modoc man, Bidwell Riddle, born c. 1892. *Photo 19(*

7

MASSACRES

Massacres, loosely defined here as mass killings of Indians, were common events. The examples presented in this chapter represent only a few of many such instances. While it may be argued that a military party such as that of N. Lyon, Brevet Captain, Second Infantry, U. S. Army, in which troops under his command killed at least 135 and possibly 250 Pomo Indians in 1850 was merely a case of "over-kill," nevertheless men, women and children were indiscriminately shot, and Lyon himself reported that in one engagement "the island became a perfect slaughter pen." Lyon's expedition was carried out by order of Brevet Major General Persifor F. Smith, Commanding Third Division, who had the intention of "chastising" the Indians for the murder of Andrew Kelsey and Charles Stone at Clear Lake in December, 1849. One version of why the Indians killed Kelsey is contained in Thomas Knight's statement (Document 7:2). Whether the Indians were too severely chastised for committing the two killings must be left to the reader's judgment after he has read Capt. Lyon's report. The Humboldt Bay episode of February, 1860, cannot be called anything other than a massacre, and we believe that groups of whites armed with rifles who attacked Indian villages and killed 25 or 30 or 40 were responsible for acts which cannot be labelled by any other term.

Headquarters Clear Lake Expd.
Anderson's Rancho, May 22, 1850

In compliance with department orders (special) No. 24, I proceeded from Monterey to Benicia, where I arrived on the night of the 4th instant, and next morning took command of the expedition designed to proceed against the [Pomo] Indians on Clear Lake and Pit river, by virtue of Major Seawell's order of that date (a copy of which is herewith enclosed), and setting out next day (6th) from Benicia, I reached this position, at the south end of Clear Lake, on the 11th. The next day the dragoon company (Lieut. Davidson) was detached round the western shores of the lake to cooperate with the infantry, to proceed by water up the lake. The Indians, on learning our approach, fled to an island at the northern extremity of the lake, opposite to which, and on the western shore of the lake, the command took position on the afternoon of the 14th, the Indians still gathering rapidly on the island. Lieut. Davidson, with Lieut. Haynes (mountain howitzer) attacked a rancho on the morning of this day, killing four and securing an Indian chief. Early on the morning of the 15th, the two shores being guarded, the landing on the island was effected, under a strong opposition from the Indians, who, perceiving us once upon their island, took flight directly, plunging into the water, among the heavy growth of tula which surrounds the islands, and which on the eastern and northern sides extends to the shores. Having rapidly cleared the island, I saw no alternative but to pursue them into the tula, and accordingly orders were given that the ammunition be slung around the necks of the men, and they proceed into the tula and pursue and destroy as far as possible. The tula was thus thoroughly searched, with severe protracted efforts, and with most gratifying results. The number killed I confidently report at not less than sixty, and doubt little that it extended to a hundred and upwards. The Indians were supposed to be in number about 400. Their fire upon us was not effective, and no injury to the command occurred. The rancheria, extending about half way around the island, was burnt, together with a large amount of stores collected in it. Being satisfied that the Indian tribes on Russian river had participated in the murders of Stone and Kelsey and were not harboring one or two tribes known to be the most guilty, I now proceeded to the headwaters of that river, seeking first a tribe whose chief is called Chapo; but finding the rancheria deserted to which my guide led me as his, I caused a thorough but ineffectual search to be made in the vicinity, and then proceeded down the river for about 22 miles to a tribe called the Yohaiyaks, among whom was Preesta and his tribe, the most active participants in the atrocious murders. I found them early on the morning of the 19th, on an island formed by a slough from Russian river, which was covered with dense undergrowth, and in the part where the Indians were mostly concealed were many trees, both dead and alive, in a horizontal position, interwoven with a heavy growth of vines. Their position being entirely surrounded, they were attacked under most embarrassing circumstances; but as they could not escape, the island soon became a perfect slaughter pen, as they continued to fight with great resolution and vigor till every jungle was routed. Their number killed I confidently report at not less than 75, and have little doubt it extended to nearly double that number. I estimate their whole number as somewhat greater than those on the island before mentioned. They were bold and confident, making known their position in shouts of encouragment to their men and defiance to us. Two of their shots took effect, wounding somewhat severely Corporal Kerry and private Patrick Coughlin, company 'G', the former in the shoulder and the latter in the thigh. A body of Indians supposed to have been concerned in the outrages at Kelsey's rancho, and who it was believed were harboring one of the tribes known to have been concerned in the Kelsey murder, lay about ten miles below; and in order that action might promptly be taken against them, according to the circumstances in which they might be found, I detached Lieutenant Davidson with his (dragoon) company to proceed hastily to the spot, so as to anticipate an alarm from the events just mentioned, and obtaining, with the assistance of Fernando Feliz, upon whose land these Indians lived, the facts, he was instructed to act accordingly. On arriving at Fernando Feliz's rancho he found the Indians had fled through fear. The intelligence that the hostile tribe was harbored by them proved unfounded, and no definite intelligence that they had participated in the murder aforsaid was ascertained.

I am, sir, very respectfully, your most obedient servant,
                    N. Lyon, Brevet Captain 2d Infantry,
Major E.R.S. Canby,   Commanding Expedition.
Monterey, California
Assistant Adjutant General

7:2   Statement by Thomas Knight

"There were a good many Indians in the Clear Lake region, a very good sort, and when I lived in Napa Valley I used to employ them to work for me. I treated them well and never had any trouble with them. Other white men employed them also. The Kelseys would sometimes go out and get 50, 60 or a hundred of these Indians, and bring them to their place, and make them work for them. They treated them badly, and did not feed them well. They should have given them a bullock once a week or so to eat, but failed to do so. The Indians were kept so short of food that they occasionally took a bullock and killed it themselves. On such occasions, if the Kelseys failed to discover the special offenders, they would take any Indian they might suspect, or perhaps one at random and hang him up by the thumbs, so that his toes just touched the floor, in an adobe house they had on the premises, and keep him there two or three days, sometimes with nothing to eat, and some of the other Indians would go and slyly feed them. Sometimes they would kill an Indian outright on the spot for some small offence. In driving them to their place they would shoot any of the old or infirm ones by the wayside. At the time of the Red Bluff excitement, the Kelseys went up into the Clear Lake region, and got some 80 Indians, and drove them down to Red Bluff to work the valuable mines that were supposed to be there. On getting them there, a long distance from their homes, it was ascertained that the mines were a sell, and there was no gold there. The Kelseys then and there abandoned these Indians, who were in a hostile country, with nothing to eat, and they were killed and starved, and finally only some eight or ten of them ever got back to their homes. In revenge they murdered Andy Kelsey, who was in the Clear Lake country, tending a large herd of cattle the brothers had there. The government troops [under Capt. Lyon] then went up and killed a large number of these Indians, and the two other Kelseys also killed a good many. They were arrested for their inhuman treatment of the Indians, many of those they had massacred being old or infirm and had never made any trouble, but through some flaw in the law or informality they escaped punishment."

7:3   Letter, Hitchcock to Adjutant General

San Francisco, Cal.
Adjutant General: March 31, 1853

. . . An Indian war may be said to exist in the upper waters of the Sacramento extending many miles to the north and east beyond Yreka, over 150 miles to Fort Reading. In making this report I cannot forbear stating that I have received similar information from 2 separate channels, making it probable that an inextinguishable desire of vengeance towards the whites exists along that border.

A party of citizens under the conduct of Captain Ben Wright last fall massacred over 30 Indians out of 48 who had come into Captain Wright's camp by invitation to make a "peace". Lieutenant Williamson, Topo. Engineers, and Captain Miller, Assistant Quartermaster, have each informed me of substantially the same particulars, derived by them from separate individuals of Captain Wright's party, to the effect that Captain Wright determined not to return to Yreka without bearing some evidence of success in his expedition against the Indians, and having failed to find them by hunting for them, he invited them into his camp by means of a squaw. Upon this invitation 48 Indians came into his camp, and while there Captain Wright directed his men to charge their rifles afresh to make a sure fire, which was done in the presence of the Indians without exciting their suspicion; and then upon a signal indicated by Captain Wright, they suddenly fired upon the Indians and succeeded in killing about 30. The signal was the discharge of a revolver by Captain Wright, by which he killed the two principal Indians with whom he had been engaged in talk.

Captain Wright returned to Yreka, which place the papers state he entered in triumph, his men bearing on their rifles the scalps of the Indians, and was received with a general welcome by the citizens of the town.

Captain Wright reported that he had demanded of the Indians a return of stolen property and that on their refusal to deliver it up he had then punished them.

General E. A. Hitchcock
Comdg. Pacific Division

7:4   Newspaper article, San Francisco, 1851

Near Cottonwood, the Indians have been punished severely by the citizens. On the evening that Mr. Curtis camped at Leonard's ranch, just on this side of the Stream, a company of men returned from the pursuit of the thieves. They had killed that day about 30, assisted by some friendly "Diggers" of the Valley. Mr. Curtis heard the relation of the affair and says the citizens gave the "Diggers" great credit for the manner of their bearing in the fight. . . .

On the day that Mr. Curtis left Leonard's, the citizens intended to cross the river and attack some thieves that had given considerable trouble in that quarter. It is only the mountain Indians that commit depredations; those in the Valley being friendly and inoffensive.

7:5   Newspaper article, Sacramento, 1851

We have just received intelligence of a battle which has taken place between a party of whites and a large party of Indians on the Coast Range. It seems that the Indians had stolen a quantity of stock belonging to Messrs. Toomes & Dye, from Leonard's Rancho, about 125 miles above this place on the Sacramento River. The gentlemen who had lost the stock, thereupon raised a party of whites, and went out to punish the Indians. They travelled back about 35 miles from the river and entered the mountains. Here they found a very large ranchedero, consisting of about 500 Indians. They attacked them, but the Indians were prepared and fought most desperately. The Indians used arrows only, and the whites had much the advantage with the rifle. Although 25 in number only, the whites killed 40 Indians, while none of their party were shot.

7:6   Newspaper article, San Francisco, 1852

The following is from the *Daily Alta California*, May 4, 1852.

The Shasta *Courier* of Saturday last contains a correspondence from Weaversville, Trinity County, which recounts the particulars of a fearful act of retributive slaughter recently committed in that district. A rancheria of 148 Indians, including women and children, was attacked, and nearly the whole number destroyed.

It appears that the Indians of that vicinity have for many months displayed uncompromising hostility towards the whites, and several murders and robberies have been daringly perpetrated. About the 15th ultimo, a Mr. Anderson, who was much esteemed in the vicinity of Weaversville, was missed, and a search being made his mutilated remains were found about six miles from that place, where he had been attacked by Indians, his cattle driven off, and himself cruelly murdered and robbed. A party of 36 armed men, under Sheriff Dixon pursued the murderers and came up with them on the South Fork of the Trinity. The scene that followed is described:

"On Thursday afternoon, the 22d, the scouts discovered the rancheria in a small valley at the base of 3 mountains on the south side of the South Fork of Trinity River. At midnight the company started from their encampment, Capt. Dixon having divided his force into 3 parties, so as to come upon the Indians from different quarters and surround them. When the day broke, all parties were in the desired positions, and on the signal being given, the attack commenced. Each rifle marked its victim with unerring precision—the pistol and the knife completed the work of destruction and revenge, and in a few moments all was over. Of the 150 Indians that constituted the rancheria, only 2 or 3 escaped, and those were supposed to be dangerously wounded; so that probably not one of those engaged in the murder of the unfortunate Anderson now remains alive. Men, women and children all shared the same fate—none were spared except one woman and two children, who were brought back prisoners.

In palliation of the slaughter of the women and children it is stated that the Indians thrust them forward as a screen for themselves, and behind their persons, as from a barricade, kept up a fire upon their assailants."

7:7　Newspaper article, San Francisco, 1852

A few days ago a man keeping a store and ferry on King's River came into our camp, under whip and spur, stating that he had been warned by a body of some 6 or 8 chiefs of the King's River tribe, to leave immediately—that the next time they warned him, they would kill him. Very soon there was a party numbering 28 men, mounted, and armed to the teeth, who left here for that river to investigate the affair.

Had they confined themselves strictly to this object, there is no doubt but the whole affair might have been settled to the satisfaction of all parties; for I believe it to be the desire of the Indians to preserve the treaty. But instead of making any inquiries regarding the threat, the whole party rode into the rancheria, and after a few words had passed, the import of which I did not understand, they commenced firing upon and killed about 25 or 30 of them . . .

(Signed) W. A. A.
San Joaquin River,
July 4, 1852

7:8　Newspaper article, San Francisco, 1853

Exciting News From Tehama—Indian Thefts—
Terrible Vengeance of the Whites

Mr. Lurk, of Adams and Co., furnished the *Union* with the following exciting news.

The Indians have committed so many depredations in the North, of late, that the people are enraged against them, and are ready to knife them, shoot them, or inoculate them with smallpox—all of which have been done.

Some time since, the Indians in Colusa county destroyed about $5,000 worth of stock belonging to Messrs. Thomas & Toombs; since which time they have had two men employed, at 8.00 per month to hunt down and kill the Diggers, like other beasts of prey. On Friday, the 25th ult, one of these men, named John Breckenridge, was alone, and armed only with a bowie knife, when he met with four Indians and attacked them. They told him to leave, and commenced shooting arrows at him; but, undaunted, he continued to advance, and succeeded in killing one, and taking one prisoner, while the other two escaped. He immediately proceeded to Moon's Ranch, where the captured Indian was hung by the citizens.

On Friday, the 25th Feb., stock was stolen from Mr. Carter of Butte county, to the value of $3,000. Mr. Carter went forthwith to the camp of the well known stage proprietors, Messrs. Hall and Crandall, and thence started with a party of twelve men in search of the Indian depredators. After a fruitless search in the vicinity of Pine and Deer Creeks, the party became impatient, and dispersed on Sunday evening. Returning home, one detachment of the party, discovered a half-breed by the name of Battedon, and took him prisoner. The man, fearing for his own life, agreed to show the cave where the Indians were concealed, if they would release him. Notice was sent round, and the people assembled again at Oak Grove on Monday, from which place they started at midnight for the cave.

Arriving there at early daylight on Tuesday morning, rocks were rolled into the cave, and the wretched inmates, rushing out for safety, met danger a thousand times more dreadful. The first one that made his appearance was shot by Capt. Geo. Rose, and the others met the same fate from the rifles of the Americans. Altogether there were thirteen killed; three chiefs of different rancherias, and three women. Three women and five children were spared; and it is but doing justice to say, that the women who were killed were placed in front as a sort of breast-work, and killed either by accident or mistake. Capt. Rose took one child, Mr. Lattimer another, and the others were disposed of in the same charitable manner among the party.

On Tuesday night, March 1st, three work oxen belonging to Messrs. Bull and Baker were stolen from a corral in Shasta city, and on Thursday morning twenty-six head were driven off at Red Bluffs; value near $4,000.

7:9   Newspaper article, San Francisco, 1860

Indian Troubles in Mendocino

The Indians have again become very troublesome to the settlers of Mendocino county. Mr. White, a resident of Long Valley, informs us that they have become so bad that the settlers have been compelled to organize themselves into a standing army, so to speak, and by taking turns keep their stock and homes under constant guard. For some time previous to this being done, the Indians had killed from ten to fifteen head of stock nightly. One gentleman alone, Mr. Woodman, has lost 100 head of horses, 74 of which were found dead in a canyon not far from his place, and upon the bodies of which the Indians were having a great feast. On the 19th of December, the settlers turned out, and attacking the enemy succeeded in killing 32 and taking two prisoners. The United States troops located in that region are represented to be pursuing, during all these troubles, a "masterly course of inactivity." The aid of the State has therefore been asked, and will we trust be granted. Petaluma *Journal*, 20th January.

7:10   Newspaper article, San Francisco, 1860

Indian Butcheries in California

The New York *Century* of 12th May has the following observations upon a matter which has been often laid, in all its terrible details, before the readers of the *Bulletin*:

We have been informed through the papers, of the murderous outrages committed on the aboriginal inhabitants of California by men with white skins. We regret to say that there is no exaggeration in these accounts. On the contrary, on conversing with a number of individuals who, to some extent, witnessed the transactions, we can bring to light no circumstance to palliate or extenuate them in the slightest degree. In the Atlantic and Western States, the Indians have suffered wrongs and cruelties at the hands of the stronger race. But history has no parallel to the recent atrocities perpetrated in California. Even the record of Spanish butcheries in Mexico and Peru has nothing so diabolical.

Humboldt county, in the northern section of the State, has been the scene of a great portion of these outrages. The perpetrators seem to have acted with a deliberate design to exterminate the Indian race. Their butchery was confined to women and children, the men being absent at the time. They were of the Digger tribes, known as friendly Indians, the most degraded and defenseless of the race, entirely destitute of the bold and murderous spirit which characterizes other tribes of red men. They were charged with stealing cattle and other property from the whites, and with selling firearms and ammunition to the hostile tribes. The attack was made in the night, when they were collected in their little settlements or villages at some sort of merry-making. The men were known to be absent—they had possibly fled on suspicion of danger. Under these circumstances, bands of white men, armed with hatchets—small bands but sufficiently numerous for the purpose—fell on the women and children, and deliberately slaughtered them, one and all. Simultaneous attacks were made on the different rancherias or encampments. Fire-arms were scarcely used, the work being done with hatchets.

In one of the settlements an aged and feeble chief collected the women around him, when they were about flying on the approach of the human bloodhounds, assuring them that white men did not kill squaws and that they would be safe. But they all perished together. One of our informants saw twenty-six bodies of women and children collected in one spot by the more humane citizens preparatory to burial. Some of them were infants at the breast, whose skulls had been cleft again and again. The whole number slaughtered in a single night was about two hundred and forty.

We have spoken of the authors of this butchery as men — white men. So they were. We can invent no logic that will segregate them from our own species. Would that it were possible to do so. The whole number engaged was probably not over fifty or sixty. They were the lowest and most brutal of the border population, such as hang on the outskirts of civilization, and possess nothing of humanity but the form and the bestial instincts.

Mendocino county, within a few days' travel of San Francisco, has been the theatre of atrocities nearly parallel, under cover of martial authority. Regularly organized bodies of armed men attacked the settlements of friendly Indians charged with stealing cattle, and murdered them in like manner, except that fire-arms were used and not hatchets. In this case, men, as well as women and children, were massacred. To defray the expenses of this heroic work, enormous claims were presented to the Legislature.

A gentleman who has spent much time in Mendocino county, informs us that the intercourse of the whites with the Clear Lake Indians, as they are called, has laid the foundation for the ultimate extermination of the race by disease, in the manner of the Sandwich Islands. Of five or six hundred squaws, from ten years old and upwards, he was assured that not a solitary individual was exempt! Civilized humanity will scarcely believe it possible for human beings to be degraded so far below savages, as are the filthy wretches who infect the frontier settlements, and commit such deeds of rapine and blood as we have here but inadequately described.

7:11   Newspaper article, San Francisco, 1860

Horrible Massacre of 200 Indians in Humboldt County

By the steamer *Columbia*, which arrived this forenoon from the North, we have tidings of a terrible butchery, by a band of white murderers, of the Indians around Humboldt Bay. Mr. Lord, the express messenger of Wells, Fargo & Co., favors us with the following statement of the massacre:

Between three and four o'clock on Sunday morning last, (26 February,) an attack was made by a party of white men, upon Indians at several villages around Humboldt Bay. At Indian Island, opposite the town of Eureka, and distant but a few hundred yards, more than 40 Indians were killed, three-fourths of the number being women and children. On the beach, south of the entrance to the bay, forty or fifty Indians were also killed. Report says all that were there—every one— was killed. It is also reported, and is no doubt true, that a simultaneous attack was made upon the villages on Eel river. From what was known in Eureka not less than two hundred Indians—men, women and children—were killed on this Sabbath morning.

It is believed that the farmers and graziers of Eel river county, who have suffered from Indian depredations, during the past year, were the men who performed the deed. The cause assigned is, that the coast Indians furnished arms and ammunition to those in the mountains, and gave them asylum, when hard pressed by the volunteers. They have been seen to take large quantities of beef from the mountains to their houses nearer the settlements. Most of the people at Eureka and vicinity were bitter in their denunciation of this wholesale butchery.

J. A. Lord

We also have the following testimony on the same subject:

TO THE EDITOR OF THE *BULLETIN*: − I learn from Mr. Van Ness, Sheriff of Humboldt county, who arrived in San Francisco this forenoon, passenger on the steamer *Columbia* that the massacre which took place on Humboldt Bay, last Sunday morning, was committed by a body of men, some 40 in number, from Eel river. They rode through to the south end of the bay in the night, hitched their horses, took Capt. Buhne's boat, crossed to the south shore, and killed all the Indians they found. They then proceeded up the Bay to Indian Island, and commenced an indiscriminate slaughter of men, women and children, and left before daylight. They gave as their reason, that the Indians of the Bay and the mountains are leagued together, and are constantly killing their cattle. When pursued, those in the mountains leave that region and go down to the coast. Parties of Indians, from ten to twenty, had been seen during the past week going to the Bay. Those men from Eel river, becoming exasperated, followed the Indians, and determined to clean out every thing that wore a red skin. Sheriff Van Ness thinks that the number of Indians (including men, women and children) who have been thus slaughtered amounts, probably to about eighty.

This is but the commencement of an Indian war in that section of the country. An intelligent Indian told the people of Eureka, that the white men had killed his wives and children, and he had nothing more to live for; and he was going to the mountains with what few of his tribe were left, to fight against the whites.

J.R.D.

7:12 Newspaper article, San Francisco, 1860

The Humboldt Bay Massacre — Statement by the
Sheriff of Humbolt County

San Francisco, February 29, 1860.

EDITOR *BULLETIN:* — In your issue of the 28th, I notice a communication relative to the recent Indian massacre in Humboldt county, purporting to be a statement furnished by me. The writer of that letter must have got many statements, and mixed them up to suit himself. This would have been well enough, had he given his information as gleanings, and not lumped it as an account from me. My account I will here give you:

On the evening of Saturday, 25th February, a simultaneous attack appears to have been made upon the Indians, on the coast of Humboldt county. About 80 are known to have been killed—the greater part of whom were women and children. The parties engaged in the wholesale killing, the writer knows not; neither does he know the number, nor from what portion of the country they came; neither does he know cause sufficient to prompt them to so bloody a deed.

In connection with this deed, it may be well to state briefly the condition of Indian affairs in Humboldt county. The greater portion of the citizens there are engaged in stock-growing. Necessity compels them to graze their stock remotely from their residences. East of the redwoods, in the eastern portion of the county, is an extensive and beautiful range for grazing. On these hills are herded between 7,000 and 8,000 head of cattle. During the last year about one-eighth of the stock has been killed by the Indians. About a year ago, James Elleson, (than whom none was more highly esteemed,) while in pursuit of the Indians who were driving off and killing his stock, was mortally wounded. From one end of the county to the other, stock has been killed, and many a lone traveler has been cut off. The commander of Fort Humboldt, partly through weakness and partly through indisposition, refuses to take cognizance of these facts. The settlers go out to give the Indians battle; the Indians disappear from the grazing country—the settlers see them daily passing down to the coast, in the white settlements. They go to the Indian ranches, find beef and one wounded Indian in the ranches of the *peaceable* Indians; the volunteers disband—their foe will not meet them, and they do not feel able to keep a standing army at their own expense, and at the same time help to support an inactive force which is cooped up at Fort Humboldt. In a short time after the volunteers disband, the Indians, encouraged with their good luck, redouble their efforts to drive off and kill stock; they are seen passing up the stream to the grazing lands; more stock is missing; in the day-time, and in the face of the settlers and herdsman, they drive off stock. Well, a call for a volunteer company, to be organized according to law, is made; the company is organized, and returns to the proper authorities are made. Immediate action is necessary; they equip themselves—expecting to be called into service at an early day; they get but little encouragement. Now, they are heavy tax-payers, and they are losing all they possess. So, they get desperate, and perhaps are prompted to deeds of desperation.

I state these facts, not as an apology for bloody deed, but to serve to modify somewhat the censure which should be cast upon the perpetrators of this terrible massacre on Humboldt Bay.

B. Van Ness.

Assistant Adjutant General:

Fort Humboldt
March 10, 1860

I have just been to Indian Island, the home of a band of friendly Indians between Eureka and Uniontown, where I beheld a scene of atrocity and horror unparalleled not only in our own Country, but even in history, for it was done by men self acting and without necessity, color of law, or authority—the murder of little innocent babes and women, from the breast to maturity, barbarously and I can't say brutally—for it is worse—perpetrated by men who act in defiance of and probably in revenge upon the Governor of the State for not sending them arms and having them mustered in as a Volunteer Company for the murder of Indians by wholesale, goaded also by Legislative acts of inquiry into such matters. At any rate such is the opinion of the better class of community as related to me this Sunday morning. I was informed by these men, Volunteers, calling themselves such, from Eel River, had employed the earlier part of the day in murdering all the women and children of the above Island and I repaired to the place, but the villians—some 5 in number had gone—and midst the bitter grief of parents and fathers—many of whom had returned—I beheld a spectacle of horror, of unexampled description—babes, with brains oozing out of their skulls, cut and hacked with axes, and squaws exhibiting the most frightful wounds in death which imagination can paint—and this done . . . . without cause, otherwise, as far as I can learn, as I have not heard of any of them losing life or cattle by the Indians. Certainly not these Indians, for they lived on an Island and nobody accuses them.

[Major Raines then describes the murdered Indians, as he found them in each lodge, the number killed being as follows: 1st lodge—2 women, 3 children; 2nd lodge—1 man, 5 women, 2 children; 3rd lodge—2 women; 4th lodge—3 women, 5 children; 5th lodge—4 women, 1 child; 6th lodge, 1 woman. In addition to these Major Raines says that 18 women and an unknown number of children had been carried away by the Indians for burial before his arrival.]

(In another letter to the Assistant Adjutant General, March 10, 1860, Major Raines says "About 188 Indians, mostly women and children have been murdered, Viz., 55 at Indian Island; 58 at South Beach; 40 on South Fork Eel River and 35 at Eagle Prairie.)

Major G. J. Raines

7:14   Newspaper article, San Francisco, 1860

The Recent Massacre of Indians at Humboldt Bay

Fort Humboldt, Cal., May 22, 1860

To the Editor of the San Francisco *Bulletin* — Sir: Attempts having been vilely made, again and again, to palm off upon the military, and mainly upon myself, the cause of the blackest crimes perpetuated on this Bay which have ever disgraced the history of mankind, by false and contemptible lies, incriminating along with me even revered gentlemen; and as some of these lies have found themselves in the columns of your newspaper, please favor me by publishing the inclosed, (a copy of which has been forwarded to Sheriff Van Nest,) in order to "disabuse the public:"

I would premise by stating that instructions similar in substance have been given to each officer on the same service, and also that up to this date I can find no excuse whatever for the horrid massacre on this Bay and the removal of Indians thereof from the county, whom I have considered as safeguards to the citizens of this vicinity and their property, by acting as spies upon the mountain tribes, to destroy small numbers and betray larger ones who might come for spoilation or murder.

Very respectfully, your obed't serv't.,
G. J. Raines
Major U.S.A. Comd't Post.

(Letter from Major Raines to Sheriff Van Ness above alluded to.)

Fort Humboldt, Cal., May 17, 1860

Sheriff B. Van Nest, Eureka, Cal. —Sir: Having been informed that a certain fiction favorable to the interests of the assassins in this county—of which you appear as spokesman—have been getting up a design apparently with a sinister view, (as the good citizens of Eureka will know that all legitimate calls upon the military in Indian matters would be properly attended to,) and as a false statement of yours in the San Francisco *Bulletin* of 5th March last, and your having taken no steps whatever to bring to justice the perpetrators of the horrid massacres on this Bay and in the county, of 26th February last, lead to an inference unfavorable to your official character, it becomes my duty, as the officer in command of United States troops at this post, to warn you and all concerned against taking any unlawful steps in the premises. I therefore transcribe for you a copy of a late order, as follows:

Fort Humboldt, Cal., May 4, 1860.

To Lieut. J. W. Cleary, 6-Infantry, U.S.A., Comd'g. Co. in the Field.
Sir: Yours of the 30th ultimo is acknowledged, and I regret much the death of Yo-keel-le-bah, killed, it is feared in his overwhelming confidence in the promises and protection of the white man. Our main dependence was upon him to communicate with the mountain tribes. His character and friendship for the settlers, and his saving of their cattle, are well known to me.

But do not give it up yet, but try and have a talk with them by the aid of Mr. Stam and the interpreter sent to you, and have some argument with the Indians that they must cease to kill cattle and agree to give up culprits, and they shall not be killed. If you succeed, inform the cattle owners that they must put a stop to "volunteers" pitching in and killing men women and children, as they often do, which necessarily frustrates all our efforts for peace and the assurity of property. The Indians being impressed with the idea that forebearance will save their lives, that *must have* its effect, and this plan of the volunteers killing all the Indians to check cattle-stealing is evidently perfectly absurd, as I have been assured again and again by different persons that there are 3,000 of these Upper Eel river Indians alone, and perhaps 10,000 in the country and its vicinity, all told.

I am informed that the volunteers under Wright were out three months, and killed all of three men, and he had, too, some active and energetic men in his company. Now if thirty-five men in three months kill three Indians, it requires just 250 years, at that rate, to kill them all on Eel river, and 700 years to rid the county, allowing nothing for increase!

The hostility of these Indians is questionable. For a year past they have killed no citizen, and the case of Ellison (not Emerson, as you suppose) could not be fairly called so, as he found the Indians carrying off meat—he followed them with some four or five men, fired into them—shot down two, and they were still at it when, in a return of fire of arrows, one hit Ellison in the groin, from which he, some days afterwards, died (as per statement of Mr. Dix, one of the party, which I have in writing.)

The Indians have been driven, as you say, from this part of the country, and your idea that they came to kill cattle, not from malice, but because they find it difficult to subsist, is probably correct. This is a sorrowful state of things, but we must stop it if possible, and punish the guilty, while hostility must be met with the like. I am aware that they have been so often shot at that they are off at the moment they see a white face; and that it would require some 300 troops to remove them to a reservation. Yet something may be done with a specific understanding.

You state that in a circle of 25 miles there are ten or twelve persons living and about 2,000 head of cattle; that the cattle are not in any inclosure, but are allowed to range over a large extent of country, nearly all of which belong to persons who live at a distance of 25 or 30 miles, and that you doubt very much if some of them have any one to take charge of them. Well, this is to be regretted, but soldiers are not herdsmen, and your camp should be moved where there is a more military demand for their services.

Very respectfully, your obed't. serv't.,
G. J. Raines,
Major 4th Infantry Comdg. Post.

P.S. — If you take any prisoners, send them in under guard to this post; and if you cannot get at the Indians otherwise, try and make it known to them that you will feed them. Then send to me, and I will come out and have a talk with them.

7:15 Newspaper article, San Francisco, 1861

Letter from the North

The steamer Columbia arrived here last night about half-past 6 o'clock from ports on the Northern coast, bringing papers from Humboldt Bay to the 23d February, and from Crescent City to the 16th.

Indian Troubles—Killing off the "Bucks."

The Humboldt *Times* is filled with notices of "outrages" by the Indians on the settlers, and the killing of large numbers of the former by the white men. That journal of the 9th February, has the following items on the subject:

About a week ago thirty-nine diggers were killed by the settlers, on main Eel river, above the crossing of the old Sonoma trail. It seems that a few settlers at Ketinshou, at the beginning of the winter, in order to avoid danger to their stock from snow, moved down on main Eel river, at the point mentioned. Not long since some of them returned to look after their houses, &c, and found that the Indians had destroyed all that they had left. Hereupon a party started in pursuit of the offenders, taking along some friendly Indians to assist them. They report having found the band that committed the damage and killed the above number of bucks.

The settlers of Upper Mattole on Saturday last made an attack on a band of predatory Indians (in fact, all the Digger tribe would come under that head) and killed seven of their number. The Indians had previously, as usual, made it a practice to run off and kill stock, but not being satisfied with that, had made an attempt the day before to take the life of one of the settlers—an elderly gentleman whose name we could not learn. They shot at him with arrows, one of which struck him, but not so as to inflict a serious wound.

The same journal of date the 23d February says

A band of Indians killed and drove off several head of cattle and a lot of hogs from settlers on Kneeland's Prairie last week, whereupon a party of men went in pursuit of the rascals, came up in the redwoods near North Yager Creek, and killed four of their number.

Ketinshou Valley was sacked by the Indians on Friday last, by watching the only settler there, John Fulwider, until he went for his cow in the evening, and then rushed into the house. They shot the dog and fired at Fulwider on his return. Having nothing to defend himself with he had to leave. He went over to Eel River, to the settlement, which was abandoned on Sunday last, for the reason that there was too many Indians about. They had killed about 300 of their hogs and a great number of stock. On their way in they came across the Indians that had robbed Larabee's house, and killed two of them. They went on to the house, or to where it had stood, and found that the Indians had burned it and killed Ann Quinn—cook at the ranch. They found the body of Ann lying about six feet from the door considerabley burnt. David King was plowing a short distance from the house at the time and when he heard the firing, started towards it. The Indians saw him coming and fired at him and attempted to cut off his retreat, but he succeeded in affecting his escape. The names of the men that came down are G. Abbott, J. Bartlett, A. Posey, John Dewey, S. Fleming and Pierce Asbill. They arrived at Larabee's place, which is on

Van Duzen Fork, about three hours after the house was attacked. The men recovered about three horse loads of plunder.

We have not received a mail from the south for two weeks, and it is the general conviction that the mail rider has been intercepted and killed by the Indians between Long Valley and Hydeville.

Pomo man, Chicken Seagull, born 1852. Photo 190

SCALPING OF INDIANS

The scalping of Indians is usually thought of as a barbaric Indian custom practiced by the tribes of the Plains and the Eastern Woodlands. Many anthropologists believe that it was not an aboriginal custom, but was a practice introduced on the east coast by the French and English, from whence it spread westward. Regardless of its origin, some whites in California practiced the custom as evidenced in the four brief accounts which follow.

8:1   Newspaper article, Sacramento, 1852

Indian Difficulties

The Yreka correspondent of the Shasta *Courier* states
that a fight took place a short time since at Wright's Camp
with 21 Indians. Two citizens were severely wounded. On the
arrival of the party at Yreka, they paraded through the
streets—the wounded being borne in litters—each of the
party, consisting of 16 whites, 2 Indians, and a negro, having
a bow and arrows, and the muzzle of his gun decorated with
a scalp taken from the enemy.

8:2   Newspaper article, Marysville, 1859

A new plan has been adopted by our neighbors opposite this
place to chastise the Indians for their many depredations
during the past winter. Some men are hired to hunt them,
who are recompensed by receiving so much for each scalp, or
some other satisfactory evidence that they have been killed.
The money has been made up by subscription.

8:3   Newspaper article, Marysville, 1861

A Bounty Offered for Indian Scalps – That sounds
barbarous, but it is true in Shasta county, as will be seen by
the following extract from the Shasta *Herald* of May 9th:

The party who started in pursuit of the Indians who committed
the depredations we noticed in our last issue, overtook them on Mill
Creek, in Tehama county, and succeeded in killing four of their
number. Mr. Waggoner recovered his horse, but the rest of the stolen
animals had been killed and eaten. A meeting of citizens was held a day
or two ago at Haslerigg's store, and measures taken to raise a fund to be

disbursed in payment of Indian scalps for which a bounty was offered. A Committee was also appointed to confer with a meeting to be held during the week at Antelope Creek. The initial steps have been taken, and it is safe to assert that the extinction of the tribes who have been to settlers such a cause of dread and loss, will be the result.

In 1850 we saw the scalps of Diggers hanging to tent-poles in the Shasta and Trinity country. The Oregon men who first settled that part of the State thought it sport to kill a Digger on sight, as they would a coyote. The Diggers can be saved from forcible extermination only by the intervention of Uncle Sam. There should be troops enough employed at each Reservation to keep them corraled.

8:4   Newspaper article, Marysville, 1862

Fight With The Indians

From private information, we learn that Capt. Good's company of volunteers overtook a party of Indians near the site of the late massacre in Butte county, near Chico, and gave them battle. Seventeen of the Indians were killed and scalped by the volunteers, who, being from the immediate vicinity of the former massacre, are highly exasperated at the red-skins. None were killed on the side of the whites. They are determined to drive off or exterminate the Indians, it is said.

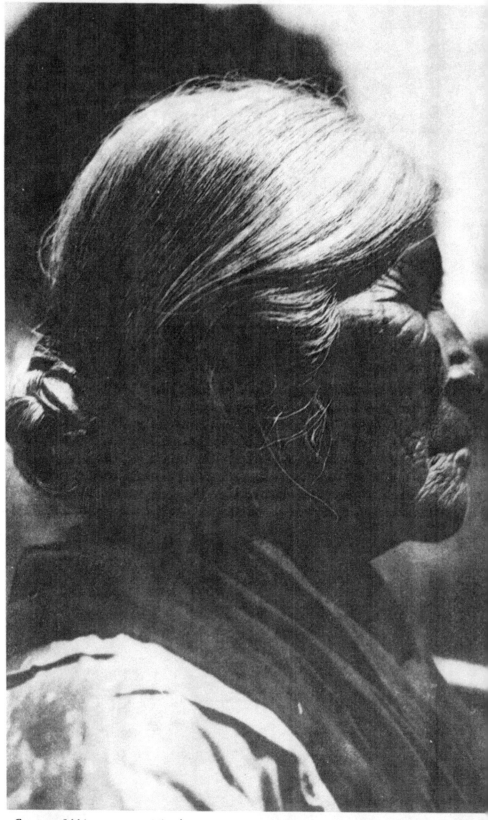

Courtesy LMA   Miwok woman, Sophie Thompson, born 1868. *Photo 1923*

DISEASE, LIQUOR AND SEXUAL
EXPLOITATION OF INDIAN WOMEN

*Some of the disadvantages to the Indians of their con-
tact with the whites are treated in this chapter. A hint of the
effect of introduced diseases on the population numbers of
the California Indians can be gained from Documents 9:1-3
and 2:2, 14.[1] Alcohol was another of the unhelpful contributions the whites made to Indians, as the instances reported in
Documents 9:4-7 illustrate (see also 2:2, 9, 14). The sexual
exploitation of Indian women by white men on a frontier
where available white women were in short supply had profound effects on native family structure and was an important factor in the genetic dilution of the Indian population.[2]
There were many instances, no doubt, of happy marriages
between white men and Indian women in the 1850s and the
1860s—two newspaper accounts of legalized marriages occur
in Documents 9:15, 16.*

1 – For a survey of this subject covering the period 1848-1870 see S.
F. Cook. *The Conflict between the California Indian and White
Civilization: III, The American Invasion, 1848-1870.* Ibero-
Americana, No. 23. Berkeley, 1943.

2 – R. F. Heizer and A. J. Almquist. *The Other Californians: Preju-
dice and Discrimination Under Spain, Mexico and the United
States to 1920.* University of California Press, 1971, pp. 75-92. S.
F. Cook. "Racial Fusion Among the California and Nevada
Indians." Human Biology, Vol. 15, pp. 153-165, 1943. S. F.
Cook. *The Conflict Between the California Indian and White
Civilization: IV, Trends in Marriage and Divorce Since 1850.*
Ibero-Americana, No. 24. Berkeley, 1943.

Fort Miller Cal
March 9, 1854

Sir

The Medical Officer of this Post having reported to me the prevalence of venereal disease among the troops of this command I have the honor to make the following report to the Col. commanding the Dept. for the information of the Indian Department—if necessary. The Indians that have for years lived in the immediate vicinity of this Post have during that time been in constant intercourse with the worst class of whites to be found in any country. They have contracted disease—to them the most fatal—and are constantly furnished by the whites—with liquor so that every day an observer may see a dozen Indians reeling drunk. The Civil law as administered here seems wholly inoperative not only to the protection of the Indians but the punishing the whites. All are diseased and from such constant intercourse with whites it must go on increasing where the case is now sufficiently mild to admit of it. These Indians are more degraded and worthless then any I have ever heard of. This is no better locality for Indians even if no whites had ever been here, than many others in the surrounding country and away from all their present bad influences: and under existing circumstances it is the worst place they could be at. It is not of course in my power to prevent their intercourse with whites or prevent their obtaining liquor. I am continually obliged now to quell disturbances among drunken whites and Indians to prevent serious results. All disturbances are caused by introduction of liquor among them and intercourse with their women. The abuse of the Indians is increasing from day to day. The Indian Agents have done nothing towards bettering their condition and the most chanted construction of this is that they know nothing of the facts in the case for if otherwise they are criminal. It is the greatest possible injury to the

Indians to allow them to remain where they now are or in this immediate vicinity, and there is no reason for it. A position two miles removed from here, or twenty, would be just as good for the Indians to collect food and the change would not only prolong their lives, but promote their happiness and welfare: and it is charitable to suppose that these are objects that the Indian Dept. desires to obtain. It will be no better if they are simply removed from the Military Reservation, and I would recommend that they be taken to the Fresno Indian Farm, fifteen miles from here. It is only by a move of this kind that they can be saved from complete annihilation in a comparatively short time. The presence of these Indians too in this immediate vicinity has the worst possible effect upon the Troops here, and had there never been any, the same state of things would exist and require the same action of the Supt. of Indian affairs. Their great injury has resulted from their intercourse with the mining population along this River, and they should be removed as soon as possible. The Indians can certainly maintain themselves elsewhere as well as here, and I think much better. They are of course naturally indolent and lazy and when they can be about a town such as we have here and obtain their living by begging or evil practices, they will not work. I hope this may incur a favorable consideration from the Col. Commanding and the Supt. of Indian Affairs for Calif.

I am Sir very respectfully
Your Obt Servant
LaRhett L. Livingston
1st Lt., 3rd. Art'y
Cmdg. Post

To Major W. W. Mackall
AA Genl. U.S.A.
Benicia/Cal/

Fort Miller California
March 9th 1857

Sir

Pursuant to a sense of professional as well as official duty I have to report the existence and continued prevalence of "Venereal diseases" among the enlisted men of this command to an extent likely to prove extremely prejudicial to its strength and efficiency. A reference to my daily morning reports and monthly reports of sick would discover a seeming discrepancy between those reports and this. I have to state in explanation that there exists an unwillingness on the part of the men to be placed on the sick report when they become the subjects of this disease, hence all of the cases are not reported. It has become within my knowledge that both non-commissioned officers and privates have become the subjects of primary disease the initial symptoms of which being slight and soon subsiding by self instituted local treatment they have not reported themselves and secondary accidents with all their direful effects have been the result—than which no disease makes greater inroads upon the constitution or more permanently impairs the general efficiency of the man.

In view of these circumstances I would most respectfully recommend that some measures be adopted which shall lessen the facilities for contracting the disease.

Very Respectfully
Your Obdt. Svt.
William J. L'Engle
Asst Surg
To   U S A
Lt. LaRhett L. Livingston
3rd Regt. Artillery
Comdg Post

9:2   Newspaper article, Sacramento, 1851

Mortality Among The Indians

Dr. Harkness informs us that a brother of his, who has just come down from the Upper Sacramento, brings intelligence that sickness prevails to a considerable extent among the tribes of Indians in the vicinity of the river. He noticed on the road a number of unburied bodies, and in the huts and woods many who were lying prostrate with disease. The ranks of the aborigines are rapidly wasting away before the onward march of the pale face; and very soon, the last son of the forest will have been summoned to the presence of "The Great Father."

9:3   Newspaper article, Sacramento, 1853

The [Nevada] *Journal* of Friday says that the small pox has prevailed to a great extent among the Indians the present season, and that it is computed by those best acquainted with the details of Indian life, that not less than four hundred of all sexes and ages of the Indians have been destroyed by this disease the past six months—that is one tenth of the whole number.

The Indians are totally helpless when thus attacked, and if anything is resorted to besides groans by the sufferers or howling of their friends, the supposed remedy generally hastens death. The most common sufferers are children, which are swept off in numbers. The Indians are very uncleanly and careless in exposing themselves, and thus easily contract disease in its most deadly shape. The ravages of small pox have been mostly confined to the Indians, and but very few whites have suffered.

9:4   Newspaper article, Sacramento, 1855

Drunken Indians

We noticed a troupe of Indians, male and female, on the Levee, yesterday, well lined with whisky, and in possession of an extra bottle or two to keep the lining intact. One of the males was particularly happy—his broad face suffused with silly smiles, and his tongue rolling in chops of broken English.

"Injun lub whisky," he said smilingly, "Injun get drunk—bad—me no lub whisky—no get drunk—ugh—you sabe—there my wife," and then ran and caught one of the drunken squaws and led her, unwillingly, back, with an air of triumph as though she were the flower of the prairie. With the troupe—about twenty in all—was an Indian boy five or six years of age, with a countenance that for intelligence would have been creditable to one of our own race. They resided somewhere above the city, on the banks of the American, and embarked in canoes near Gay's saw-mill. The embarcation was attended with nearly as much difficulty as the landing under Scott, at Vera Cruz, and occupied a proportionate time. One of the women wept and scolded before she ventured on the precipitate descent of the bank, but on securing a permanent seat on the bottom of the canoe, commenced and continued singing till her voice was lost in the distance. The boy, on arriving at the craft, dexterously hauled it to the shore, jumped in and paddled away impatiently like a high-pressure steamer on the point of a start. We saw one boat load under way, and some distance up the river. The balance of the troupe was left sitting on the bank passing around the bottle, getting "tight" as fast as possible. Who sold the whisky?

9:5   Newspaper articles, Butte, 1856

A Villainous Outrage

We saw on Sunday afternoon, a poor Indian boy apparently about ten years of age, so drunk as to be almost unable to walk. Judge Jones had him in charge when we saw him, and said he had learned from the boy, who speaks English, that he had obtained the liquor from a Chinaman. Perhaps Chinamen know no better than to sell spirits to Indians, but they should be prosecuted, nevertheless, as should every one else who is guilty of doing so.

Good

The chinaman who sold the liquor to the Indian boy on Sunday was arraigned before Judge Jones yesterday, and found guilty of the offense. He was fined seventy-five dollars for his rascality, but through his lawyer, appealed the case to the Court of Sessions. Perhaps this will prove a good lesson to others who have been in the habit of furnishing liquor to those poor defenceless creatures. We believe this is the first case of the conviction of any person of this crime that has occurred in the State since the law making it a crime to sell ardent spirits to Indians was passed.

9:6   Newspaper article, San Francisco, 1858

Digger Killed in a Drunken Brawl—
Verdict of an Indian Jury

On 8th June, a number of drunken Indians came to the ranch of Mr. Taylor, at Penn Valley, Nevada county, during his absence from home. There was one sober among them, and he advised the family to close the doors, stating that his comrades were all insane from the effects of liquor. The doors were accordingly closed and fastened, and a general fight soon commenced among the savages, which resulted in one of them shooting another in the back with an arrow, killing him instantly. The point of the arrow, it is supposed, must have penetrated the heart. The murdered Indian belonged at Penn Valley. The murderer was afterwards regularly tried by the Indians, who decided that it was a case of "justifiable homicide"—the fact that he was drunk being considered a good defence.

9:7 Newspaper article, San Joaquin Valley, 1858

Indian Fight

The Volcano *Ledger* says that a few days since, some twenty miles above that place in the mountains, and a considerable distance from any settlement, a collection of drunken Indians, male and female, enacted among themselves a horrible tragedy. There were about twenty in the party, and by some means they had managed to procure a large jug of liquor. After becoming crazy and furious from drinking, they engaged in a desperate fight with each other. When discovered by our informants, one Indian and two squaws were found dead, with their bodies badly bruised and mangled, while the living were in a state of beastly intoxication, and many of them bleeding profusely from the cuts and bruises they had received.

9:8 Newspaper article, San Francisco, 1856

Some of the agents, and nearly all of the employees, we are informed, of one of these reservations at least, are daily and nightly engaged in kidnapping the younger portion of the females, for the vilest of purposes. The wives and daughters of the defenceless Diggers are prostituted before the very eyes of their husbands and fathers, by these civilized monsters, and they dare not resent the insult, or even complain of the hideous outrage.

9:9 *Newspaper article, San Francisco, 1857*

Looking After the Squaws

In the Red Bluff *Beacon*, of 3d September, John Breckenridge says:

While myself and three other men were in charge of the Indian prisoners on Butte creek, that had been captured by Gen. Kibbe's command—one Cain, a miner, came to them and claimed a squaw, one of the prisoners—and undertook to take her away. When he was prevented from doing so by my men and myself, said Cain then went down the creek, and in about two hours returned with a mob of forty-five men, and Deputy Sheriff Cheesman, and took H. S. Sadorus, G. M. Stratton and M. Amesby and myself prisoners, and released all the Indians. Said Cain took the squaw he claimed, on the 27th of August, to Dogtown, and was married to her while her "Buck" was still alive, although shot. I am of the opinion that the only motive the mob had was to secure the squaws and keep them on the creek.

9:10 *Newspaper article, Sacramento, 1858*

Indian Troubles in the North

We yesterday met a gentleman, for whose veracity and judgment we can vouch, who has been long a resident of the Klamath river country, and enjoyed the best possible means of information on the subject, who gave us some intelligence concerning the reported Indian hostilities in that region, which should be regarded by the authorities in whatever steps are taken in the premises. He assures us that there has been no hostile disposition manifested by the Indians towards the whites in general, and that the only depredations that have been committed have been provoked by a parcel of abandoned characters who live in the vicinity of the villages, and who are in the constant habit of committing the grossest outrages upon the squaws. In a few instances these outrages have been avenged by the Indians, by shooting the aggressors or killing their stock. These acts of retribution are called Indian outbreaks, and are made the pretext for fresh outrages upon the poor redskins. Our informant has been in the habit for years of making weekly trips, in the prosecution of his business, through the heart of the country in which the hostilities are reported, and has seen no disposition manifested to molest the whites who behave themselves as white men should.

9:11   Newspaper article, Nevada City, 1858

Squaws

We observe, says the Shasta *Courier*, that the recent rains have had the effect of increasing the female portion of our "native" population. They may be seen gathered in small groups squatted along our side walks during the day, especially from sundown to a late hour of the night. It is a pity and a shame that these poor degraded beings are, through the negligence of the general government, forced to procure their bread and clothing in a manner the most infamous. We call the attention of the Agent at Nome Lackee Reservation to these degraded creatures. They are a disgusting sore upon the face of this community—a most vile nuisance, calling loudly for abatement.

9:12   Newspaper article, San Francisco, 1859

Interfering with the Indians

A white man named Downs, living at Spanishtown, Butte county, is causing great disburbances among the Digger tribe, located in the vicinity of Shields' Gulch, in Butte county—so much so, that the miners at that place have petitioned to the Indian Agent for his intervention in the matter. The Indians are at present very kind to the miners and disposed to be friendly, but there is danger that, if they are allowed to be imposed upon, in the manner that this man Downs is doing it, they will become exasperated and cause trouble. It appears that Downs once lived with a young squaw and had a child by her. She afterwards went back to her people and married an Indian. Downs wants her as his wife again, but she does not like him, and prefers to remain where she is. Downs swears that he will have her back, if he has to kill the whole tribe. Several times the squaw has been compelled to fly from the rancheria in order to escape him. A day or two ago, the miners, at the request of the Indians, actually went to the Indian camp in order to prevent Downs from forcibly carrying off the squaw; and finally, to protect her from his violence, were compelled to give her and her husband shelter at their own cabins. This state of things they represent to the Agent as being very annoying to them, and they desire it remedied.

9:13   Newspaper article, San Francisco, 1859

Soldier Killed by Squaw

A party of four soldiers recently abused a squaw at Hoopa, and the squaw resisted, stabbing one of the party fatally. An investigation was to take place.

9:14   Newspaper article, Red Bluff, 1862

Outrages in Tehama County

Editor *Beacon:* — It is well known that there is, or has been, a body of soldiers in this county for several weeks past, for the avowed object of defending and protecting the citizens of the county against Indian depredations. It is equally well known that the depredatory Indians were on the east side of the river. By the neglect, carelessness, mismanagement or something worse, of the present Superintendent of Indian Affairs for the Northern District of California, it is known that there has been nothing raised either on Nome Lackee or Nome Cult for the subsistence of the Indians. Under the belief, and with the facts to substantiate it, that the Indians at Nome Cult were either to starve to death, or kill off, or be killed off, by the settlers, both Indians and settlers came to the conclusion that it was best for the Indians to leave the valley; and in this they were advised, counseled or favored by the Government employees at Nome Cult. Pursuant to this open, or at least tacit understanding between the Indians and the Government authorities, two tribes, the Hat Creeks and Con-Cows, left Nome Cult undisturbed, and without resistance or remonstrance, to make their way to their old haunts, in the hope of escaping death by starvation. With the morality or the policy of this, the writer has nothing to do. But to the sequel.

After these Indians had left Nome Cult—in starving condition—and made their way into the Sacramento valley, an effort was made by the Agent's employees to stop them. To do this they summoned to their aid Company E, 2nd California Cavalry, or a portion of it. The command promptly obeyed, and on the 1st day of October, they left the town of Red Bluff, on their mission. The command, or a portion of it, arrived in the neighborhood of Nome Lackee, to arrest and re-capture the Hat Creeks on Thursday or Friday. So far was their duty.

On Friday night a party of these soldiers visited the ranch of Col. Washington, and made themselves annoying to the Indians in the rancheria. This party was small, only three, as reported.

Saturday night, the 4th of October, 1862, was made memorable by the visit of a portion of this command, headed, aided and abetted by the commanding officer, Lieut. ____, (or some one assuming his title,) to the farm of

282

Col. Washington, and to the rancheria of peaceful and domesticated Indians resident thereon. Not one of the soldiers, private or Lieutenant, (or pretended Lieutenant, if such he was,) called at the farm house, but rode by and entered the Indian rancheria, with demands for Indian women, for the purpose of prostitution! They were requested to leave and ordered off the place. They answered they would do as they pleased, as they had the power. They were then told that it was true they were the strongest, and no force at hand was sufficient to contend with them, and they were left in the Indian rancheria. Most of the young squaws in the rancheria had by this time ran off and concealed themselves, and were beyond the reach and brutal grasp of the ravishers. They, however, were to be satiated, and like brutes dragged the old, decrepit "tar-heads" forth, and as many as three of the soldiers, in rapid succession, had forced intercourse with old squaws. Such was the conduct of the portion of the command of Co. E, on the night of the 4th of October, 1862, who visited the Indian rancheria at the Old Mill Place, about 3 miles from N. L. headquarters.

It is but proper, after consulting with those who are acquainted with the outrage, to say that the Lieut. (or pretended Lieut., if such he was,) did not arrive at the scene of action until after the larger portion of his men were on the ground – But it is absolutely certain that he was there—that he put his horse in the stable to hay, and then prowled around and through the Indian rancherias in quest of some squaw. Whether he found a fit subject upon which to practice his virtuous and civilizing purposes, the writer is not informed. He, however, saddled up and left the scene of moral exploit about daylight.

In justice to decency, humanity and civilization, these brutes should be punished. It is due to the honor, the reputation, the chivalry of the army of the United States, that the insignia of rank and position should be torn from the person of the Lieutenant (if it was he who was there,) as an officer unworthy its trust and confidence.

Oct. 6, 1862.   Foot Hills

9:15 Newspaper article, San Joaquin Valley, 1858

White Men Marrying Indian Women in Fresno County

Indian women, says the Mariposa *Gazette*, have been married to white men in numerous instances in Fresno county. They are said to make excellent wives; are neat, and tidy, and industrious, and soon learn to discharge domestic duties properly and creditably.

9:16 Newspaper article, San Francisco, 1859

Marriage—Digger Squaw and White Man

The Rangers are busily employed in the neighborhood of the Cow Creek, in securing the natives, and transferring them to the Reservation. Household ties have been ruthlessly destroyed on several occasions. Justice Stephenson performed the marriage service for the benefit of a white man and a red daughter of the soil, whose affection had somehow become entangled. Her name appears on the certificate as Miss Limotona Digger. She is said to be a daughter of the once famous Chief Witosh.

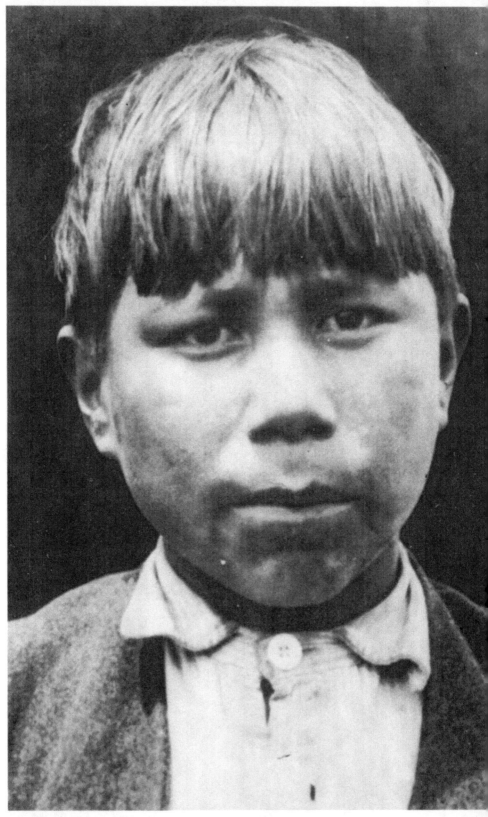

Hupa boy, W. Smoker, born c.1895. Photo 190_

10

INDIAN MISTREATMENT OF CHINESE

The only group which had equally few rights as Indians in Gold Rush California was the Chinese.[1] It is small wonder, then, that the Indian on occassion "picked on" people who had no defenders, and to judge from the newspaper accounts presented in this chapter the whites were only amused by all this. The Miner's Tax referred to was an effort by the State Legislature to discourage gold mining by non-whites and was aimed mainly at Chinese and Mexicans. While the state rarely enforced the act, it appears that the Indians on occasion used this as an excuse for extortion of Chinese.

The Chinese and Indians, despite the fact that they were both members of despised groups, did not make common cause. They did not intermarry and a true antipathy seems to have prevailed (cf. Document 10:3).

1 – S. M. Lyman. "Strangers in the Cities: The Chinese on the Urban Frontier," *in* C. Wollenberg (ed.), *Ethnic Conflict in California History*. Tinnon-Brown, Los Angeles, 1970, pp. 61-100.

A writer from Sonora to the *Republican* gives the following ludicrous anecdote:

It is reported that a party of six "digger" Indians came down from the mountains a few days since and when near Jesse Brush's residence, on the Tuolumne, they met an equal number of Chinamen. The chief advanced and demanded their poll-tax. This they obstinately refused to pay. The chief then demanded of them to show their receipts. They refused to do this also. The Indian then shot one of them, whereupon they capitulated and paid over $18. The "diggers" then returned, evidently well satisfied.

10:2 *Newspaper article, San Joaquin Valley, 1858*

A High Old Camp of Diggers in Calaveras County

On Central Hill, about two miles from San Andreas, says the *Independent*, is a Digger rancheria, containing in the neighborhood of three hundred souls, men, women, and children. A friend informs us that they have of late been cutting up some "high old tricks," impelled thereto by the fleeting aristocratic impulses which rare decoctions of "red-eye" and "forty-rod" usually generate. One day last week, a party of "bucks" went down to a neighboring claim where three Chinamen were at work, and levied a license-tax of three or four dollars a head on the frightened Johns, who demurring to the procedure, were forthwith marched up to the "campo," and put under strict guard until such time as their avarice should relent. The Johns held out until nightfall, when the Diggers, becoming sleepy, placed a solitary squaw upon duty to watch the prisoners during the night. The Chinamen were wet and muddy from the labors of the day, but they doubled themselves up as best they could, and slept or shivered until morning. In the morning the Diggers proposed to compromise for four bottles of brandy. A treaty to that effect was readily concluded, and the prisoners released. On Friday, a week from yesterday, twenty or thirty of those same fellows assailed three white men in the camp of the latter, beating and injuring one of them very severely. They used clubs and bottles in the fray, and so exasperated did one of the savages become in the heat of battle, that forgetting every thought but slaughter, he actually threw a full bottle of brandy at one of the white men, knocking him down and severely cutting his scalp. We are informed that some reckless scamps, keeping a whisky-shop a mile or two from the rancheria in question, are in the habit of associating with these Diggers and trading them intoxicating liquors. They should be closely watched and brought to punishment. Knowing the extent to which liquor stimulates the revengeful passions of a savage, the man who would be guilty of selling them any, should be treated as the common enemy of society.

10:3   Newspaper article, San Francisco, 1860

The Digger Indians "Down" on the Chinamen

In the vicinity of Kanaka Bar, one day recently, says the Weaverville *Journal*, a party of Indians entered a China cabin with thieving intent, and indignant at not finding any money, proceeded to chop the Celestial occupants up in a cruel manner. One of them has died since. Instances are related where Diggers have taken the cue from the Sheriff, and compelled Chinamen to pay license, but never before of so unceremonius and sanguinary proceeding, because they failed to make a raise. "Lo, the poor Indian," is fast becoming civilized.

Last Saturday, eight Indians visited Fairfield Bar, on Middle Feather river, as Chinese Tax Collectors. Two old Chinamen were politely requested to pungle down their "Poll Tax," when they presented their receipts. The "lords of the forest" assured the Johns that said paper was "no good," nothing short of cash would satisfy the demand. The Johns having no money, the tax collectors knocked them down and appropriated all the rice, pork and other valuables in their cabin.

Maidu man, Johnny Bob, born 1880. Photo 190

11

INDIANS AND THE
WHITE MAN'S LAW

Indians were prohibited from giving testimony for or against whites in Section 394 of the California Civil Practice Act of 1850 and were, therefore, deprived of the ordinary means of legal protection. Some of the ways in which Indians were punished or not provided protection under the white man's law are illustrated in this chapter.

Fort Humboldt Cal.
May 24th 1856

Sir.

An express recently arrived from Lieut. Rundell on Klamath river represents the Indians as perfectly quiet in that section. A circumstance that occurred on the Bay last week seemed likely at one time to create trouble. "Coon Skin" the principal chief of the Indians hereabouts, complained to me that a squaw with her two children, the daughter of his brother, had been stolen from his rancherie by a party of white men headed by one Spear who lives some seven or eight miles from here, and that the brother of the squaw in attempting to defend her was badly beaten. The Indians had already applied to several of the citizens of Eureka for redress, and they appeared to be determined to seek it by some methods of their own, if neither they nor myself would act for them. My first impulse was to take the squaw by force from Spear's house, but on reflecting that I had no power to punish him, and also that my right to take the squaw, even on the Indian's representation might be questioned by the civil authorities, I took the Indians with me to squire Hanna, an intelligent lawyer on the Bay. With his assistance a complaint in proper form was made out, sworn to in a manner by the Indians, and a warrant obtained from a Justice of the Peace and placed in the hands of the Sheriff. In the meantime, Spear and his associates, learning that proceedings had been initiated against them, fled taking with them the squaw and her children before the Sheriff could reach the house. I learned the next day that Spear had communicated with the authorities and finding that they were in earnest had agreed to compromise the matter by delivering up the squaw and paying the costs. Although anxious to have the man punished, I doubt whether even so much would have been effected had he been brought to trial. Much is the sympathy with the "squaw men" as they are termed among many people living on the Bay. Although many of the good citizens were loud in their denunciations of the outrage committed and affecting to fear disastrous consequences, there were few ready to give me any assistance in the matter, some ridiculing the idea that an attempt even should be made to do the Indian justice.

I am, Sir, very respectfully
Your Most Obt. Servt,
F. H. Bates
1st Lieut., 4th Infy.
Comdg. Post

To
Capt. S. R. Jones
Asst. Adjt. Genl. U. S. A.
Benicia, Cal.

11:2   Letter, Dillon to Mackall

Fort Bragg, Cal.
May 16th 1860

Sir

I have the honor to report that in obedience to an order from your Office, I arrived at this Post on the 5th inst. and relieved Lt. Carlin in command.

In leaving the Detachment at Round Valley in charge of a Sergeant, I deem it proper to report the condition of affairs in that valley. It might have been supposed that the settlers, being satisfied that it is the intention of Government to reserve the entire valley, would have stayed the hands of slaughter, and permitted the starving Digger to remain unmolested in his mountain retreat, until the Government shall have provided for him, a home in his nature valley. But not so. Several parties have recently been on expeditions against him, and only a short time before leaving, I was informed by an Indian that a large camp near the forks of Eel River had been attacked on the day previous, and that he alone had escaped. The monster Hall, so frequently reported for his atrocities, was said by the Indian to have been of the party. This man of devilish attributes, assisted for a time by Jarboe's Company, has well nigh depopulated a country, which but a short time since swarmed with Indians. Indeed I was told by this Indian that in this last attack, was consummated the entire destruction of the particular band to which he belonged.

Only a day or two after this attack, a man named Dodge fell upon an Indian and with a hatchet literally chopped him to pieces. The only charge against the Indian was that he had stolen a knife.

This same Dodge, a few weeks previously, blew out the brains of a squaw, charged with killing a pig. The same day, on which the butcher Dodge made mince meat of this Indian, a wretch called Vaughn, alias Texas, once before reported for the same offense, violated the person of an Indian woman, as I am informed, in the presence of a white man.

These facts are universally known in the valley, but I was unable to obtain evidence sufficiently strong, to justify me in the arrest of these men.

These people will not testify against each other, and in most cases of this nature, Indians are the only witnesses.

I am not aware of any recent depredations on the part of the Indians, though there is reason to suppose that an animal is occasionally made away with. In this connection it is worthy of remark, as evincing the general character of these people, that while it was stated to the investigations committee of the Legislature, by various persons, under oath, that from one hundred thousand, to one hundred and fifty thousand dollars worth of property had been destroyed by Indians, yet the list of taxable property in the valley, also sworn to, exhibits only the sum of about thirty thousand dollars.

From this it would appear that five times the entire quantity of stock now in the valley has been destroyed by Indians. This glowing absurdity needs no comment. . . .

For information concerning affairs in the vicinity of

Fort Bragg, I can only refer you to a recent report of the Officer commanding this post.

Very respectfully
Your Mo ob svt
Edward Dillon
2nd Lt. 6th Inft. Comg.

Maj. W. W. Mackall
Asst. Adjt. Genl. U.S.A.
San Francisco
Cal

11:3   Newspaper article, Sacramento, 1851

Murder in Santa Barbara

An Indian was murdered in Santa Barbara, recently, under circumstances which call loudly for the establishment of a Vigilance Committee in that place. He was called from his house by a Sonorian, whose name we did not learn, and who without any provocation whatever, plunged a knife into his heart, killing him instantly. Some four or five Indians were present, witnesses to the transaction, and they pursued the murderer, caught him and carried him before a magistrate. Will it be believed that he was almost immediately released from custody, because our laws will not allow an Indian to testify against a white man? The Indians in this part of the State, in the main a harmless race, are left entirely at the mercy of every ruffian in the country, and if something is not done for their protection, the race will shortly become extinct.

11:4   Newspaper article, San Francisco, 1858

Flogging An Indian

The Santa Rosa *Democrat* gives the following account of the punishment inflicted on an Indian criminal in that town on the 20th April:

On Monday last, an Indian was convicted before Justice Pyatt of this place, by a jury, of stealing, and sentenced on Tuesday morning to be publicly whipped—fifteen lashes with raw hide. The Indian was a confirmed thief, having been before detected in thefts at various times. After the sentence of the Court, he attempted to escape by running, and when overtaken by the officer, turned to fight, and had to be re-captured by force. He was brought back, however, and the sentence of the law inflicted upon him. There is certainly a strong tincture of barbarism in this manner of punishment that should be avoided in a civilized community, even though inflicted upon a savage. It would be difficult, we admit, how-ever, to devise a judicious and sufficient substitute. These Indians are indolent and poverty-stricken, so that fines can-not be collected; they are lazy and filthy, so that incarcera-tion in prison, where they must be fed without labor, has even a charm to them; they are indolent, treacherous and mischievous, so that no one would take the responsibility of guaranteeing their conduct, and pay their fine for their labor.

11:5   Newspaper article, San Francisco, 1858

Indian Trouble and Slaughter in the North

The Red Bluffs *Beacon* (Tehama County) has received a communication from E. W. Inskeep, dated Cold Spring Valley, April 28th, as follows:

A few day's ago, George Lane's squaw divorced herself from her lord and master, by running away, and taking with her his Indian boy and a good revolver, a lot of ammunition, etc.; since which time Indians have stolen all the provisions, blankets, powder, lead, etc., from a ranch a little north of Lane's, called Elmer's ranch. They have also attempted to steal Klotz and Co.'s horses, but the whites were too fast for them. They took a yoke of cattle from Ferguson & Co. on the 20th April. To-day, (28th April), several persons will start in pursuit of them.

The *Beacon* says, that subsequent to the receipt of this letter, it had been ascertained that the party who went out in search of the Indians came upon them somewhere on Butte creek, (which divides Shasta and Tehama counties,) and killed some fifteen of their number.

11:6   Newspaper article, San Francisco, 1858

Execution of an Indian

White men are not usually hanged for killing Chinamen, but Indians who commit such a crime are strung up with little ceremony. Last week a Digger was hung at Jackson, Amador county, for having last summer murdered some Chinamen at Rancheria. The execution was conducted in comparative privacy, there being only about 150 persons around the gallows, among whom were some 20 Indians. The Jackson *Ledger* says of the behavior of the culprit upon the scaffold:

The Indian confessed his crime, and acknowledged the justice of his punishment. He had a great deal to say about the Indians not aiding him in getting clear. He thought they ought to have assisted him. He sent word to his mother to go to the other side of the mountains, as he thought the Indians on this side would mis-use her. He had a great desire not to be hung till twelve, when the sun had commenced going down. Three Indians were on the scaffold, to whom he talked a great deal. One of them took his hat, coat and shoes after he was hung, and immediately put them on. He expressed a desire for the minister to pray for him as he wanted to go to a better country; he was tired of this one. He said he was sorry for what he had done, and requested that his body be given to the Indians for burial. He died with courage, the fatal drop falling at 12 minutes after 12 o'clock—just as the minister closed his prayer.

Atrocious Cruelty to Indians

A correspondent of the Marysville *Democrat,* writing from Clear Lake, of date 3d May, says:

An occurrence took place in this vicinity, about a week ago, which I would not call anything but willful murder. An old Indian and his squaw were engaged in the harmless occupation of gathering clover on the land of a Mr. Grigsby, when a man named Frank Harrington set Grigsby's dogs upon them, (which, by the way, are three very ferocious ones,) and before they were taken off of them, they tore and mangled the body of the squaw in such a manner that she died shortly after. It is said the dogs tore her breasts off her. The Digger man escaped without any serious injury, although bitten severely. Of course, it was the dogs' fault, although Harrington had lived with Grigsby over a year and knew full well the character of the dogs, for this is not the first instance of their biting persons. But he only set them on for fun, and they were only Diggers! There is a talk of having him arrested, but no doubt it is all talk.

11:8   *Newspaper article, San Francisco, 1859*

The Lynching of the Indian Boy in Tehama County

A few days ago, the Indian boy who set fire to the house of Col. Stevenson, was taken from the custody of Sheriff Dunn, by a number of citizens, and hanged. The Sheriff had taken him to the Court House and left him in a room adjoining the Court room, and while absent for a few moments, the boy was taken by the mob. This is really horrible, and reflects no credit to the parties concerned. The *Beacon* condemns the act in a very severe manner, by alluding to it in "eloquent silence." The boy was but twelve or fifteen years of age. (The Tehama *Gazette* says that he was only ten years old.) What good will the hanging of the stripling accomplish? Will it deter other Indian boys from committing a similar act? If so, the act is defensible. If not, what then? That the boy deserved hanging, if he was capable of appreciating the magnitude of his crime, is very true; but why not let him be hung in a legal manner? There was no danger of his escaping. Shasta *Courier.*

11:9   Newspaper article, Sacramento, 1860

Digger's Opinion of Jail Life

Four Digger Indians who were convicted some thirty days since of malicious trespass, in firing Cloyd's pasture field near Upper Calaveritas, whereby a good part of his fence and other valuable property were destroyed, last Monday completed their sentence of twenty-five days imprisonment in the county jail. They came directly to San Andreas after being liberated, to claim their bows and arrows, left in charge of the constable. Being playfully asked their opinion of jail life, they honestly replied: "Moquelune Hill mucha bueno; Pink 'im bueno hombre; get 'im heap chummuck; jail mucha bueno, heap like 'im, me!'"

11:10   Newspaper article, San Francisco, 1861

Indian Lynched in Shasta County

On the 5th of March, says the Shasta *Courier,* an Indian, known as To-an-yo-la, was hung by some of the citizens about Dry Creek, in Shasta county, after a fair and impartial trail for the murder of one Larkins, in the fall of 1854. He was apprehended on information given by other Indians. He made a full confession of his guilt, and in mitigation of the crime, said he was induced to kill Larkins by other Indians, who gave him glowing accounts of the amount of money, clothing, grub, etc., he would obtain by the murder.

11:11   Newspaper article, Marysville, 1862

Indian Murder

On Sunday last the body of a Digger squaw, about 30 years of age apparently, was found lying face downward, and partially covered with dirt, in a dry ditch just beyond the Field property, on the corner of D and Ninth Streets. Examination showed that the woman had been stabbed with a knife in as many as 20 places around the neck, breast and arms, of which four or five of the wounds were of a character sufficient to cause death. The body was taken in charge by Coroner Hamilton, and at the inquest held by him yesterday it appears that a party of Diggers were seen about the place Friday afternoon and one fellow, known as "Yates," was seen to beat and abuse this woman, who was one of his wives. Some persons took him off, but he was very wrathful and drew a knife. Afterwards, the creatures were seen trying to force this woman to drink whiskey from a bottle, which she refused to do, and there was a general row among them. Groans were heard from there during the evening; and the evidence being strong against Yates, Captain Cook tracked him to the campoody of his tribe on the other side of the Feather river, thirteen miles above this city, where some of his men acknowledged that Yates had killed the woman. Cook tried to secure the fellow, but he got off, though wounded in the leg by a pistol-shot from the officer. The coroner's jury returned a verdict in accordance with the above facts. This Yates is a dangerous and bad Indian, having threatened the life of white men before now, but like most of those miserable creatures, he probably thinks that he had a right to kill his own wife, or else there is no use in having one, as we once heard one of those heathen remark.

Crescent City, April 15, 1862

Since my last letter to the *Bulletin* we have had considerable stir in our usually quiet town. Several burglaries
have been committed here during the last three months, and
though the authors of them were well known to be a gang of
fellows of the basest sort, who have long consorted with
"diggers" here, yet no one had been detected, till about three
weeks ago. Bacon, flour, liquors, drygoods, boots, etc. have
disappeared—three houses, at least, being broken op :n in the
process, and no fixing the crime on any of the parties, till
three weeks after the latest of the robberies—which was that
of a drygoods store. About three weeks after it happened
some of the goods were seen about the premises of a man
known as "Ed Buckner" who has been but a few months
here, and is believed to be the most experienced operator and
chief leader of the gang. He was arrested and bound over for
trial. Last week he was indicted, tried, convicted, and sentenced to two years confinement in the State Prison at San
Quentin.

Directly afterwards, a public meeting of citizens was
convened and a committee appointed to notify one Freeman,
(one of the most obnoxious of the "squaw men") that he
must leave by the first opportunity. He gave a defiant refusal;
and, as he is a desperate and very powerful man, it is not
unlikely there will be trouble soon after the steamer goes
down.

For all these evils which constitute almost the only dis-
turbing element in our little community, there is but one
remedy—the removal of every Indian to the Reservation, and
the stationing of a body of U. S. troops between here and
there, to keep all red-skinned diggers from coming this way,
and all white-skinned diggers from going that way. Superintendent Hanson has power to remove the Indians, and Gen.
Wright has power to make the separation effectual and permanent. The people will give every possible aid to both.

303

When his operation is carried out, this community will be rid of a gang of men whose only inducement to stay here is to be with the squaws, and who live on the fruits of honest men's labor.

11:13   Newspaper article, San Francisco, 1863

White Boy Shooting an Indian Chief

Correspondence from Woodbridge, San Joaquin county, to the Stockton *Independent* says:

A shooting affair occurred at Lockeford on Sunday. A boy about 17 years old deliberately shot and seriously wounded an Indian, José Piñon, chief of a tribe residing in the vicinity of Lockeford, discharging the contents of two barrels into the right hip and thigh. The Indian was seriously hurt, and now lies at the Lockeford House. The boy was taken before a "Justice" next morning, who summoned a jury, and by some Dogberry hocus-pocus set the guilty party at liberty. I am credibly informed that the boy lay in wait for the express purpose of killing or shooting the Indian.

11:14   Newspaper article, Sacramento, 1865

Outrage in Mendocino County

A correspondent of the *Union*, writing from Ukiah City, Mendocino county, August 13th, relates the following case of outrage:

Allow me to inform you of a most inhuman outrage that took place here last Wednesday morning. A young man living here in town hired an Indian to go with him after a load of barley. When about one-fourth of a mile on their way, they met one Bob Hildreth, who claimed the Indian as his property and asked the Indian where in h-ll he was going. The Indian answering, after barley, he told him to get out of the wagon d--d quick; that he would show him the way to come home. He made the Indian cross his hands behind, when he fastened them with his rope, swearing he would drag him to death. Then mounting his horse and taking two half hitches around the logger head of his saddle, he put the spurs to his horse, throwing the Indian eight or ten feet, with a hard fall—the Indian screaming and begging for his life. The horse, after going some few jumps, became frightened and threw Hildreth off. The rope being tied would not come loose, the horse running zigzag across the road and crossing two different ditches before he was caught. The Indian was terribly mangled, his arms being twisted off in his shoulders. So much for slavery in California. Jarboe, the great Indian hunter of Humboldt, who is now dead, claimed to have had those Indians bound to him by one of the most cursed of all laws that ever were passed in this State. Hildreth, buying the property of Mrs. Jarboe, now claims these Indians are part of his estate. She setting the Indians free to go where they please, they will not stay with Hildreth, nor has he any right to them. The Legislature has done much blowing concerning the Indians in this county, but every Act hits them harder. They are held here as slaves were held in the South; those owning them use them as they please, beat them with clubs and shoot them down like dogs, and no one to say: "Why do you do so?" James Shores, an Indian slaveholder here, shot one the other day, because he would not stand and be whipped, inflicting a severe wound, but not killing him. Hildreth is bound over in the sum of one thousand dollars for his appearance, but I have my doubts of finding a jury that will convict a man for killing an Indian up here.

Horrid Murder of an Indian Boy

The Shasta *Courier* of November 18th describes a recent tragedy in its county, as follows:

Near North Fork of Cottonwood, week before last, a most cowardly and barbarous murder was committed. It seems that two white barbarians went to an Indian rancheria in that neighborhood for the purpose of getting possession of an Indian girl about ten years old. This attempt at forcible possession was resisted by the mother of the child, assisted by a crippled Indian boy, the only one in the rancheria. The resistance of this poor cripple so exasperated the villians that one of them seized him by the top of the head, while with his knife he first cut his throat and then stabbed him to the knife hilt, and to wreak his vengeance fully, turned the knife in the wound several times, then withdrawing it, again stabbed his victim, turning the knife as before, repeating the act until life was extinct. While this butchery was going on, the girl and her mother made their escape. In a few days after the fiends burnt the rancheria. There is nothing but the dead body and Indian testimony to prove the above, and though it is convincing, it is not enough, under the law, to punish the miscreants. White men who live with Indians habitually should do so subject to Indian testimony; and we think a law to that effect would be wise and proper.

Courtesy LMA
Yurok woman, Alice Spott, born 1880. *Photo 19*

12

INDIANS AS THE
BUTT OF JOKES

As towns developed in California and the number of Indians decreased, those native survivors who frequented the urban areas were often viewed with amusement and ridicule. Taking Indians as comic characters, however, seems to have prevailed only where the miserable remnants of population survived. In the country where "wild" Indians could still be hunted and killed or captured and indentured, they were still "savages."

A Dressed Indian

To one who has crossed the plains, or been much among the Indians, there is something extremely ludicrous in seeing one of them sporting the cast-off toggery of a white man. Our city is visited daily by the remnants of a Digger tribe, whose sole occupation appears to be the eating of watermelons and searching closely in the vicinity of the curbs, to pick up such articles of clothing as may chance to have been cast there by the purchaser of a new suit. After one of these perambulating excursions, they repair to the shade of a large sycamore on the levee, where they dress themselves, after the most ornamental fashion permitted by the quality of the goods in their possession; and again repair to the public thoroughfares to make an exhibition of their spoils. A muchacho, for instance, whose age embraces the cycle of 15 or 16 years, puts on the coat of a man of six feet in height, deficient a sleeve, having lost its buttons, and genteel in nothing but the length of its skirts, which reach to the ground, and in its collar, which covers the ears. Now imagine one of the old hats thrown from the store of Steph. White, covering the boy's head—the brim resting behind upon his shoulders, and in front upon his eyebrows, his feet bare, so much of his countenance as is visible suffused by a broad grin, his hands scaled with dirt, his pantaloons of a dubious character, and the picture is complete. The squaws and old men walk behind this portable figure, to form its perspective, and in the excess of their parental admiration, preserve a stoicism of feature which comports highly with the nature of the great triumph achieved in setting the Digger fashions!

John Digger at Marysville

The Marysville *Appeal* of 6th August says:
A tall, corpulent, pox-marked Digger, with bones half an inch thick through his ears, and a shocking bad hat on his head, stalked into the *Appeal* sanctum yesterday and informed us in a solemn manner as follows: "Me bluth'n-law—Wahketaw—Captain Yuba Ingin—he mucha dead; Sacramento Ingin poison he. No good. Welly bad Ingin—poison no good. By'm bye kill 'em." Saying this, and uttering several mournful grunts, John Digger helped himself to a seat and gazed wonderingly at our active scissors. We ascertained that he is a Hock Form Indian. He stuck to his story that the Chief of the Yubas was dead, poisoned by Sacramento Indians, and claimed to be his brother-in-law. Wahketaw was a "good Ingin," and the sorry remnants of his tribe have been for many years the inoffensive aboriginal bummers of this city and vicinity. Wahketaw himself was a frequent visitor at the *Appeal* sanctum, and always applied for a letter or recommendation and two bits to get beef whenever he went to the fandango of a neighboring tribe. He also fell heir to the editorial cast-off hats and coats. He disliked Chinamen and dogs, and when asked if he was a good Union man replied promptly: "Yes onion welly good." He was reported to be dead once before, and we still hope to learn that he has not swallowed the poison intended for some miserable cur. We had a suspicion that coppery "bluth'n-law" of his was playing on our sympathies; nevertheless we gave him a bright new dime and charged him to go and buy a watermelon—not whisky.

12:3   Newspaper article, Marysville, 1864

"Big Ingin Mr."

Captain Sutter alias Lampacker, the Indian Chief of the Yubas, called yesterday to pay his respects to the editor—same as other big injins sometimes do. The Captain is always in trouble—always in want—family all dead, as usual—no coat or shoes—and very cold nights. The Captain is an inveterate beggar, and as he always gets something when he calls at the "sanctum,"—he makes his visits regularly—like other office-seekers. We asked the Captain about the weather, when he replied—"Very dry, no more rain, all gone." We made this inquiry out of respect to many people who have great faith in Digger meteorology, and of course among this scientific class the question of rain or no rain is settled by the authority of Captain Sutter. Flour speculators can now press upward prices, and the careful and precautionary heads of families will see that they lay in a full supply of breadstuffs for the year. We gave the Captain a "quarter" for imparting this important information, and he departed a happy Indian.

12:4   Newspaper article, San Joaquin Valley, 1858

A Fancy Digger

One of the young aborigine ladies, who have been promenading the levee for a week or two, made her appearance yesterday in a brand new fitout, and marched down the levee to the great admiration of the beholders, with the air of an upper-ten young lady through the New York Broadway, with a hundred dollar silk, fresh from Stewart's. This Hiawatha sported very jauntily one of the style of hats so very popular with the Seminary young ladies, and a dress which was actually clean, and fitted well. The waist of the dusky wearer, it is true, was not of quite so small a span as that of those who from childhood have been squeezed by corsets and other instruments of torture.

DOCUMENT SOURCES

Abbreviations Used
OIA – Office of Indian Affairs
RWD – Records War Department
USNA – U. S. National Archives

Chapter 1

1:1. USNA, RWD, RG98. Letters received, 10th Military Dept., 1847. (Document No. 26).

1:2. USNA, RWD, RG98. Letters received, 10th Military Dept., 1847. (Document No. 21).

1:3. USNA, RWD, RG98. Letters received, 10th Military Dept., 1847. (Document No. "M"-4-1847).

1:4. USNA, RWD, RG98. Letters received, 10th Military Dept., 1847. (Document No. "2" enclosure to "N" 1/47).

Chapter 2

2:1. USNA, RWD, RG98. Letters received, Dept. of Pacific, 1854. (Box No. 2, Document No. W2).

2:2. USNA, OIA, RG75. Letters received, California, 1856. (Document No. 27).

2:3. USNA, RWD, RG98. Letters received, Dept. of Pacific, 1854. (Box No. 2, Document No. W12).

2:4. USNA, OIA, RG75. Letters received, California, 1854. (Document No. H703).

2:5. USNA, OIA, RG75. Letters received, California, 1854. (Document No. H758).

2:6. USNA, OIA, RG75. Letters received, California, 1854. (Document No. H760).

2:7. USNA, OIA, RG75. Letters received, California, 1854. (Document No. H776).

2:8. USNA, OIA, RG75. Letters received, California, 1855. (Document No. H829).

2:9. USNA, OIA, RG75. Letters received, California, 1855. (Document No. H982).

2:10. USNA, RWD, RG98. Letters received, Dept. of Pacific, 1856. (Box No. 4, Document No. 0/10).

2:11. USNA, OIA, RG75. Letters received, California, 1858. (Document No. H1254).

2:12. Sacramento *Union*, Feb. 3, 1855.

2:13. San Francisco *Bulletin*, Sept. 23, 1858 (Quoting from Tuolumne *Courier*).

2:14. San Francisco *Bulletin*, Sept. 23, 1858 (Quoting from Amador *Sentinel*).

2:15. Sacramento *Union*, Aug. 29, 1859 (Quoting from Napa *Reporter*).

Chapter 3

3:1. USNA, RWD, RG98. Letters received, 10th Military Dept., 1850. (Document No. 334).

3:2. USNA, RWD, RG98. Letters received, Dept. of Pacific, 1854. (Box No. 2, Document No. W7).

3:3. USNA, RWD, RG98. Letters received, Dept. of Pacific, 1854. (Box No. 1, Document No. B93).

3:4. USNA, RWD, RG98. Letters received, Dept. of Pacific, 1854. (Box No. 1, Document No. W32).

3:5. USNA, OIA, RG75. Letters received, California, 1854. (Document No. W403).

3:6. USNA, RWD, RG75. Letters received, Dept. of Pacific, 1858. (Box No. 8, Document No. J7).

3:7. USNA, RWD, RG98. Letters received, Dept. of Pacific, 1855. (Box No. 3, Document No. J16).

3:8. USNA, RWD, RG98. Letters received, Dept. of Pacific, 1855. (Box No. 3, Document No. I11).

3:9. USNA, RWD, RG98. Letters received, Dept. of Pacific, 1855. (Box No. 3, Document No. J18).

3:10. USNA, OIA, RG75. Letters received, California, 1856. (Document No. H22).

3:11. USNA, OIA, RG75. Letters received, California, 1854. (Document No. I552).

3:12. USNA, RWD, RG98. Letters received, Dept. of Pacific, 1856. (Box No. 4, Document No. B45).

3:13. USNA, RWD, RG98. Letters received, Dept. of Pacific, 1856. (Box No. 4, Document No. L31).

3:14.. USNA, RWD, RG98. Letters received, Dept. of Pacific, 1857. (Box No. 8, Document No. R2).

3:15. San Francisco *Bulletin*, Aug. 6, 1859.
3:16. San Francisco *Bulletin*, Jan. 21, 1860.
3:17. San Francisco *Bulletin*, July 15, 1864.

Chapter 4

4:1.   USNA, RWD, RG98. Letters received, Pacific Division, 1852. (Box No. 5, Vol. 2, Document No. P13).
4:2.   USNA, RWD, RG98. Letters received, Dept. of Pacific, 1856. (Box No. 5, Document No. W104).
4:3.   USNA, RWD, RG98. Letters received, Dept. of Pacific, 1857. (Box No. 6, Documents M54, M61).
4:4.   USNA, RWD, RG98. Letters received, Dept. of Pacific, 1858. (Box No. 7, Document No. C3).
4:5.   USNA, OIA, RG75. Letters received, California, 1858. (Document No. B615).
4:6.   USNA, OIA, RG75. Letters received, California, 1858. (Document No. B622).
4:7.   USNA, OIA, RG75. Letters received, California, 1858. (Documents No. B637, B638).
4:8.   USNA, OIA, RG75. Letters received, California, 1858. (Document No. H1335).
4:9.   USNA, OIA, RG75. Letters received, California, 1859. (Document No. B697).
4:10. USNA, OIA, RG75. Letters received, California, 1859. (Document No. V25).
4:11. USNA, OIA, RG75. Letters received, California, 1859.(Document No. M90).
4:12. USNA, OIA, RG75. Letters received, California, 1859. (Document No. B99).
4:13. USNA, OIA, RG75. Letters received, California, 1860. (Document No. R779). Newspaper clipping from *The Northern Californian* April 18, 1860.
4:14. San Francisco *Bulletin*, Sept. 22, 1857.
4:15. *Daily State Sentinel*, November 1, 1857.
4:16. San Francisco *Bulletin*, July 22, 1861.
4:17. San Francisco *Bulletin*, Nov. 6, 1862.
4:18. Sacramento *Union*, Nov. 7, 1862.
4:19. San Francisco *Bulletin*, Jan. 6, 1865.
4:20. San Francisco *Bulletin*, Jan. 7, 1865.

Chapter 5

5:1.   USNA, OIA, RG75. Letters received, California, 1850. (Document No. J463).
5:2.   USNA, OIA, RG75. Letters received, California, 1850. (Document No. W419).

5:3. USNA, OIA, RG75. Letters received, California, 1851. (Document No. C672).
5:4. USNA, RWD, RG98. Letters received, Pacific Division, 1852. (Box No. 4, Vol. 2, Document No. C 10/12).
5:5. USNA, RWD, RG98. Letters received, Pacific Division, 1852. (Box No. 5, Vol. 2, Document No. P14).
5:6. USNA, OIA, RG75. Letters received, California, 1854. (Document No. H697).
5:7. USNA, OIA, RG75. Letters received, California, 1854. (Document No. H765).
5:8. USNA, OIA, RG75. Letters received, California, 1856. (Document No. W120).
5:9. USNA, OIA, RG75. Letters received, California, 1856. (Document No. H259).
5:10. San Francisco *Bulletin*, Sept. 1, 1856.
5:11. San Francisco *Bulletin*, Oct. 27, 1858.
5:12. Sacramento *Union*, Feb. 25, 1860.
5:13. San Francisco *Bulletin*, Mar. 12, 1860.
5:14. San Francisco *Bulletin*, May 11, 1860.
5:15. San Francisco *Bulletin*, Oct. 25, 1861.
5:16. San Francisco *Bulletin*, April 29, 1864.

Chapter 6

6:1. Chapter 133, Statutes of California, April 22, 1850; Chapter 231, Statutes of California, April 8, 1860.
6:2. USNA, OIA, RG75. Letters received, California, 1855. (Document No. H933).
6:3. USNA, OIA, RG75. Letters received, California, 1855. (Document No. H1018).
6:4. USNA, OIA, RG98. Letters received, California, 1855. (Document No. H1025).
6:5. USNA, RWD, RG98. Letters received, Dept. of Pacific, 1861. (Box No. 9, Document No. D24).
6:6. USNA, OIA, RG75. Letters received, California, 1861. (Document No. H275).
6:7. USNA, OIA, RG75. Letters received, California, 1856. (Document No. H109).
6:8. USNA, OIA, RG75. Letters received, California, 1855. (Document No. I1109).
6:9. Marysville *Appeal*, Oct. 17, 1861.
6:10. Marysville *Appeal*, Oct. 18, 1861.
6:11. Marysville *Appeal*, Oct. 19, 1861.
6:12. Marysville *Appeal*, Oct. 24, 1861.
6:13. Marysville *Appeal*, Jan. 4, 1861 (Quoting Red Bluff *Independent*).

6:14. San Francisco *Bulletin*, Mar. 2, 1861 (Quoting Humboldt *Times*, Feb. 23).

6:15. San Francisco *Bulletin*, Mar. 27, 1861 (Quoting Napa *Reporter*).

Chapter 7

7:1. USNA, RWD, RG98. Letters received, 10th Military Dept., 1850. (Document No. 329a). (Also Printed in Senate Executive Document No. 1, 31st Congress, 2d Session, 1850, pp. 81-83).

7:2. Thomas Knight, Statement of Early Events in California, 1879 (pp. 15-16). Original in Bancroft Library.

7:3. Adjutant General's Office, Old Files Division. (Document No. H185/R133, 1853).

7:4. *Daily Alta California*, April 19, 1851.

7.5. Sacramento *Daily Transcript*, April 28, 1851.

7:6. *Daily Alta California*, May 4, 1852.

7:7. *Daily Alta California*, July 11, 1852.

7:8. *Daily Alta California*, March 6, 1853.

7:9. San Francisco *Bulletin*, Jan. 21, 1860.

7:10. San Francisco *Bulletin*, June 18, 1860.

7:11. San Francisco *Bulletin*, Feb. 28, 1860.

7:12. San Francisco *Bulletin*, March 2, 1860.

7:13. Adjutant General's Office, Old Files Division. (Document 75C, 1860).

7:14. San Francisco *Bulletin*, May 24, 1860.

7:15. San Francisco *Bulletin*, March 2, 1861.

Chapter 8

8:1. Sacramento *Union*, Dec. 4, 1852 (cf. Doc. 7:3).

8:2. Marysville *Weekly Express*, April 16, 1859 (Quoting Red Bluff *Beacon*).

8:3. Marysville *Appeal*, May 12, 1861.

8:4. Marysville *Appeal*, August 9, 1862.

Chapter 9

9:1. USNA, RWD, RG98. Letters received, Dept. of Pacific, 1857. (Box No. 6, Document No. L7).

9:2. Sacramento *Union*, November 5, 1851.

9:3. Sacramento *Union*, May 28, 1853.

9:4. Sacramento *Union*, Feb. 27, 1855.

9:5. Butte *Record*, Nov. 29, 1856.

9:6. San Francisco *Bulletin*, June 22, 1858 (Quoting Nevada *Journal*).

9:7. San Joaquin *Republican*, Sept.___, 1858.

9:8. San Francisco *Bulletin*, Sept. 13, 1856.
9:9. San Francisco *Bulletin*, Nov. 9, 1857.
9:10. Sacramento *Union*, Oct. 1, 1858 (Quoting Marysville *Express*, Sept. 29).
9:11. Nevada *Journal*, Nov. 12, 1858.
9:12. San Francisco *Bulletin*, May 31, 1859 (Quoting Marysville *Democrat*).
9:13. San Francisco *Bulletin*, Nov. 14, 1859.
9:14. Red Bluff *Beacon*, Oct. 9, 1862.
9:15. San Joaquin *Republican*, Sept.___, 1858.
9:16. San Francisco *Bulletin*, Nov. 30, 1859 (Quoting Shasta *Herald*).

Chapter 10
10:1. Sacramento *Union*, June 6, 1853.
10:2. San Joaquin *Republican*, Sept.___, 1858.
10:3. San Francisco *Bulletin*, Sept. 12, 1860 (Quoting Weaverville *Journal*)..
10:4. Marysville *Appeal*, July 30, 1865.

Chapter 11
11:1. USNA, RWD, RG98. Letters received, Dept. of Pacific, 1856. (Box No. 4, Document No. B57).
11:2. USNA, OIA, RG75. Letters received, California, 1860. (Document No. W123).
11:3. Sacramento *Union*, Nov. 14, 1851 (Quoting Los Angeles *Star*).
11:4. San Francisco *Bulletin*, April 24, 1858 (Quoting Santa Rosa *Democrat*).
11:5. San Francisco *Bulletin*, May 8, 1858.
11:6. San Francisco *Bulletin*, Dec. 7, 1858 (Quoting Jackson *Ledger*).
11:7. San Francisco *Bulletin*, May 12, 1859 (Quoting Marysville *Democrat*).
11:8. San Francisco *Bulletin* May 31, 1859 (Quoting Shasta *Courier*).
11:9. Sacramento *Union*, Sept. 27, 1860 (Quoting San Andreas *Independent*).
11:10. San Francisco *Bulletin*, March 23, 1861 (Quoting Shasta *Courier*).
11:11. Marysville *Appeal* April 8, 1862.
11:12. San Francsico *Bulletin*, April 24, 1862.
11:13. San Francisco *Bulletin*, March 16, 1863 (Quoting Stockton *Independent*).

11:14. Sacramento *Union*, August 19, 1865.
11:15. Sacramento *Union*, Nov. 21, 1865 (Quoting Shasta *Courier*, Nov. 18).

Chapter 12
12:1. Sacramento *Union*, Sept. 6, 1863.
12:2. San Francisco *Bulletin*, Aug. 10, 1863.
12:3. Marysville *Appeal*, March 27, 1864.
12:4. San Joaquin *Republican*, ___ 1858.

CPSIA information can be obtained at www.ICGtesting.com
Printed in the USA
BVOW03s0237031014

369314BV00013B/175/P